POWER UP

POWER UP

MAKING THE SHIFT TO 1:1 TEACHING AND LEARNING

Diana Neebe and Jen Roberts

FOREWORD BY JAIME CASAP

Stenhouse Publishers

Portland, Maine

Stenhouse Publishers

www.stenhouse.com

Library of Congress Cataloging-in-Publication Data

Neebe, Diana, 1984-
   Power up : making the shift to 1:1 teaching and learning / Diana Neebe and Jen Roberts ;
   foreword by Jaime Casap.
        pages cm
   Includes bibliographical references and index.
   ISBN 978-1-62531-013-2 (pbk. : alk. paper) -- ISBN 978-1-62531-061-3 (ebook) 1. Individualized
   instruction. 2. Transformative learning. I. Roberts, Jen, 1972- II. Title.
   LB1031.N36 2015
   371.39'4--dc23
                                          2015002874

Cover and interior design by Lucian Burg, Lu Design Studios, Portland, ME
www.ludesignstudios.com

Manufactured in the United States of America

PRINTED ON 30% PCW
RECYCLED PAPER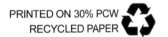

21 20 19 18 17 16 15   9 8 7 6 5 4 3 2 1

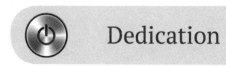

Dedication

To our students — past, present, and future.

Contents

How Technology Is Transforming Learning

For most of history, where you were born, the family you were born into, and your proximity to books and libraries all affected your educational opportunities. This was true in my lifetime. Growing up in Hell's Kitchen, New York, attending PS 111, I had the use of the Columbus Library on Fifty-First Street and Tenth Avenue. It was a small space with limited hours, serving the needs of a diverse community. I was there a lot, but the resources were limited, and when I couldn't find the book I needed, there was nowhere else to turn.

Today, we walk around with a hundred million Columbus libraries in our pockets. In just a few short years, how we access, interact with, and take advantage of information has changed forever. Technology, the Internet, the cloud, and apps are all here to stay. Currently, about 40 percent of the world's seven billion people have an Internet connection. In 1995, it was less than 1 percent. By 2005, the Internet had its first billion users. Five years later, that number was two billion, and by 2014, three billion people were online.

I believe this is the most exciting time in education history. The potential to deliver innovative instruction has never been so great. Amazing teachers are transforming traditional learning models. In just the last few years, we've seen examples such as distance learning, blended learning, personalized learning, and flipped classroom models take off. Many in the education world believe we're just getting warmed up. And yet, my eleven-year-old son's classroom looks pretty much the same as it did twenty years ago. Although I understand that change takes time, I also believe that educators must seize the opportunities available to their students.

Today, we have much more information about the science of learning. We know students vary in their capacity to learn, even in different subject areas. We know that relevance and engagement are critical to the learning process. And we are just starting to scratch the surface of how technology can help us enable and support new learning models that take advantage of research.

Second, most of our students in K–12 today do not know the world that existed before Google. Many of them can't imagine life without a smartphone. Technology and the web are this generation's electricity and house phones. We assumed those conveniences were a regular part of life. Likewise, our students see technology and the Internet as normal necessities.

Third, the way our students think about learning is fundamentally different from the way previous generations did. We waited for someone, usually one of the responsible adults in our lives, to teach us. We depended on those adults to tell us what to learn. This generation doesn't comprehend those limitations. With technology and the web, they learn when and where they want. They learn more about subjects they are interested in. When they don't understand something or want to learn something, they do not go to the adult in the room. They explore. For this generation, learning happens all the time.

For example, my son wanted to learn how to code in Java. Instead of asking me where he could take a class or waiting until it showed up as an option at school, he simply went to Khan Academy and began teaching himself. My oldest daughter wanted to learn how to play the ukulele, and instead of buying an instruction book or video, she found a lesson on YouTube that resonated with her. When we teach students how to access the tools for learning, they can pursue their passions and invent their own possibilities.

My children are representative of their generation, but they also are among the lucky ones. They have Internet access and technology at home, even if they do not have it in their classrooms yet. But what are we doing for the students without Internet at home? They are part of a growing digital divide that will perpetuate a cycle of poverty if we do not give them access to digital resources in their classrooms. The increasing number of 1:1 programs in schools is a democratizing force that needs to spread to every corner of our country and every continent of our planet.

As we innovate, we have to make sure we aren't just automating education or simply making it more efficient. It is critical that we keep our focus on learning, not on technology. Turning a textbook into an e-textbook or moving from delivering a lecture in a class to delivering a lecture on video are not examples of transformative education. To truly prepare our students for their futures, we must embrace pedagogy that gives students responsibility, leads them through inquiry, and allows them to create based on their own ideas.

Just as important, we have to let teachers develop the knowledge, skills, and abilities to take advantage of the resources that are now at their fingertips. At the end of the day, once the students are inside the classroom, the teacher is the single most important factor in a child's education. As great as technology can be, it will never replace a great teacher in the classroom. Today's teachers are the ones who are going to create the new learning models we will use for generations to come. Neebe and Roberts have made some great leaps toward determining what those models could look like in our classrooms.

Effective professional development has never been as important, but we also know that face-to-face training in digital pedagogy is only a small part of what transforms classrooms. Educators also must have access to and take advantage of instructional coaches, online resources, and professional trade books.

Power Up: Making the Shift to 1:1 Teaching and Learning is a great place for many teachers to start. Neebe and Roberts share personal stories from their own classrooms about learning to teach with a laptop or tablet for every student. They also explain very clearly how pedagogy changes when every child has access to digital tools. This book will help you navigate the transition you are about to experience as you enrich, extend, and transform learning in your 1:1 classroom.

Although it is true that my son's classroom is pretty much the same as it was when I was in school, I do not believe this will be the case for much longer. As one of my favorite teachers likes to say, "You can't opt out of the twenty-first century."

Jaime Casap, Google
Global Education Evangelist

Preface

Change is the end result of all true learning.

—Leo Buscaglia

This book was born from the many conversations we have had with educators new to teaching in a technology-rich environment. We see a tremendous need when we work with colleagues at our own schools and especially when we present our work at conferences. Inevitably our presentations provoke questions and comments that begin with "Our school is getting a computer/laptop/tablet for every student next year, so I need to know...."

Every teacher and every classroom is as unique as every student. We can neither anticipate all the needs nor provide all the answers. You will undoubtedly need more training, resources, and practice in addition to reading this book, but we hope to show you that your efforts will make a difference for your students. We've organized the book around the principles of pedagogy that have guided good teaching for years—communication, engagement, collaboration, audience, differentiation, feedback, and creativity. We have also included chapters on rethinking the way we use time during class and on ways we connect with other educators. This book will guide you through the early stages of a 1:1 environment, but we also encourage you to come back to it as your comfort level with technology integration increases. Eventually, we hope to meet you and hear about how you have enriched, extended, and transformed your own classroom environment.

Starting a 1:1 program involves doing something you've never done before and figuring it out as you go. We are reminded of a passage in Anne Lamott's *Bird by Bird* in which she discusses the process of writing:

E. L. Doctorow once said that, "writing a novel is like driving a car at night. You can see only as far as your headlights, but you can make the whole trip that way." You don't have to see where you're going, you don't have to see your destination or everything you will pass along the way. You just have to see two or three feet ahead of you. This is right up there with the best advice about writing, or life, I have ever heard. (1994, 18)

Lamott's advice can apply to our 1:1 classrooms and the journey that is teaching with technology. There's no way to predetermine every pothole we will encounter or foresee every roadside attraction that may distract our students, and that's okay. But there's also no reason for traveling alone. We have provided a road map for you, informed by our successes and failures and written with the success of you and your students in mind. (We have used pseudonyms for all students mentioned in the book, as well as for any teachers who requested that we not use their names.) We hope you are making this journey with your colleagues. If you are collaborating, please see the study guide for professional learning communities, a free resource that you can download from www.stenhouse.com.

PlugInPowerUp.com

At our companion website, pluginpowerup.com, you will find links to the resources we reference in the following chapters. We will keep the site up to date with the latest resources as the tools, technology, and pedagogy for 1:1 learning evolve. You will also find our blog, links to current presentations, and our contact information posted there.

About the Authors

We both teach in a 1:1 environment and coach colleagues about technology integration. Although we are English and social science teachers, we find that the pedagogies afforded by 1:1 are cross-curricular. We spend much of our time assisting teachers in other subject areas, so we are ready to help you, no matter your specialty.

Jen Roberts has been teaching with 1:1 since early 2008 in a large, urban public high school in Southern California. (She also taught for twelve years before 1:1 in both middle and high school.) As one of the first teachers in her district to have 1:1, she had to figure out how a laptop for every student would work in her classroom. She experimented, refined, and reinvented her pedagogy, learning as much as her students along the way. When her whole district began to go 1:1 a few years later, Jen became a district trainer and eventually a Google Certified Teacher. Although she has a release period in her day to support colleagues, her focus is still on the teaching and learning that happens daily for her students.

Diana Neebe started teaching with 1:1 in 2009 at a large, suburban public high school with access to a computer cart that she could check out and roll into her classroom. Despite the long trek to get the cart to her classroom, Diana wanted her students to have access to a wider world. She currently teaches in an independent high school in the Silicon Valley with 1:1 iPads and has been one of the lead teachers for instructional technology since her school's pilot program rollout in 2011. Diana is also a Google Certified Teacher and, like Jen, spends part of her day supporting colleagues. She continues to innovate in her classroom so that her students can change the world.

Just a few years ago, we both started where you are now. Our best advice: take a deep breath, and take comfort in knowing that tens of thousands of other teachers are learning along with you. We know you are ready to plug in and power up!

Acknowledgments

A book is born from an idea. We owe the idea for this one to Heather Lattimer, who first introduced us to each other, then encouraged us to collaborate on presentations about 1:1 learning in our classrooms, and finally, over dinner in Las Vegas at NCTE 2012, said, "You two need to write this book."

An idea leads to a creation, and though we are the creators of this book, we owe a huge thanks to the many educators who welcomed us into their classrooms as observers, mentored us formally or informally, and supported our vision: Adam Bellow, Alison Black, Alyssa Black, Jaime Casap, Chris Chiang, Deenie Clinton, Jon Corippo, Eric Cross, J R Ginex-Orinion, Kavita Gupta, Roni Habib, Troy Hicks, Rushton Hurley, Carol Jago, Diane Main, Dan McDowell, Teddy Meckstroth, Fehmeen Picetti, Meenoo Rami, LeeAnn Rupley, and Mike Salamanca.

Our creativity was also supported by the wider community of connected educators all over the globe, who share generously in the spirit of learning. Specifically, we would like to thank the many colleagues who contribute to the learning communities that challenged us to refine our thinking, question our assumptions, and improve our practice: Google Certified Teachers, California Ed Chat (#CAedchat), ISTE, NCTE, MERIT, CUE, SDCUE, and our local Ed Camps.

A creation needs caretakers, and the phenomenal people at Stenhouse have taken care of this book from the moment they opened our first e-mail. Holly Holland, our amazing editor, read and reread every word for clarity and concision. All of what you are about to read makes more sense because she guided our revisions. Chris Downey and the entire production team made sure every detail was perfect from cover to cover and all the pages in between. The marketing team, led by Chuck Lerch, made sure teachers and administrators knew this book would help them in their mission to educate students for the future.

Authors need caretakers, too. We are both eternally grateful to our families, friends, and colleagues who have supported us through this process.

From Diana

I have had the privilege to work with and learn from a number of incredibly talented teachers, and the blessing of being paired with outstanding partners at each school in which I have taught. Thank you to my partner teachers for making me a better teacher, providing me perspective, and helping carry the load of teaching multiple preps and many students. I couldn't have made the journey without Fehmeen Picetti (my "work wife"), David Smock, David Clarke, Michelle Balmeo, Andrew Sturgill, and Matt Brashears.

To my English department colleagues at Sacred Heart, thank you for inspiring me with your creativity and dedication to your students, and for pushing my thinking about how and when to use technology. Special thanks to Stephanie Bowe Ullman, Mary Fitzsimons, Barb Intersimone, Jake Moffat, Colleen O'Donnell, Bridget Stefanski, and Connie Solari.

To my colleagues in our first 1:1 Certified Teacher Cohort, thank you for stretching my thinking through conversation, and for reminding me how innovative teachers can be when we set them loose with all the right tools: Marisa Beck, Elaine Cavalin, Gus Elmashni, Christiane Gautier, Clint Johns, Dana Jordan, Lisa Karna, Ana Maria Lasala, Lindsay Phillips, Jesus Ramos, Pati Ruiz, Sophie George Steplowski, Mike Taverna, and Serene Williams.

To my USF design team buddies, Melisa Kaye and Colette Roche, thank you for asking questions that made me think deeply, for offering resources that made me thirsty to learn more, and for accelerating my creativity with your own.

To my mentors and guides, thank you for leading the way, and for giving me opportunities to learn and grow: James Everitt, Heather Lattimer, Joy Lopez, Mary McBride, Mathew Mitchell, and April Scott.

To my dear friends Kate Dunkelberger, Teresa Filice, and Christy Utter, who have read draft after draft and who have endured long walks and talks over tea, brainstorming and refining ideas for chapters: thank you for the thoughtful insights you brought to the book—gleaned from your own teaching experience and given generously.

To my parents, Cathy and Steve Combs, who have believed in me and have been preparing me for this experience from the very start. For your fervent dedication to my education, your deep interest in the work I do, and your willingness to read every word of every chapter to check for commas . . . I am so grateful.

To my incredible husband, Steven. My contributions to this book simply would not have been possible without you. Thank you for the time to write and think, and for believing I could get it all done before the baby arrived. Encouraging me to write this book was a tremendous act of love, lived out daily through dinners made, loads of laundry completed, and dishes done.

From Jen

I am very grateful to have had the privilege of knowing and working with many amazing educators. I owe special gratitude to the colleagues with whom I have worked alongside at Point Loma High: Laura Baker, Ann Baltrushes, Hans Becker, Jenny Gardham, Hortencia Garcia, Kevin Gormly, Lisa Graham, Michele McConnell, Jaime Medina, Jeannine Milan, Jennifer Murphy, Anthony Palmiotto, Darren Samakosky, Bobbie Samilson, Chris Sparta, and many more.

To my ed tech tribe of Google Certified Teacher colleagues, who have taught me, entertained me, and made me rethink everything more than once: Alice Chen, Holly Clark, Nicole Dalesio, Jeff Heil, Lisa Highfill, Reuben Hoffman, Elizabeth Calhoon, Alice Keeler, Kelly Kermode, Will and Julie Kimbly, Mike Lawrence, Karl Lindgren-Streicher, John Miller, Kate Petty, Ken Shelton, John Stevens, Adina Sullivan, David Theriault, Catlin Tucker, Mark Wagner, and the MB Voxstars.

To those in our educational technology department (past and present) who answer my e-mails and even take my calls when I am stumped—Leigh Murrell, Mike Senise, Kelly O'Brien, Renea Jaeger, and Dan Stoneman—thank you for listening and understanding the vision.

To the people who have shown me what is possible with a new perspective: Bernie Dodge set me on the path toward this book before I even began teaching, by showing me early that technology makes a difference in education. Matt Spathas talked me into trying a 1:1 classroom pilot, which gave me a huge push to learn and innovate. Mary Lange constantly reminded me that it's the pedagogy, not the tools. My students, those in high school and those in graduate programs, have helped me by learning, growing, trying new things, and telling me what they really think. Over and over it is my students who have inspired me to reflect, try again, and find what works best for them.

To my parents-in-law, Judythe and Jim Roberts, for believing in my potential long before I saw it myself and also for the babysitting, dinners, and understanding that books don't write themselves.

To my parents, Anne and H. J. Brown, for letting me make my own decisions and then supporting them. For understanding when I used more bandwidth in a few days than they used in a month, and then buying more. For reading to my children when I was writing, and for reading to me when I was a child.

To my splendid husband, Kris Roberts, and our bouncing, brilliant boys. For your technical advice and your ability to fix anything. For backups restored, fences built, cats fed, and homework done. You all pitched in to keep our home and lives running while I disappeared behind an imaginary door to write. I couldn't have done it without your love and support.

CHAPTER 1

We Have 1:1; Now What?

Adding a digital device to the classroom without a fundamental change in the culture of teaching and learning will not lead to significant improvement.

—Alan November

Step into a 1:1 Classroom

Teacher: Jen Roberts
Class: Honors American Lit

It was a normal Wednesday in late May five years after I started teaching with 1:1. Students were streaming into my third-period class. I greeted them as they picked up their computers from the cart and headed for their seats. Philip balanced his laptop in one hand so that he could open it and hit the power button as he walked. Getting booted up and online as fast as possible is a daily mission for my students. A few of them glanced at the four extra adults in the back of the room, but then went back to their business. They are accustomed to visitors in our classroom.

With only a few weeks left in the school year, students were wrapping up their final projects. All year long, in short three- to five-day bursts between our other units, they had been researching a topic or question of interest to them. We referred to this as our Expert Project (Burke 2011). They went back over their previous blog posts and the feature articles they had written about their topics. In addition to publishing their writing, they would also present to the class, complete a video, make a pamphlet, or find some other creative way of sharing their learning.

To check on their progress, I asked them to complete an online form that I had added to the class blog. Besides telling me what they still had to work on, I wanted them to think through their next steps before completion. I watched their answers roll in on my spreadsheet and made a list of which students I would be checking on first. As I moved about the room answering questions and making suggestions, the visitors began to approach my students and ask what they were working on. I smiled as I watched Francis confidently explain how he had used news archives to find an article about the first use of an autopilot in 1929 for his project on the history of aviation.

"Mrs. Roberts had a video about how to use the news archive on the class blog," he said. "After I watched it a few times, I tried looking up *airplane* in different decades. I didn't know you could get news that far back."

Figure 1.1 Students work in a 1:1 classroom.

If you have never visited a fully functioning 1:1 classroom, seeing one for the first time can be a challenging experience. You may notice that students don't all have the same thing displayed on their screens, and that the teacher spends less time talking to the group and more time with individual students and small groups (see, for example, Figure 1.1). Instructions, tasks, and workflow may not be transparent to you because they are coordinated through an online platform. You will likely see students and the teacher using online tools you've never worked with before. Stay a little longer and talk to the students about the work they are doing. Ask the teacher questions about pedagogy and preparation. Remember that like all flourishing classrooms, the culture of a 1:1 classroom is built over time. The changes in process and pedagogy may seem overwhelming at first but will become transformative.

Common Questions About 1:1

Many teachers feel some "digital anxiety" (Kajder 2003) about teaching with 1:1. Even those who consider themselves very tech savvy know that there is a difference between feeling personally proficient with technology and feeling confident about using educational technology with students. The following questions are typical of what teachers new to 1:1 programs ask when we are mentoring them.

What is 1:1?

The ratio indicates that there is one computer, laptop, or tablet for each student. Some of the ways you use devices in your classroom will depend on the type of 1:1 program your school or district has adopted. Ideally, students will be able to use the computers all day at school and then take them home in the evening. Diana's school uses this model with iPads. Jen's school uses a classroom-only model, in which the district provides a cart with a class set of laptops. At the end of the period, students return the devices to the cart. A third and growing trend in some states is known as the bring-your-own-device model, or BYOD. Students provide their own devices and are supposed to bring them to school daily. By now you probably already know what kind of model your school will be using, so we won't go into the pros and cons of each in detail, but the chart in Figure 1.2 may help you anticipate some of the benefits and challenges of the structure with which you are working. The +/− row indicates things that can be both positive and negative, depending on the point of view or situation. For example, some teachers may think it is a positive that they control when students can access devices, but it may be a negative if it means students never open the cart.

	ALL-DAY 1:1, SCHOOL PROVIDED	CLASSROOM-ONLY 1:1, SCHOOL PROVIDED	BYOD (BRING YOUR OWN DEVICE)
Pros	• Students have the device at home and at school. • All students have the same device, same software, and so on. • School/district IT department supports needs and problems.	• All students have the same device, same software, and so on in the classroom. • Students always have a device because it is stored in the classroom.	• Students have the device at home and at school. • Low or no cost for schools because they aren't buying devices.
Cons	• Some students may forget to bring their device. • Students may forget to charge their device. • Loss and damage rates may be higher.	• Student can use the device only in the classroom and may not have access to a computer at home. • Instructional time can be lost distributing and returning equipment.	• Students bring a range of devices with different capabilities. • Some students may forget to bring their device. • Some families may not be able to afford a device or there may be a disparity in devices because of family income. • District IT department cannot easily provide tech support to all devices.
+/−		• Teachers can restrict student access to devices.	• Students have to master the capabilities of their particular device. • Some states currently limit BYOD policies and practices in public schools.

Figure 1.2 Types of 1:1 Models in Schools

Why do we need 1:1?

There is a common misconception that our students know all there is to know about technology because they have grown up in a digital age. Many students know how to post a status to a social network, but that is not an indicator that they will be able to critically evaluate online sources, effectively gather and process information for a research project (either personal or professional), or collaborate to produce high-quality content material, the skills that most employers want (Jerald 2009) and that colleges expect. Businesses have been sounding the sirens, warning us that students are "woefully ill-prepared" for the future that awaits them (Casner-Lotto, Barrington, and Wright 2006). No matter what their future plans are, students need to practice and learn with the tools that will enable them to function well in college and careers. We also believe, based on our experience in our own classrooms, that a 1:1 learning environment can be more efficient, deliver richer content, and provide greater support for students than traditional setups.

Educational researchers have long been making the case for computers in the classroom. Technology in the classroom creates the opportunity for students to experience authentic learning, to explore as well as implement ideas, to collaborate and problem-solve with peers, and to hone skills critical for their success (Partnership for 21st Century Skills 2014). These 1:1 programs also "[offer] educators effective ways to reach different types of learners and assess student understanding through multiple means" (Edutopia 2008). Moreover, educators increasingly recognize the value of incorporating digital content into their schools and classrooms, with 74 percent of administrators reporting that digital content increases student engagement and 50 percent reporting that it helps to personalize instruction (Project Tomorrow 2012).

Our classrooms become more relevant and purposeful spaces when we have a laptop or tablet in front of every child, every day. Students need us to show them how to use technology to learn, evaluate, and process information; to create, publish, and share their productions; and to help them see how their digital actions can have a ripple effect, both positive and negative, that spreads far beyond the classroom. Teachers, by nature of their clientele, need to be futurists, and the future is digital; we must prepare our students for that.

How is this going to change the way I teach?

The possibilities afforded by 1:1 are exciting and immeasurable. When all of our students have the tools to do high-quality work right there in the classroom or at home, they can get more done. It means more collaboration and differentiation in the classroom. For example, in Figures 1.3a and 1.3b you will see the differences in Jen's classroom dynamics, from the first year of 1:1 learning to the most recent year.

We will show you other examples of how 1:1 has changed our classrooms and others, but you will decide how to change your instruction. Don't worry, though. Having the technology in your classroom doesn't mean you have to use it every second of every day. Step into our classrooms and you will still see kids huddled around butcher paper, markers in hand, or students sitting in small groups having a face-to-face conversation, or goofy teenagers putting on a paper-bag-puppet show. We use technology when we know it is the right tool for the job.

Education is going to change, and it's probably redundant to mention that change can be scary. You can make changes as you are ready. We encourage you to be thoughtful about how you adapt your teaching to the 1:1 environment and how you can make 1:1 adapt to you. What works for the teacher

Figure 1.3a In 2008, students had their own computers in Jen's first 1:1 classroom, but their learning setup was still very traditional.

Figure 1.3b Currently, students in Jen's classroom are more likely to use the tools of 1:1 learning to collaborate and engage.

down the hall might not work for you, but it is important to take the time to find out why it is working for him or her. Research indicates that it take three to five years for a teacher to effectively integrate a new technology into his or her classroom (Mosley 2013). In general, it means less you and more them. This will change the way you teach, but you can change at your own pace.

How am I ever going to catch up and learn what I need to know to teach with technology?

There is a lot happening in the educational technology field right now. It's really a very exciting time to be a teacher. We adopt new tools that improve our teaching and learning on a regular basis, but we can't learn about everything. No one can. We have just adjusted ourselves to a new mind-set—accepting ongoing change as part of the learning process. You don't have to catch up; you just need to plug in. You don't need to know everything that came before, just find out what's happening now.

There are many ways to start learning more about what is happening in the world of 1:1 teaching; this book is just one of them. Look online for diverse and flourishing groups of teachers sharing resources, having conversations, and blogging about their 1:1 classrooms. See if there is an Edcamp conference being organized in your area. These are free "unconferences" (http://edcamp.org/), where the participants determine the discussion sessions. They offer opportunities to network with other innovative teachers, and they often have a technology focus. Look for an online group specific to the subject area you teach. If you already belong to a national organization for your subject, they probably have an online group you can join. And take a look at Chapter 10 on becoming a connected educator. The teachers who are already a part of these groups enjoy helping others get started.

When it comes to pesky technical questions such as "How do I add collaborators to a Google Doc?" try searching on YouTube. You'd be amazed by how many short, user-friendly tutorials are available on a wide range of technical subjects, ranging from videos for beginners all the way to very advanced tricks and tips. A few minutes of searching and watching can save you a lot of time and frustration if you need to learn how to do something.

We use our learning about educational technology as a way to model lifelong learning for our students. We keep up with new developments through our professional connections, conferences, and professional reading. It requires time and effort, but the "aha" moments are worth it. Learn as you go, add new pedagogy and tools to your classroom when they work for your students, and share what you discover with the next teacher wondering how to get started.

What if I just don't have time for all this technology?

We are teachers too, and we know that you are very pressed for time. We aren't going to lie to you: learning what you need to know and setting up the digital parts of your classroom will take time. Yet we have both found that "going digital" has also saved us time, so much so that we found time to write a book about it! Diana finds a lot of time saved in assessment. Jen finds a lot of time saved in lesson preparation. We both find time saved through differentiation, which allows us to facilitate and coach all students individually. There are still only twenty-four hours in a day, and the other parts of your life aren't going away. Keep in mind that some tech tasks require a big time investment to get started but will save you time in the long run. Also, some things that take you a long time to do the first time become easier and faster each time you use them.

Beyond the learning curve, many teachers worry that "all this technology" means that we are always on—that we no longer get a break from school like we once did. As we place devices in the hands of students, we run the risk of allowing their questions and needs to seep into all of the free space in our lives. But just because students, parents, and colleagues *can* e-mail us at all hours of the day and night doesn't mean that we need to respond immediately or feel tethered to our smartphones and laptops. We know plenty of teachers who observe e-mail-free evenings, or who only check the learning management system once at night after their kids go to bed. How you define your boundaries is up to you. Communicate those boundaries with your students; in doing so, you are modeling a more balanced approach to navigating today's tech-centric world.

What about distractions on the Internet?

Yes, there are many. Students want to check their e-mail, view sports scores, or, here in coastal California, see what the waves are like, but they still have work to get done. In our classrooms, this is another teachable moment. Students, like adults, need to learn to manage their online behavior, and teachers can help. If you set clear expectations and respond appropriately to off-task students, you will find this is a minor issue. Separate the behavior from the technology. A distracted student is nothing new. Students choose their Internet destinations and can learn to choose wisely. You can set up policies for your classroom, such as asking students to turn their screens to face you when you are giving instructions, and you can establish expectations about on-task behavior. You can offer students a list of acceptable sites they can spend time on when they've finished their work and tell them they must ask before going anywhere else. You cannot eliminate distractions, but you can set clear expectations about the work that needs to get done while students are in your class.

What about students who don't have Internet at home?

We know that not all families have reliable or regular access to the Internet. However, the number of students who tell us they don't have Internet access at home gets smaller every year. When the rare parent expresses concern, Jen's response is always the same: "If you don't have a computer or Internet access at home, that's the best reason to make sure your student stays in my class. Where else will he or she learn those skills?" Parents always walk away from these conversations persuaded that Jen will be supportive and flexible and that using a computer in the classroom will ultimately benefit their children.

Make sure there are ways for students to get online after school on your campus. Open your classroom at lunch. Allow multiple days to complete online assignments, so students without Internet at home have time to work at school. A student without Internet access at home *or* at school is truly being left behind.

How do I keep students from searching the Internet for answers?

This is a very common concern among teachers, with good reason. We have all seen student work that included poorly cited material from a website or, worse, was lifted entirely from an essay-selling clearinghouse. World language teachers are coping with the vagaries of online translation, especially when they ask students to write papers at home. These new electronic capacities create challenges for both what and how we teach. This is not new. Socrates, as quoted by Phaedrus, said of writing, "It will introduce forgetfulness into the soul of those who learn it: they will not practice using their memory because they will put their trust in writing." He could have been talking about Internet searches today. So, just as Jen required her sixth-grade son to do his math homework at the kitchen table to be sure he did not rely on a calculator, teachers in an Internet age will have to adapt their teaching and assessment practices to account for Internet-aided student work.

The answer, we think, is to turn the problem into a solution. Having easy access to an Internet search means students can focus on analyzing and synthesizing information. Yes, students need to have certain basic knowledge, but what that knowledge is (or should be) is a cultural construct of each generation. Search is here to stay, and we can teach students to use it to answer basic questions. But search is not the same as research (see Appendix B, "Teaching Search Skills"). Having basic answers at their fingertips means students can move on to higher-level investigations. Students can quickly look up the dates of a presidency, but can they gather evidence about which president made the most effective social reforms and then make an argument based on their findings? Several of our lesson examples later in the book model how to leverage search and other online tools to encourage critical thinking.

How do I get started?

Planning is the key to the success of any lesson, and it is key to the success of a 1:1 implementation in your classroom. Begin if you can by visiting other classrooms where students are already using devices daily. You don't have to stay long, and if you can stop in for a short time over several days or weeks, that's even better. Try to be there for the beginning and end of class if you can, and be sure to ask the teacher and students questions about what they are working on. Gather ideas, see how the teacher manages the students and the technology, and decide how those techniques will apply in your own classroom. Initial visits will probably give you more questions than answers. Keep learning.

In the middle of each chapter, we offer you some suggestions and challenges to get started. We call this the Plug In. These are usually short-term, concrete steps you can take to adjust to teaching with a 1:1 classroom. When you get to the end of each chapter, you will find the Power Up, more suggestions and challenges to take you even further into your exploration of the concepts in the chapter. We encourage you to try at least several of the things in each Plug In and Power Up section.

PLUG IN Some Simple Steps for Getting Started

1. **Know what type of 1:1 program** you will be working with. Will your students be given a device or will they bring their own? Do they get to have them at home and at school? How does your school or district leadership envision the way students will use 1:1 in the classroom? Spend some time considering the pros and cons of the 1:1 program you will be working with.

2. **Connect with other teachers** online. Many online teacher groups are devoted to helping support you and your colleagues as you make this transition. We recommend starting with Twitter or an online group specific to your subject area. There is more information about becoming a connected educator in Chapter 10.

3. **Visit a 1:1 classroom**. If possible visit one similar to the 1:1 model you will be working with. Talk to the students and the teacher. We think you'll have plenty of questions of your own, but you might also try asking some of the questions that we tried to answer for you in the section above. See what another 1:1 teacher thinks about those queries.

Before You Begin

Getting ready to use computers or tablets or any device with all of your students is a big step. Here are some points to consider before you hit those power buttons:

Know Your District's Acceptable Use Policy (AUP)

This is a document that you and your students should all be expected to sign before using a computing device in the classroom. A typical AUP lists the types of prohibited behaviors that students should not do with the device. Usually, this includes not visiting inappropriate websites, not downloading copyrighted material, and not defeating the district Internet content filters. Ideally, your district already has an acceptable use policy. If not, you can visit pluginpowerup.com, where we offer several sample AUPs in the Resources section of the site. How you review the AUP with your students will depend on their ages and their previous experience with using technology in the classroom. This is an excellent time to set your own expectations as well.

In addition to the acceptable use policy you should be familiar with the types of material and websites blocked by your school or district's Internet content filters. See Figure 1.4 for some information about content filtering for schools.

The federal Children's Internet Protection Act (2000) requires schools and libraries to filter obscene Internet content. So, almost all schools and districts have some kind of Internet content filter. The filter will prevent students from visiting prohibited websites, such as those that include pornography, but will also likely block sites that refer to drugs, and social media sites like Facebook and Twitter. Some districts have very strict policies and others are more open. It is a good idea to check that a site you want to use with students is not blocked at your school site. The easiest way to check is to try to access the site while you are at school. It is also a good idea to know who you should contact to ask to have sites "white listed" or added to the list of acceptable sites. Be prepared to make a case for the educational value of the site you are asking for access too. We suggest you develop a good working relationship with the people who oversee the content filter.

Figure 1.4 Internet Content Filters

Know Your Own Expectations

In addition to familiarizing yourself with the district policy, you should create and review classroom expectations with students about using devices. Asking other teachers about their rules is a great way to gather ideas before writing or co-creating your own. Having a school or grade-level set of expectations is also helpful. There are obvious rules, such as prohibiting food and drinks other than water. But there are also less obvious rules to consider, such as asking students not to touch each other's computers or tablets. We both include that rule not only to prevent mischief, but also to encourage students to use words and explain the steps to solve a problem when they want to help a peer. This benefits both students, because the helper has to be clear and articulate about the solution, and the student being helped gets the hands-on experience of fixing his or her own issue. We'd also suggest that you ask the students about their expectations. How do they expect to use their devices in the classroom? They probably have some great ideas to share.

Know Your Management Style

Think about how you want to manage devices in the classroom. Your answer may depend on the type of 1:1 program at your school. We recommend revisiting the following questions several times during the year as you become more comfortable with 1:1 implementation.

- Where will student devices be at the beginning of class? On desks? Still in the cart? Powered on or off? If you teach multiple periods in a day like we do, you may find this answer changes depending on the period.
- How will you signal to students that you want their eyes on you?
- What should students do with their devices to signal that they are listening?

- How and when will students pack up their devices at the end of class?
- Are there traffic flow patterns to be considered? (This is an especially important consideration with a cart model.)
- What are your policies about headphones, volume, and music sites? (If you have limited Internet bandwidth, you should limit the use of sites that stream music because they will slow down access for other students.)
- How should students handle a technical problem with their device?
- What are the rules and expectations about printing?

Get to Know the Device Students Have

If your school or district is providing students with devices, then the device your students have is likely different from the computer you already use and know. Borrow a student device from your IT department or ed tech office and try using it for some of your authentic tasks. Send some e-mail, open available applications, see how the camera works, and play with it. Make sure you know how to control the sound, turn the wireless on and off, save work, and turn in work. Attend a training session specific to that device, if possible. Search the name of the device and "tutorial" for helpful videos that might teach you some timesaving tips. See if you can figure out some tricks for quickly hiding what you are working on when someone else walks in. This will help you recognize those behaviors when you see students try them. Let some students use the device while you watch to see what they do with it. Ask them how this technology could be used in class. What can they teach you? Ask them what kinds of problems you should watch out for. Consider training them to be your tech experts, responsible for helping you maintain the equipment.

Rethink Your Classroom Routines

How would your daily routines for students change if they were doing them digitally? Diana swapped paper reading logs for Goodreads updates online when her classes went 1:1. Jen was able to have students move the spiral notebook they usually kept for class notes and journal entries into a Google Doc. A science teacher with tablets now has her students take lab notes in an app that lets them include pictures of their experiment as they go. Exit slips can be collected electronically, and assessments can be done digitally as well. Each of these adjustments requires some learning time for you and for students, but they ultimately save you class time and preparation time, not to mention a lot of paper.

Commit to One Small Solution

Many new-to-tech teachers find temporary solace in assigning one job to the device in students' hands, such as "We will use it to type when they finish their handwritten drafts" or "We just use it for Internet searches." Once you get the basics down, start brainstorming challenges you have in your classroom and look for ways that the computer/tablet can provide your solution. We have seen baby-step breakthroughs in classrooms of tech novices who commit to one small adjustment. Here are some examples of real teachers who have recently walked in your shoes:

- A Spanish teacher had high hopes of conferencing with every student each grading period, but couldn't find the time for oral exams. She switched to video conversations in which she gives students a prompt, and they send her a video recording of themselves speaking. She still gets to hear students' accents and conversation skills but is no longer confined by the hours of the school day.
- A resourceful biology teacher, constrained by the school budget, was tired of offering only one dissection per year. He now runs virtual experiments and dissections on a regular basis, using the 1:1 devices in his classroom.
- A veteran English teacher was frustrated that vocabulary instruction always got bumped at the end of each class. She now asks students to compete online as they play vocabulary games on Quizlet.com.
- A teacher of special education, watching her students struggle to remember due dates, set up "tasks" and "auto-reminders" to send prompts and reminders the night before important deadlines.
- A math teacher knew his students struggled with homework. He set up an Edmodo class so that students could post questions. He found they often answered each other before he had returned home from school.
- A history teacher, tired of calling on the same students over and over, decided to try a class discussion app that allowed all students to answer the questions he was asking and brought new ideas into the conversation.

In each of these cases, the teacher saw a need and found a way to use 1:1 technology for a solution. You'll also notice that, with the exception of the dissection example, most of these small solutions could be applied in almost any classroom. We have been delightfully impressed by how well tablets and laptops work to supplement a tight budget, extend instructional time, increase engagement, and support students outside of the classroom. A problem is a great place to start!

Tips for Day One with Devices

We suggest teachers set a low bar for the first few days with student devices. Don't expect to launch a project, cover curriculum, or even have things go smoothly. When Jen uses laptops with her students for the first time each year, her main goal is to get them all logged in (really!). Between tech issues and passwords forgotten over the summer, this can be a stretch. Her second goal is to have all the students visit and bookmark her class blog. That means students have to launch a browser, type in the URL correctly, and figure out how to make a bookmark for it. When they get to the blog, they find links there to take them to other activities. Meanwhile, Jen can help anyone who is still stuck. During the first week of class, Diana teaches her students how to use one note-taking app (Notability) and one organized storage system (Google Drive). They practice using those two essential apps every day for a week before she tries more. Students will quickly get the hang of these basic steps when they practice them daily, but to begin with, start small.

During Class Time and Beyond

Most of the rest of the book focuses on planning for instruction and what to do when students are in your room with their laptops or tablets. That is the work of teaching and learning. Here, we offer just a few general tips about the nuts and bolts of running a 1:1 classroom.

Expect the Unexpected

We guarantee you that lessons will not always go smoothly. The website you used last week could be blocked by the content filter this week. The power will go out. The app you were sure was free no longer will be. Your display cable will fail. The bulb in your projector will burn out. The school Internet will shut down. Your students will find something inappropriate. Someone will copy (or delete) someone else's work. We could go on, but we think that's enough to terrify you for a while. All of these issues are temporary, solvable, and rare, but they might slow you down for a day or two. Have a backup plan, and don't panic. It is tempting to give in to frustration and vent a bit when things like this go wrong, but remember: your students are watching you. To them, you are a model of how to cope with adversity. Remain calm. Switch to your backup plan. Shrug your shoulders. Tell them you have some ideas for troubleshooting, but you don't want to waste any more of their class time. Express disappointment, and let them know you will try again tomorrow.

But, just as often, the unexpected can be fabulous: a student finds a great site that the class can all use, a student teaches you how to do something new, an app or website you've been using gets a redesign and adds new features that make it possible to create in new ways. Educational technology innovators are constantly making their applications better. There are hundreds of ed tech startup companies working daily to create new tools to improve education in some way. All of them are aimed at helping teachers and students be more efficient, communicate more effectively, manage information gathering, or master material. Change is the new normal. Most of it will come when you least expect it, and in most cases it will be awesome!

Walk Around

We want to trust our students, and we know that most of them are on task most of the time, but a little adult supervision goes a long way. Knowing what is on our students' screens is part of our process. Jen is lucky to have some fancy software that would let her monitor her students' laptops from an underground bunker in an undisclosed location, but even that is a poor substitute for being out among the students. In her first week with 1:1, a student in Jen's class complained that he was having trouble reading the projected text from the back of the room. Jen walked to the back to see it from his perspective. She discovered that the text was a little too small, so she fixed that problem, but she also noticed what a great view she had from the back of the room. From the middle of the back row she had a clear view of almost every student's screen. This place became her new favorite spot. She bought a remote clicker so she could control her own computer from the back when she needed to, and started spending the period *among* her students. Whatever you do, get up and get out there. Students are much more likely to ask for help if you are closer. You will have a better idea of what they are doing. Your presence will reduce distracted behavior and solve many of the management problems people worry about with 1:1 programs.

Some other suggestions for classroom management:

- Diana uses iPad mirroring software (Reflector App) and requires off-task students to show her what their devices are displaying on their screens through AirPlay.
- Jen replaced the comfy desk chair that came with her new digital classroom with a stool. The uncomfortable seat at the front of the room reminds her to get up.
- Some teachers hang a big convex mirror in the back of the room, like those used in convenience stores to deter theft, to help them see student screens.
- Electronic management products such as LanSchool will let you see all student screens at once and even take over a student's laptop if you need to.
- Set up a cue to have all students show you their screens on demand by holding up their tablet or turning their laptop.
- If you must be at the front of the room, watch the faces of the students. A student doing something off task with his or her computer will attract the attention of other students.
- When you are planning to conference with a student or work with a small group, position yourself so you can see other screens at a glance. (This is why we both hold writing conferences in the back of the room.)
- When students are working in groups, move around. There is no electronic substitute for your presence among them.

Give Students Time to Work

In the old paradigm of school, students were expected to passively absorb information by day and then go home and produce their own response or regurgitation alone as homework. Okay, that is vastly oversimplified, but we also think it is basically true. In a 1:1 classroom your students have the tools to produce high-quality work in your classroom. Let them work.

This is a good time to investigate the process of project-based learning and to remember that manipulating and synthesizing material is a far better path to retention than listening to a lesson about the same content. The Common Core State Standards focus on what students can do, so you likely will devote lots of class time to letting students get something done. You can find more information about the ways we have been rethinking our class time in Chapter 9.

At the End of the Day

We know teachers aren't finished when the last bell rings. The tasks and reflective processes in a 1:1 classroom aren't so different from what we did before 1:1. We are still going to assess, reflect, and plan next steps for our students. Our workflow just might be a bit different.

Jen at the End of the Day

My room gets pretty quiet at the end of the day, if you don't count the music from the dance team practicing in the mezzanine outside my classroom. This is my chance to sit down and look at how my student projects are going. At the moment, they are working on an article about their research topics. My students share all of their articles with me in Google Drive, and I want to see what they need. I'm looking to assess their progress as well as to find examples I can use as models. I'm also looking for trends that could indicate the need for a specific intervention or mini-lesson. With the preview feature in Google Drive, I can use the arrow keys on my computer to move through the students' documents as if I were flipping through a stack of papers. (It's one of those unexpectedly fabulous features that Google added one day.)

Very quickly I can see that most of my students have a good start on a draft. I make some notes about a few who seem stuck so I can check with them directly tomorrow. I notice that many have articles that read more like research papers. There is a "just the facts" quality to almost all of them. My students and I have read feature articles that integrate nonfiction narratives with expository passages, and I have emphasized the dual nature of a feature article in both our reading and writing lessons. But they are used to seeing narrative and expository as separate genres and don't know how to blend them. Finally, I come to a paper that leads with a narrative about a piece of trash flowing into the storm drain and out into the ocean. The writer buttresses the story with statistics about trash in the ocean and then comes back to that piece of trash as it turns in the great Pacific Ocean garbage patch. Written by a second language learner, the draft has numerous mechanical errors, but the ideas and voice are right. I know the student well, and I smile, knowing she will be pleased to see her writing used as an example.

Here I pause and ponder how best to structure this mini-lesson. I could share a copy of her paper with everyone in a view-only folder. Or I could project it in class and talk about what is working well. Sharing a copy means students can see the document, but they may not realize what they should be looking for in the article. I decide that projecting it on the screen and discussing it would be better, but still, absent students will miss that discussion. So instead, I launch my screencasting software and made a quick recording of my computer screen with the model article on it. I scroll through her paper and talk about how effectively she uses the narrative to draw the reader into her article. It takes only a few minutes. Although far from perfect, the two-minute video will be featured on the class blog to show students, and they can refer to it later. At the end of the video, I challenge them to go to their article and try adding some narrative about a person or event related to their topic.

Within this short after-school session, I have rediscovered the value of 1:1 learning. I was able to quickly see my students' work in draft form and draw conclusions about the next lesson they need. Because they all have access to the class blog, they can watch and rewatch the writing lesson I will show them tomorrow. And because they all have laptops, they can begin substantial revisions to their own writing during class, a process I will be able to view both during class and at the end of the day tomorrow.

Diana at the End of the Day

The last of my students walk out the door, and I can feel myself joining the collective exhale of teachers everywhere as I sit down and put my feet up. The end of the day feels self-indulgently mine. After scrolling through my e-mail and responding to anything that seems urgent, I spend a few moments reflecting on the day. Updating my class website is my meditation on today's victories and flops. I start by typing in our agenda, and fill it out with links to handouts and pictures of our notes from the whiteboard. I know that a few of the students who were absent today will be looking to get caught up tonight. I love knowing that every class of the year has been recorded in this fashion, so our fleeting sixty minutes will be preserved in a time capsule for next fall when I'm desperately trying to remember how many days it took us to read each text. My freshmen just started *The Odyssey* and usually struggle with the first few nights of reading even a hundred lines of the epic poem. I take a few minutes to set up their online support network for the evening's reading: a quick paragraph that previews the plot, a link to a funny YouTube video called 60-Second Recap that will put the section in context when they are finished, a couple of comprehension questions, and a public domain painting of Odysseus stranded on Calypso's Island. I update the start and stop times for the audio track if they are listening while they read, and click to make the post "live."

Confident that students will be equipped to complete the homework tonight, I pull up their exit slips to figure out what I need to know for tomorrow. At a glance, I have responses from all of my students on one page: 70 percent of my students can explain what an epithet is and how Homer uses it in the prologue, 32 percent understand the allusion to the Trojan horse and can connect it to their history classes from middle school, and 86 percent predict that Odysseus will eventually find his way home. I also have a list of questions that students have so far about Greek cultural terms; I'll address those in class tomorrow. My greatest concern right now is finding ways to support reading comprehension and to make my support present when they walk out my door. I will check the class reading support discussion board tonight before I go to bed to clear up any confusion, but in the meantime, I will trust my students to help each other out.

What's Different?

We both have immediate access to our students' work through shared documents and surveys, so we don't have to wait until the next class before looking at their progress. Daily, we can look at samples of student work and questions and adjust accordingly. Not all 1:1 programs support this kind of interaction, but having students interact with you digitally means that it is quite simple to gather multiple formative assessments of their progress and to make sure your lessons are timely and, if needed, differentiated based on students' needs. It becomes much easier to incorporate student work and questions into your lessons, often in real time. And both of our models for supporting student learning—whether in reading or in writing—are completely paperless, thus saving us from the purgatory of the copy room.

What's the Same?

We still spend time looking at student work to determine students' needs. We still plan lessons and student conferences to meet those needs. We still use a variety of formative and summative assessments. Good teaching is still good teaching. The devices in our classrooms do not separate us from our students; rather, they put us in closer collaboration.

Shooting for the Moon

The path to a digital classroom is long. As we have said, it usually takes three to five years for a teacher to make the transition. Try thinking of this as your own personal Apollo program. NASA specialists used each mission in the program to add and test some capability that they would need to get Apollo 11 to the moon. First, they had to prove that they could get a spacecraft into orbit and back to Earth. Then they had to prove they could dock two spacecraft in orbit. Each mission built capacity.

Apply this concept to your classroom. Think of your initial steps for your digital classroom as getting into orbit. At this stage you are mastering the basics, testing tools you may want to use in a more sophisticated way later. In many ways you are creating a digital copy of steps you now do on paper. That's fine. As you learn to use digital tools to duplicate what you already do, we know you will begin to see possibilities in those tools to go beyond what you already do. With each project you do with your students, you will be testing a new capacity that you will likely build on with the next project.

TECH for Teachers and Students

Handoff: Students' interests drive the learning experience with teacher guidance and the flexible choice of tools and technologies to achieve an authentic and exemplary product.

Choice: Teacher sets broad goals for student learning and offers a choice of tasks using a specified range of available tools.

Enhanced: Teacher integrates multiple tech tools to create an enhanced learning experience for students.

Traditional: Teacher designs the task using traditional pedagogy with technology supports.

Created by: Jen Roberts @JenRoberts1

Figure 1.5 We explain the acronym TECH for teachers and students.

You might find our TECH model helpful (see Figure 1.5). Jen created this after one of our conversations about the SAMR model by Dr. Rueben Puentedura. SAMR categorizes classroom tasks that use technology as substitution, augmentation, modification, or redefinition, but we didn't find the language of the SAMR model to be supportive of teachers new to technology. TECH may help you rethink your classroom practices as you move with your students from traditional pedagogy into technology-enhanced activities that will eventually give students more choices and more responsibility.

The early chapters of this book will show you some of the ways other 1:1 teachers have taken their students into orbit. The latter chapters will show you some instances of teachers doing projects they could not have done before a 1:1 program. These folks have had time to adjust to their digital classrooms, and now they are shooting for the moon.

POWER UP! Taking Your Preparation to the Next Level

1. **Read your school's or district's Acceptable Use Policy (AUP).** It might have another name like "Student Use Agreement." It's important to know the rules for student use and consider how you will explain and enforce those expectations with your students.

2. **Test drive the student device.** If all of your students will have the same device, get your hands on one as far in advance as possible. Call your IT department or Technology Coordinator and ask to borrow a student device. If that fails, it may even be worth picking up a similar model used through an online reseller or running a Donor's Choose project to fund the purchase of a new one.

3. **Commit to one small solution.** Think of one problem or friction point in your classroom that might be smoother with a tech solution. Talk to other 1:1 teachers if you need help with what that solution might be. Ask about it on Twitter and include hashtags like #edchat and #edtech to reach a wider audience.

Part I

ENRICH

En·rich (v): *To improve or enhance the quality or value.*

How does a 1:1 classroom improve the value of the education we provide our students so that the process of learning enriches their lives?

CHAPTER 2
Communication and Workflow

Com·mu·ni·ca·tion (n): The imparting or exchanging of information or news.

Teacher: Connor McGee
Class: 7th Grade Science
Observer: Jen Roberts

The human heart is a miraculous thing. It beats constantly for our entire lives, and we hardly ever think about it. The students in Connor McGee's seventh-grade science class were thinking about it, though, and learning in the process. Their school is in southeast San Diego, a lower-socioeconomic neighborhood where most students do not have Internet access at home. Although McGee's students represent those on the disadvantaged side of the digital divide, they are ready to use computers in the classroom to learn.

Their day began as usual with a warm-up question on the board and their spiral science notebooks on their desks. "What structure makes the sound of your heart?" McGee echoed the question on the board. After students had identified valves as the source of the *lub-dub* noise in their chests, he asked some further questions. "Do you think all hearts sound the same? What might make one heart sound different from another? Did you know doctors can use heart sounds to diagnose heart problems?" He gave students a chance to think about and answer these questions before sending one student from each table to the computer cart to bring back a laptop for each person at their four-person table.

A list on the board outlined the tasks for students. The first task was the warm-up question, and the second directed students to log in to McGee's Moodle page. On the screen up front, McGee flipped through several links and pages of his site to get down into the material he wanted students to focus on. I'm not a regular Moodle user, and the navigation process moved too fast for me to follow, but the students were familiar with it, and they all seemed to land on the right page within a few moments.

I found a student working alone in the back of the room and asked her what she was learning about. She smiled shyly, unaccustomed to visitors, but showed me the chart she had in her notebook and explained how she would take notes about what she found online. McGee had set up the page in a grid that matched her notes. For each of four different heart valve problems the student read website descriptions (most were from the Mayo Clinic) of the condition and then returned to her teacher's web page to click a link and listen to an audio clip of what a heart with that condition sounds like. She put in her earbuds to listen to the first clip. She played it several times and then wrote "*Lub Dub Dub*" in her notebook to describe the sound.

Another student had finished his exploration of the four conditions and moved on to the next step in the assignment. He was looking at another page of McGee's site that had four sound links; he had to correctly identify which condition he was hearing for each link. A boy next to him was rapidly taking notes from another web page. He explained that he had been absent the day before and wanted to catch up on his notes so he could get to the heart sounds that his classmates were exploring.

McGee and I wandered the room. He spent a minute or two to check in with each child and redirected students who wanted to socialize instead of listen to heartbeats. I stopped when I came to a student who had something entirely different on her screen. She was using her computer track pad to direct an animated scalpel across an animated heart, to complete a virtual heart transplant. The animation told her what to do at each step, but it used very specific anatomical vocabulary. I asked the student why she was doing the transplant instead of listening to the heart sounds. She showed me her notes about the heart sounds and explained that the virtual heart transplant was the next activity on McGee's Moodle page. When I asked him about it after class, he said, "I know they won't all get there, but for the students who finish faster, the heart transplant seemed like a neat experience for them to get to have. I found it on a medical school website."

Just a few years ago these students would have been learning about the human heart from a textbook. They might have heard the sounds if the teacher had brought in some speakers and played each example at his discretion. They would not have been gathering current facts from websites or listening to each heart sound as many times as they needed to hear it. A skilled teacher had transformed this learning experience with access to some simple online resources available to anyone with an Internet connection. What made this lesson work so well was McGee's Moodle site. From one central starting point students could reach the resources they needed to do the investigation in class. The teacher had already invested the time to build a site using Moodle, but he could have used a variety of learning management systems. The platform is not crucial, but the centrality of a consistent, online starting point for students makes the management of a 1:1 classroom much more efficient. You might call it the heart of a 1:1 classroom.

Using a Learning Management System

In a 1:1 classroom, having an easy-to-use communication system simplifies the exchange of information among teachers and students. The mantra in Jen's classroom is "Turn on, log in, go to the blog." Her class blog provides the daily directions, links, reminders, and resources that students need. Alternatively, because Diana's students take their devices home with them, her web-based classroom hub serves its purpose when students walk out the door. She uses Schoology as her learning management system. Having one place where students can easily access the links and information you have provided is an indispensable part of a 1:1 program.

Learning management system (LMS) is the generic term for an online classroom hub. You may have a choice about the LMS you use, or your school may require you to use a specific platform. Some are paid services with a lot of options and some are free, generally with fewer options. Usually, an LMS is limited to the instructor and the students enrolled in the course, a walled garden to protect students and keep class communications private. Schoology, Canvas, SchoolLoop, Edmodo, Blackboard, Moodle, and Google Classroom are some of the common systems. Each is a bit different, but all perform the same basic functions. Students log in to the LMS to see the work assigned to them, access course resources, contribute to online discussions, turn in assignments, and sometimes, take assessments.

Most 1:1 implementations include an adopted LMS. Your school or district should be able to give you training and support to use it. Despite the initial learning curve for teachers and students, a robust LMS will save you time in the long run and can facilitate class communications. Ask other teachers to show you how they use the LMS, and search online for video tutorials. Although courses can be conducted entirely online, your students will still be attending class with you. Your physical classroom space is augmented by the LMS and becomes a "blended" learning environment. (See Chapter 9 for more on blended learning.)

A great advantage of using an LMS with students is the ability to share the digital version of your course with collaborating colleagues and duplicate it for yourself in other years. Although we all make changes and improvements to our courses year after year, we find it nice to have an easy-to-revise platform. Jen has a great story of a student teacher who wanted to know more about teaching *Walden* by Thoreau. Jen suggested she search [Walden] on the class blog. Four previous lessons Jen had taught related to *Walden* came up, each a bit different. The student teacher was able to view the options and then craft her own lessons based on the ideas she found on Jen's classroom blog.

We encourage you to use the LMS supported by your school or district, but you should also consider whether you are likely to change schools in the near future. We know several teachers who have lost access to all the content they created on a particular LMS when they changed schools or districts. Of course, your school administration may mandate a particular LMS for the sake of consistency, but if you have a choice and think you may move schools, consider managing your class through a blog, Edmodo site, or something else to which you will still have access after you move.

Communication Is Crucial

To use an LMS well, teachers must communicate effectively about both subject content and classroom logistics. Students must know the material they need to learn, but they also need to know assignment expectations and procedures for submitting work, understand grading policies, and know how and when to seek assistance.

Begin by taking a hard look at how your classroom runs. What is your teaching style? What are your beliefs about how students learn best? What is already working in your classroom that you want to keep or improve? What do you wish you had more time or resources to do? We would love to sit down with you, discuss those questions, and help you customize a digital version of your classroom that works for you and your students. Because we can't be there in person, we hope this chapter will get you started.

Having a robust LMS, class blog, or website should be your primary communication piece. We have trained our students to check online before coming to ask us what they missed while they were absent. Parents can also check the class site to find more information about projects, due dates, and course materials. Students can help each other with questions if the LMS you use allows for discussions. Teachers frequently tell us stories of students asking and answering each other's homework questions before the teacher has a chance to get online.

In addition to an LMS, you could try other communication tools, such as the ones listed here:

- **Remind.com:** Safe and private, Remind offers one-way text messaging to your classes. Students and parents can sign up to get text or e-mail messages from you. Remind is great for sharing important reminders and for sending messages to groups you may not see often, such as school clubs you advise or a team you coach. Students and teachers never see each other's phone numbers, so Remind will work with almost all privacy policies. Teachers can log in to the Remind.com website or a mobile app to send and schedule messages.
- **Google Voice:** It allows two-way communication and keeps a record of all messages. This free service does not count as a text message with your wireless carrier. Best of all, text messages also appear in our e-mail, and when we respond to students, they receive it as a text message. Google Voice allows you to set do-not-disturb hours and block harassing calls, but we've never had to use either of those features. We find that students are incredibly respectful and grateful about being able to text us for a quick bit of help after school.

- **Facebook Page:** A community Facebook page is different from a personal account. When students "like" the class page, they do not become your Facebook "friends." You will be able to see only what is public on their profile, but the students will see the posts from the page in their activity feed. Check that your school or district social media policy does not exclude this option.
- **Twitter:** Many teachers are setting up class Twitter accounts to tweet short messages about what the class is learning and to connect with other classes. Again, be aware of social media policies, and remember that your tweets are public.
- **Photo Sharing:** Instagram, Vine, and other photo- and video-sharing sites can also be fun communication tools for students and parents. We know a teacher who takes a picture of the homework on the whiteboard daily and posts it to Instagram with the class hashtag for parents and students to see.

Digital Citizenship

When we begin to ask our students to communicate with us and each other in online spaces, we also need to begin teaching about digital citizenship: the etiquette, behaviors, and laws that govern our online behavior. As educational technology coaches Tanya Avrith (2014) and Kim Meldrum like to say, "You can't inoculate students with digital citizenship." In other words, teaching about digital citizenship is not a one-time lesson that should guide students forever. Helping our students successfully navigate a digital world is something we work on in our classrooms every day. It means teaching them good manners for online interactions with their classmates and others. It also means teaching them to protect themselves—from online predators, sure, but also from computer viruses, spammers, hackers, and even their own friends. We also need to be sure they understand the importance of respecting copyright, Creative Commons, public domain, and fair use. To raise our digital citizens we will have to give them an education in maturity, caution, and respect along with the content of our courses. You can find more information on digital citizenship terminology in Appendix A. There are also links to a variety of materials related to supporting digital citizenship in your classroom at pluginpowerup.com, under the Resources tab.

The Workflow Has to Work

How do you get material from your computer to your students? Once students do work digitally, how do they turn it in to you without having to print it? How do you share feedback with students after you have evaluated their work? These are questions of workflow. How you solve them will depend on the devices your students have and the tools you are comfortable using. Expect your workflow to evolve and become more efficient as you get more comfortable with 1:1 teaching and learn more about online options (see Figure 2.1). Also, whatever system

Figure 2.1 Diana uses 1:1 technology to check and send work to students.

you use to distribute and collect materials this year inevitably will be better in subsequent years because companies are continually updating products.

Your students will help too. Over and over, we find that our students produce solutions we had not thought of before. They find ways to share information with each other and with us even more efficiently (see Figure 2.2). They suggest apps and websites we haven't tried. Also, our students move from class to class all day long, so they often spread ideas other teachers haven't had a chance to share. It may be frustrating to hear, "Well, Mrs. V. shares documents by using . . . ," but before you get frustrated with the comparison, remember that this student is making a suggestion about efficiency that might be worth looking into.

Figure 2.2 A student views her assignment on a tablet.

Teacher: Eve Gardner
Subject: Tenth-Grade English
Coach: Jen Roberts

Eve Gardner stopped by my classroom after school in early September. "I want to use less paper this year," she said. "I know there is a way to send things to my students digitally, but I need help." Gardner had a team vocabulary activity that she wanted to send to her students. It was a Word document that she had uploaded to Dropbox, an online file-sharing service. I started by asking her some questions.

"Would you like to send this to them as a Word document?"

She considered that: "If I do, how will I get it back from them?"

Great question! She was thinking ahead. I knew she wanted minimal complications, so I suggested that students could e-mail their completed assignments or print them out and return them to her.

"No," Gardner said. "I don't want all that e-mail. How can I get it so they work on it in Google Docs?"

"We could send it to them as 'view only,'" I said. "They would make their own copy, do their work, and share it back to you." (There are better solutions using Doctopus or an LMS that integrates with Google Drive, but we didn't have that with our LMS at the time, and Eve was not ready for the technical expectations of running a Doctopus add-on.)

"That's what I want," she said, perking up. "How do I do that?"

I walked her through the steps of making her document viewable to anyone with the link and adding that link to her existing class blog. When students clicked the link, they would be able to make their own copies of the document to edit and share with her. She wrote down all the steps very carefully, and then stayed to try it with a few other documents while I helped another teacher and checked in on her progress.

Learning and practicing the steps to make her document viewable to her students took some time, but after doing it daily for a few weeks, Gardner was a pro. She told me later that she had saved herself lots of paper and a lot of time in the copy room.

The Tools of Workflow

Google Drive is an incredibly powerful resource for teachers using 1:1. Within Drive you can create, share, and publish documents, presentations, spreadsheets, and forms. We share folders with our students, watch their writing projects develop, have teams collaborate on presentations, and collect data with forms. Anything you create in Google Drive can be published to the web for easy linking to your LMS. Students can share their work with you while they are still working on it, which makes for amazing formative feedback opportunities. Shared folders make it easy for groups to collaborate. Google Drive is browser based, so you and your students will need Internet access to use it, but that also means that students can easily access their projects from home. Google Drive automatically saves work and keeps a record of all previous versions. You can see who wrote what on a shared document using the revision history. We have written every word of this book using shared documents in Google Drive, allowing us to collaborate on drafts, leave each other comments, and revise together in real time. If you are not already familiar with the power of Google Drive, consider learning more about it. You will see Google Drive referenced often in the examples in this book.

Dropbox is another very useful workflow and sharing tool. Teachers at Jen's school share folders in Dropbox for curriculum collaboration. Some students at Diana's school use Dropbox to send files from their iPads and also as an "off-device" storage backup. Dropbox can be a useful workflow tool if you create shared folders with students, but Dropbox also allows you to right-click on any document and get a link to share that document. You can add the link to your LMS so that students can click the link and download the document to their computers. To get the work back from students, you can ask them to submit it through an LMS or upload it to your Dropbox using one of several services for that. At the moment we like DROPitTOme (http://dropitto.me). A few notes about Dropbox: storage space is generous, but it might not be enough if all of your students are sending you large files. Also, it is not possible to collaborate simultaneously. If two people open the same document at one time, they won't see each other's changes and might end up saving parallel copies.

Workflow is a process of solution finding. There is always a way to get information from point A to point B. The challenge is figuring out the easiest way to make that happen. For a single file, e-mail often works fine, but it may not scale well for a teacher with 180 students. In this case, we have two solutions. At the beginning of the year, we have our students share a document with us in Google Drive. We call it their English Journal, and they use it to do all the bits of small work that happen daily in class: answers to warm-up questions, vocabulary notes, reading reactions, character charts—the things they used to do in a spiral notebook. After they share the document with us, we can see the work they do in it all year long. An important trick is that we ask our students to add their new work *at the top* of the document and date each entry. At first, working from the top feels awkward to them, but after a few days of not having to scroll past their previous work, they begin to understand why. For us it means that we can open their English Journal anytime and see their most recent work right on top. The Google Docs preview feature lets us flip through their documents with the arrow keys on our computers to see all of their work very quickly. Because they share this one document early in the year, we don't have to deal with little bits of work coming in via separate files every day. For larger, more formal projects, such as an essay or article, we create a new document just for that purpose.

When we want to get an answer from all of our students, based either on an activity or assessment, we use a Google Form (a feature available through Google Drive). A form enables us to ask a variety of questions and see all of our students' responses in a spreadsheet. This is a useful way of assessing progress on a project, collaboratively gathering data for the whole class to use, or having students submit the URL for work posted somewhere else. Google Forms simplify our workflow and make it easy to collect, organize, and evaluate information from all of our students quickly. Visit pluginpowerup.com for more information about these tools.

PLUG IN   Make Some Communication Decisions

1. **Find out what kind of learning management system (LMS)** you are encouraged or required to use. Conduct an online search of the name and read about it. You can also type the name of your LMS+tutorial on YouTube and see how it works. Make plans to attend a training about the LMS and/or visit a teacher already using it.

2. **Survey your students about their Internet access** at home. Find out how many have cell phones or e-mail addresses. Ask them about their communication preferences and about their experiences with social media. Sample student survey questions are available in the Resources section of pluginpowerup.com.

3. **Create a Google account** if you don't already have one. (A Gmail account is a Google account too.) This will give you access to a huge range of educational tools, including Google Drive, Google Voice, Blogger, Maps, and YouTube.

Logistics

A few tips about managing a digital 1:1 classroom:

Naming Conventions: Teach your students to name their digital files using a specific pattern and you will be happier. In our classrooms, students are required to name every document like this: *period last name first name assignment title*. For example, if John Smith is in period three and working on his argument essay, he will name his paper 3 Smith John Argument Essay. In this way we can tell at a glance to whom the paper belongs, which assignment it is, and in which period we see that student. This process also enables us to sort papers by title, with the results being grouped by period because the number comes first. If you can, get your school to agree on a common naming convention for student work. It will make things easier for the students as they share work with a variety of teachers.

Creating Accounts: Many websites require you and your students to create accounts before using them. Most ask for an e-mail address and a password (see next bullet). In almost all cases, students must be thirteen years or older to create online accounts. Some services allow teachers to create student accounts without e-mail addresses, but we know of only a few. Your school or district may provide your students with e-mail accounts and/or access to district resources with a district log-in. When creating accounts with students, be sure to teach about privacy, security, and online identity. Diana teaches students to use their first name and last initial only for creating accounts. You may want to have a similar convention.

Passwords: Teach students basic password literacy. They should know not to repeat important passwords, and not to use real words or obvious choices. Stress the importance of not sharing passwords even with close friends. You can count on some students forgetting passwords. Happily, most sites are equipped with a "forgot password" link. Diana has students save passwords in their phones. Jen keeps a spiral notebook in which students can write down school-related passwords. Jen keeps the notebook in a secure place, but any student can ask to look at his or her page for a password reminder.

Single-Log-In Websites: If a group of students needs access to a site that doesn't allow collaborators, we ask the project manager or team leader to create a log-in that will be shared with a password specific to their group.

Saving Work: We have witnessed a few lost work disasters on tablets and classroom computers. Sometimes a web server shuts down because an "error" occurred or an app quit unexpectedly. For these occasions, it is critical that students back up their work as they go. We encourage students to work in Google Docs, which saves automatically every few seconds, and periodically export their manuscripts by downloading them. Dropbox works well for most apps, and is the backup location of choice for many of Diana's students. Even with the possibility of technical glitches, we still see a lot less student work go missing in the digital world than we did when they used only paper.

Uploading Work: Sometimes uploading work can cause a website to time out and quit, which is a big reason for saving documents elsewhere. It's important to have the document live somewhere other than in the fragile type-in box on the computer screen.

CAPTCHA (Completely Automated Public Turing Test to Tell Computers and Humans Apart): These computerized tests are meant to thwart hackers, bots, and spam, protecting the work of real people. But sometimes, the CAPTCHA letter and number arrangements are difficult to interpret and repeat appropriately. The secret is to use the refresh button, which is usually at the top left of the screen. If students can't re-create the CAPTCHA, encourage them to refresh the page for a new set of words they can identify. It may take a couple of tries.

Navigating New Tools: Most of the time, students adopt an "I'll figure it out" attitude. For them, fiddling around with unfamiliar apps or sites is the preferred method of acquiring new skills. The first time Diana used Google Sites with her students, she wrote a very thorough, multipage handout that explained the linear steps for creating a website. But she found the stack of handouts still in the center of each table while students huddled around a single screen to watch a YouTube video explaining the same process. They figured it out, and she wasn't the one to teach them.

Prioritizing Versus Playing: As teachers, we want to hold students to a firm list of priorities and make sure they meet deadlines. Allowing for an initial "test-drive" assignment with a new app or website ("Spend ten minutes with this site. What did you find?") is a way to meet students in the middle and allow their play to have purpose in shaping their vision for the project. Consider grading student projects by process checkpoints. This is a useful strategy for forcing focus.

Public Criticism: Not all interactions online are positive. Occasionally, by publishing to a public audience, students are subject to harsh criticism or snarky comments. This is an opportunity to teach students not to respond to Internet trolls and also how to comment on each other's work appropriately. Encourage your students to participate online only on sites that post a commenter's name. Anonymous responses tend to be the most damaging.

Internet Filters: It is very likely that your school has an Internet filter. It is frustrating to plan a lesson at home only to find that the site you wanted to use is blocked on your campus. Check to make sure the website you want to use is accessible at school before you invest too much time planning how you'll use it. (See Figure 1.4 in Chapter 1.)

Monitoring Digital Student Work

Consider the paper-based classroom for a moment. To see student work, you either walked around and looked over their shoulders or waited until they turned in work for evaluation. It's possible that some students never turned in anything because they didn't finish. It's pretty hard to evaluate nothing.

In a 1:1 classroom, you still get to look over their shoulders as you move through the room, and we encourage that, but you also get to look over their shoulders digitally when work is shared with you online. Even better, in our classrooms, students share their work in Google Drive (using the big blue "share" button) on the day they start a project, so we can watch their writing and research process evolve. If a student does not complete an assignment, we can still see what he or she did accomplish and what that student might be struggling with. Because we can check their work in progress, we can provide early intervention to students who are falling behind or have been absent from school. When content lives on a single device, such as on an iPad app, it is more cumbersome to oversee progress. In these situations, we rely on updates from students through cloud backups that are shared with us (as on Dropbox or Google Drive), and in-class spot checks.

Organizing Student Work

Where do you put all those digital files students are sending you? We use Google Drive and find it's best to group the files by assignment regardless of the period in which we see the student. Our naming convention of *period last name first name assignment* makes it easier to search for documents in Google Drive. If Diana wants to see all the papers her students have written on *The Great Gatsby*, she can just search [Gatsby]. If Jen wants to review all the work Michael Davis has done this year before meeting with his case manager, she can search [Michael Davis] and see all of his documents. We know some teachers like to keep separate files for each class and then subfolders for each assignment or a folder for each student, but grouping by assignment works for us.

Pacing in a 1:1 Classroom

Teachers often ask us how we decide how long a digital project or unit will take. The most honest answer is that many assignments and projects involving 1:1 technology take a little longer than their paper-based counterparts. Often this is because students are doing more work to complete higher-quality products. The difference in the outcome seems worth an extra couple of days. At the beginning of a unit, we try to strip the project to its core components. Will students be doing research, data collection, writing, or something else? Will they be using images or video? What tools will they be using that they have or have not used before? How will they present or publish their work? Each of those variables will affect the length of the project.

Diana schedules a unit using tasks with which she is familiar, which makes it easier to estimate the time allotment. She always adds in a night's worth of homework at the beginning of the unit for students to explore the new tool(s). We suggest a day or two in the middle of the unit for catch-up. Diana deliberately plans *nothing else* on that day to accommodate the unexpected (assemblies, computer meltdowns, and bad timing). Finally, she tacks on two days at the end of the unit for polishing—time students need to professionalize the product. During those final days, Diana plans other assignments and lessons that are "flex lessons"— enrichment pieces that would be great to get to but that she can scrap if necessary. When planning a unit-pacing guide for a project, make an educated guess and then factor in some room to breathe.

Another crucial aspect of planning a unit for a 1:1 class is considering the digital tools students will use. First and foremost, we are responsible for teaching our students the content of the course. Digital tools can absolutely enhance that process, but too many can get in the way of learning. Jen tries to limit new digital tools to just one or two per unit and to always make sure those tools are going to have a use beyond the current assignment. By circling back and reusing tools, students become familiar with them and can more easily add to their repertoire and extend their thinking. "Remember when we made a word cloud of Red Jacket's speech?" Jen might say. "Today I want you to make word clouds of these two other speeches and then compare them." By the end of the year, students can choose the appropriate tools for their projects and also use multiple tools in the same project.

The Teacher's Role in a 1:1 Classroom—Diana Explains It Best

A 1:1 environment offers options for what students can do during class. *But what will I do?* I wonder if my high school swimming coach ever asked herself before practice, *What will I do while the team is in the pool?* A single glance across the pool deck would confirm that Mrs. Knock was a fantastic coach: timing us, cheering us on, modeling proper form while perched on a diving block, even lying down on wet concrete to remind us (*hup!*) to breathe on cue. But it was a rare day that Knock would don a Speedo and jump into the pool with us.

The first time I turned total control over to the students to work on their writing for publication I felt a bit like a fish out of water. If I wasn't going to be the one leading discussions about the latest chapter, or creating journal topics, or prompting reticent readers, what *would* I do? I was no longer their target audience; I had become their coach. Stix and Hrbek (2006) explain that when teachers serve as classroom coaches, they promote creativity and innovation while empowering students to own their learning.

During class, I do my very best to coach. Many days, I start class by setting the objectives for the hour and reminding students about upcoming deadlines. Then, I let them work. In the meantime, I pull students aside to meet individually or in small groups. It turns out that I still have plenty to do.

The Students' Role in a 1:1 Classroom—Jen Explains It Best

At the end of my second semester teaching American literature with a 1:1 classroom, final exams were approaching and students kept asking what they should study. I contemplated going back through our class blog and making them a study guide, but then I had an idea. All of our lessons for the semester were archived on the class blog. Why should I be the one to make the study guide? I broke students into groups and asked each group to create a Google document to share. The groups reviewed different segments of the class blog and pulled out the things they thought would most likely appear on the final. Collaboratively, each team built a study guide that included links to the readings and then brainstormed questions I might ask them about those texts.

By wandering the room and reviewing their guides, I could see what each group thought was most important from the semester. I asked the students to publish their study guides and share them with the other groups. Each student left that period with six possible study guides to review. This was during the pilot phase of 1:1 for my district. My colleagues did not have computers in their classrooms yet. I was excited about how well my students had done with their group-created study guides when I ran into Mr. Sanders. When I told him about the work my students had done, he ran his hand through his hair in frustration. "I spent five hours on Sunday making my students a study guide," he said. I believed him, but I felt bad because I know his hard work ended up at the bottom of backpacks. Even if my students didn't review for the exam any more, at least they had reviewed a lot just by making the study guides.

It's not that a teacher has less to do in a 1:1 classroom, but it is true that the students have more to do. The adage told to me while I was student teaching holds true: "The person doing the most work is doing the most learning." In a 1:1 classroom, the students have the tools to do the work.

Finally, consider the communication and workflow tools students will use in college and in the workplace. Online classes and online training modules will be a part of their lives in almost any path they choose. Students who study in teams have been shown to perform better in college than those who go it alone (Ender 1985). Being able to read and annotate online texts and e-books will give them wider and easier access to course materials. Students will need the digital skills they develop in your classroom to excel in the future.

 POWER UP! Prepare to Launch a New Version of Your Classroom

1. **Add some content to your LMS** and get familiar with how students will join your online class. Some systems use a code. Some have students added automatically by the IT department.

2. **Consider how you want to digitally distribute and collect** student work. We prefer Google Drive, but Dropbox or your LMS might work better for you.

3. **Go digital.** You probably have a lot of course resources that are only on paper, including articles you've saved or materials other teachers gave you as hard copies. We don't recommend scanning your entire filing cabinet, but you will want to figure out how to scan or create digital versions of the crucial items you will need. It is also worth taking a moment to search for something similar online. An old newspaper clipping is now probably available in an online news archive. A book you used to copy a chapter from could be online now.

CHAPTER 3
Engagement

En·gage·ment (n): The state or act of being engaged. Also the state of being in gear. An intense attention to the task at hand.

Teacher: Deenie Clinton
Class: Freshman Biology
Observer: Diana Neebe

On a warm afternoon in the beginning of May—the time of the year our administrators have dubbed "Mayhem" because of all the AP exams, athletic events, graduation to-dos, and raging hormones—I observed a freshman biology class, interested to see what all the commotion was about. Two students were pumping their fists in the air and cheering; another was standing up at his desk, fidgeting with nervous energy while excitedly looking down at his iPad. Students on the left side of the room were turned completely around to watch a grinning Deenie Clinton as she paced back and forth, iPad attached to her hand with a leather Grabbit strap. The air was warm and still, and in my own classroom an hour before, that had been enough to lull my flock of fourteen-year-olds into a poetry-inspired trance. Some of these very same students were now sitting (quite literally) on the edge of their seats, completely engaged.

I moved to a lab table in the back of the room and settled in to observe Clinton's review of organism and animal dissections, which would lead to an actual rat dissection later in class. All of the students had used their iPads to log in to Nearpod, a free website (and corresponding app) that lets teachers create or download a collection of presentation slides (known as a slide deck), share interactive lessons, and then monitor and evaluate students' responses. As Clinton clicked from one slide to another, all of the tiny iPad screens in the classroom changed simultaneously from a picture of a sponge with labeled parts to a grid with a matching question.

"Ladies and gentlemen, next question!" she said. "Notice there's a column to the left. Put the letter of the correct phylum there to match the organism. Show me what you remember."

As the students' responses popped up on her screen, she sifted through them to find one set that was close to being fully correct but had a few wrong answers. She pushed that set out to her students anonymously and asked them to consider the answers.

"With your partner, what's right with this one? And what can we correct?"

Students turned to their tablemates and, in hushed voices, discussed where (and why) the person answering the question may have gotten confused. A student from one of the groups called out, "Shouldn't grasshopper be G—Arthropoda—and jellyfish be B—Cnidaria?"

"Yes, perfect! Now . . . what type of symmetry is shown in the organism on your screen: no symmetry, radial symmetry, or bilateral symmetry?" (See Figure 3.1.)

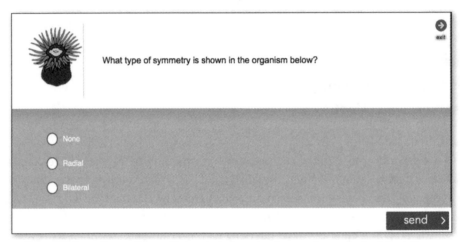

Figure 3.1 A question on Nearpod helps students review for organism and animal dissections.

The review lesson continued for fifteen more minutes, during which students asked clarifying questions such as "Could you go over the difference between endoderm and ectoderm again?" Clinton took the opportunity to help students make connections among the five dissections they had completed so far in the unit, and when everyone was able to answer all of the prompts in the Nearpod slide deck, she knew that the class was ready to move on to their final dissection.

There is no doubt about it: Clinton's lesson was engaging. But what stood out to me was that instead of involving only a few competitive and quick students who blurt out answers before the rest of the class is ready to respond, the lesson engaged *all* students. At each question, every student had a chance to think, write, label, ponder, and review. The teacher got to see all of the responses right away, and no one was left out.

The Science Behind Engagement

Engagement is the holy grail for teachers, an almost mythical, nirvana-like state that we achieve in our classrooms when all the elements fall into place perfectly: just the right activity, at just the right time, with just the right grouping of students and boom, a classroom of kids so engaged, we could take a bathroom break and they wouldn't even notice we were gone. Beginning teachers are likely to attribute an engaging lesson to luck. Over time they learn which teaching strategies are more energizing to students, and begin to see the patterns in their teaching that lead to increased student engagement.

Let's take a quick look at the research about student engagement and see how we can put it to use in the 1:1 classroom: Students report higher levels of engagement when they have caring teachers who create active learning opportunities (Cothran and Ennis 2000). We know that higher levels of student engagement also have been associated with greater academic achievement and decreased dropout rates (Griffiths et al. 2012). A 1:1 classroom creates the opportunity to make all learning experiences active and productive, and to transition from the old paradigm in which one student would participate at a time to a new normal in which everybody does the thinking and everybody contributes to the learning. A 1:1 classroom is an excellent way to facilitate engagement, because it places three key conditions—connection, perplexity, and curiosity—within reach for every student.

Connection

When students believe that their input is valued and will earn a response, they are more likely to participate actively. This is the essence of a participatory culture (Jenkins et al. 2006) and the allure of social media—the idea that what we say matters and that others will respond, almost instantly sometimes. We can use digital tools to create connections for our students within the classroom and beyond while simultaneously teaching the etiquette of written communication. (See Figure 3.2.)

New standards and the ease of global communication create opportunities for connecting our students with other students and authentic audiences for their work. At the same time, there are lingering concerns about student privacy and safety online. If your school or district accepts federal funding, you may also have to follow legal requirements for filtering content and limiting access. Based on our conversations with teachers nationally and globally, customs about publishing student work, pictures, and names varies widely. Therefore, we can't give you guidelines about what you can and cannot put online with regard to student work. We encourage you to communicate with parents and administrators about the kinds of connections you want to create for your students and why. When in doubt, get parent permission in writing.

Figure 3.2 The Tension of Connection

Perplexity

Perplexity drives inquiry. As explained by Dan Meyer, former high school math teacher and Stanford researcher, perplexity is the process of being interested in something you don't know about yet, but would like to investigate, and believing you have the tools to find out

(Meyer 2014). When we create perplexing situations for our students, we inspire them to seek answers that will deepen their understanding of concepts and topics they care about. Perplexity helps learners move beyond the extremes of boredom—"I don't know, and I don't want to know"—and confusion—"I do want to know, but I can't figure it out." In class, teachers can foster perplexity by starting with a specific and interesting problem to explore and providing the right amount of modeling, scaffolding, and confidence building to help students solve it.

Curiosity

Finally, curiosity also provides a crucial path to engagement. Think about the book you can't put down or the television drama you are compelled to watch. You are curious about the characters' outcomes. Whereas perplexity focuses on solving a problem with the tools you have, curiosity involves waiting for an answer you know is coming. A missing piece of information or a surprising outcome drives you to stay tuned (Musallam 2013). Our students rarely come to us already curious about the things the content standards expect them to learn, but we can cultivate their curiosity by providing bread crumbs of information that will encourage them to follow the path to knowledge. A history teacher might give students excerpts from a soldier's diary leading up to D-day. A science teacher might pause the video of an experiment just before the chemical reaction takes place. A 1:1 environment makes it even easier to cultivate curiosity and also to satisfy that curiosity, because, as experienced educators know, the answers to one question often lead to the next question.

Engagement in Action: Connection, Perplexity, and Curiosity

Engagement Strategy: Connection
Shared Reading Experiences

Reading is, and likely will remain, a primary method of providing students with academic content material. We know that students make more meaning out of what they read when they can talk about their reading with a peer (Beers 2003). In a 1:1 classroom, students can interact with the text, their peers, and their teacher in a variety of ways that will increase their engagement and boost their comprehension.

Shared reading experiences with digital texts enable multiple students to read and interact with the same text simultaneously. A shared text can now include discussion threads about aspects of the text, links to additional content, polls, and comprehension-check questions to help teachers gauge students' needs and hold readers accountable. Teachers can create their own interactive texts or download e-books with interactive aspects; many are free or low cost (see Figure 3.3).

Interactive books are great, and can help connect students to content that seems out of reach—whether because of language, time period, or topic. But taking on an entire text is a behemoth of a task. Trust me. I rewrote *The Scarlet Letter* as an iBook. I learned a ton in the process of teaching myself iBooks Author and copyright law for works in the public domain. But it essentially monopolized my entire summer. I'm glad I did it, and my students respond very favorably each year. But I wouldn't recommend starting off with something as comprehensive as a novel. Before you commit to twenty-four chapters of built-in reading questions, glossary notes, and video footnotes (whoops), consider test-driving an article or a short story. Learn the tool first, and then tackle the tomes. If you are unsure what you have the rights to use and reproduce, please read Appendix A, "Copyright, Creative Commons, Public Domain, and Fair Use."

Figure 3.3 Diana's First Experience Making an E-book

Getting started with digital texts will likely be a challenge for you and your students. For many of the teachers we work with, the hardest part of 1:1 learning is the transition from print to digital texts. At first, giving up paper texts can feel limiting. We see most teachers initially switch from a paper copy to a scanned digital copy for each student, without adding any of the advantages of interactivity to the reading process. Try to view your switch to digital texts as a series of phases. Begin by digitizing your paper copies. Once you become comfortable creating electronic texts, push yourself to make those texts interactive. It's worth the time to learn how to use collaborative reading tools and create interactive texts. In addition to saving yourself a trip to the copy room, you will increase engagement because students appreciate the interactive elements and collaborative discussion threads of digital texts.

To send students a digital copy of an article, you can scan it and save it as a portable document file (PDF). Most modern copy machines and some printers can scan documents and e-mail them to you. Once you have a PDF version of the text, you can upload it to your learning management system for students to access. Students with iPads can annotate a PDF using an app such as Goodreader or Notability. Students with laptops can annotate a PDF with one of several web tools (search [annotate PDF] to find the latest). Alternatively, the text you want students to read might already be available online (see Figure 3.4).

Having each of your students read a digital text is a good first step, but it does not really represent a shared reading experience, although it does save a lot of paper. To go further, we suggest sharing a document with groups of four to six students using Google Drive. Through the chat window built into every Google Doc, students can "discuss" the text one section at a time and add margin notes about the meaning. Jen uses this process to have her students do close readings of short but complex excerpts of texts, such as the writings of Emerson and Thoreau. This shared reading strategy also works well with science articles and primary sources.

Diana can't imagine teaching Shakespeare without her *Shakespearience* iBooks, and some of her science colleagues swear by their interactive science textbooks. We know many teachers who have become adept at finding additional readings for their students online. To see whether the reading material you need is already online, search the title and author, or look by subject. It can also help to add the words *full text* to your search.

The great thing about these sources is that the text is already digital— no need to print or scan it. You can direct students straight to the link where you found the source, or you can use a Google Doc to reformat the text into something that fits your purpose better. As always, we encourage you to be thoughtful when giving students online texts. Some readings work great just the way they are on the web. Others you might want to modify, to remove ads and other distracters. There are several great tools that strip distractions from text. (We like Readability and Clearly as options.)

We also encourage you to teach students how to navigate online texts in their primary form. Model your thinking as you look at an article online and show students how you separate the important information from the distractions. Much of our print experience is now online, and students will need to know how to get the most out of their reading experiences in all formats.

Figure 3.4 Online Readings

Before class, Jen makes six copies of the text in Google Drive and shares one copy with each group of six students. (She uses a spreadsheet to place her students in groups and can then easily copy and paste their e-mail addresses for quick document sharing.) Sometimes she is sharing an identical document with each group, and sometimes she is sharing modified texts based on students' needs. (For more on differentiation, see Chapter 6.) The students in each group have editing rights on the document shared with their group. Although each student is part of a team, the group members will not sit together. Their discussion will be conducted by typing in the document chat window. The classroom remains whisper-quiet except for the rapid clicking on small keyboards. If you walked into Jen's classroom during this activity, you would think she was running some kind of silent typing competition, because her students are so focused on their screens.

As the students read and discuss the text, Jen keeps the six group documents open in different tabs of her browser and can switch among them to answer questions and see what is happening in the various discussions. Students know she is monitoring their chats, so their conversations remain focused. From the transcripts of the conversations, Jen can see their thinking evolve from confusion to clarity and respond to process questions, if needed.

In Figure 3.5, you can see an excerpt of one such conversation. Notice how excited the students get when they start to comprehend what Emerson is saying. Yet, even as they congratulate each other, they quickly move on to the next paragraph. The text is perplexing, and the process connects students with each other as they make meaning from Emerson's words.

Maria: Okay, I am confused with the first paragraph.

Alejandro: i dont get it

Maria: Oh I think I get it now

Alejandro: what do you think?

Maria: Its about being original

Angelica: idk he is getting convicted??

Juan: self confidence ? i think ..that's what I think are we supposed to mark the text ?

Maria: envy is ignorance; that imitation is suicide; doesn't that mean to be original and decide for yourself?

Juan: yeah , wouldn't that also mean like self confidence ?

Alejandro: when he says "imitation is suicide" i think hes saying to be your self dont imitate others

Juan: ye

Maria: exactly.

Juan: * yes .

Angelica: haahaha yehhh

Juan: alright alright I get this :)

Angelica: okay AGREE

Juan: amen .

Maria: Okay so we get it then?

Alejandro: then wen he says "that he must take himelf for better for worse as his portion" i think hes saying to take responsibility for your own actions

Juan: agree

Angelica: dam Al Helluh smart or what hah;)

Alejandro: haha thanks

Juan: I know right :D alright well this one is difficult |:

Angelica: every heart vibrates to that iron string.

Maria: I think this is the on that says to be yourself and make your own decisions.

Angelica: what about that?

Juan: idknow , I'm lost on this one

Alejandro: in the first lines hes saying to trust your self like your gut feeling

Juan: highlight it and post on comment on it

Maria: to accept life as it is and go on living life with confidence?

Alejandro: thats a better one

Maria: :)

Juan: yeah it is

Figure 3.5 Excerpt from a Google Doc Group Discussion of "Self-Reliance" (Typos Included)

We have found that students understand text much better through online discussions than through face-to-face conversations. Because students have to jointly annotate the document, they feel more accountable for the results and work together to figure out the meaning. Through the chat windows, Jen can see students quoting the text, proposing possible meanings, and negotiating and debating alternatives. In short, she can collect evidence of their developing understanding. Students tell Jen they love the online chat because the room stays quiet and they can concentrate on what they are reading before adding their thinking to the chat window. In a more traditional setup, where students discuss text face-to-face and we walk around and listen, we know they veer off topic fairly often, and we can't stay with one group long enough to hear their thinking evolve.

At the end of the period, Jen makes a copy of the chat from each document that she can look at more closely later. She wants her students to learn to talk to each other about texts, too, but when she really wants them to focus on what a text says, an online collaborative reading engages them more fully while also giving them more thinking space. Often she has used their chat transcripts to show students the kinds of things she wants to see them doing in face-to-face conversations.

We have also been using collaborative reading tools such as Actively Learn to engage students in reading both short and novel-length texts. Actively Learn is a free tool that enables groups to share the same digital text. Everyone in the group, which could be a whole class or subgroups within a class, sees the annotations made by others. Teachers can add discussion questions and polls right into the text. These embedded reader- and teacher-created items make the reading a more social experience. Instead of a drama teacher sending students home with a paperback copy of the play and an assignment to read the first act, students can open the play in Actively Learn and read Act I while adding their thoughts to discussion questions about character motivation, watching related videos about staging and blocking, seeing fellow classmates' annotations, and voting in polls about the play. There is an ever-growing list of tools for collaborative reading. Most support a variety of text types and can be used in almost any subject area.

Jen's use of a shared Google Doc for a discussion about a text is a *synchronous* reading experience for students. It works only because the group is on the document all at once. Sometimes an absent student will join from home, but most of the action is happening in the classroom at the same time. Our common use of Actively Learn is *asynchronous*. Students don't need to be reading all at once. They can jump into the discussion whenever they have time for that homework, see the additional content, and add their thoughts to the discussion threads. Both methods engage students with the reading, but when and how students participate differs. Collaborative reading can be synchronous or asynchronous, depending on your purpose, technology availability, and student readiness for real-time interaction while reading.

Engagement Strategy: Perplexity
Short-Term Research
Teacher: Jen Roberts
Class: American Lit

When I taught American literature, before I had computers for my students, I introduced the Harlem Renaissance with a short slide lecture about the people and places relevant to the era. I was preparing to do that again the year my students first got laptops when I had a lightbulb moment. What would happen, I wondered, if I left the pictures but stripped the words from my slides, replaced them with questions, embedded the presentation on the class blog, and let students work in partners to find the answers by their own online research? (In a classroom without computers, this lesson would include a worksheet of questions that students would answer, using a textbook. Not the worst lesson, perhaps, but probably not something my students would get excited about.) I was not sure if this type of scavenger hunt research would interest my students. All I really had done was add a picture to the questions and swap the textbook for some online resources. Still, it meant my students would be finding answers for themselves instead of listening to me.

I admit I was a little surprised when I saw my students get so engaged with this process. They didn't need me. Students happily absorbed themselves in working through the slides with their partners, looking carefully at each image and searching for answers to questions such as "What was the Great Migration, and what impact did it have on the Harlem Renaissance?" and "What was this place? What happened there?" next to a picture of the Cotton Club. My goal was to help my students gain basic background information about New York City in the 1920s, but along the way, they also honed their search skills, found answers through diverse resources, and became completely engrossed in the process. "Can we do this again?" was the question I heard most often. (See Appendix B for more on teaching search skills.)

This was one of the first lessons my students gave me about the ways learning changes in a 1:1 classroom. I knew then that my job was no longer to transfer knowledge to my students, but rather to establish the conditions that would encourage and support them in creating knowledge for themselves.

What made this strategy so engaging for my students? They enjoyed that they could work in pairs; collaboration provided some connection. Yet, I also believe that perplexity was the primary catalyst. Students knew that the answers to the questions existed, and finding the information was a matter of having the right search terms and skimming the right sources. This process provided the right level of perplexity to make the task interesting and doable. Also, each question came with an image. The images provoked curiosity. When they saw the pictures, students wanted to know more about what was going on. Why were those policemen in old-fashioned uniforms posing for a picture in front of stacks of alcohol?

There is growing consensus among students, teachers, and administrators that integrating technology into the curriculum increases engagement because students can explore topics in greater depth beyond what is provided by traditional textbooks (McDowell 2013). With a textbook, students know they will eventually find the answer and that the teacher probably already knows the page on which they will find it. With the aid of the Internet and some decent search skills, different groups may find the same information in various ways from various sources. Or, better, they may find *different* information from different sources. When the answers are less clear-cut, students learn about credibility and the importance of verifying the information they read online (see Figure 3.6).

When I first made the move to 1:1, my mentor Diane Main (@Dowbiggin) told me that I'd have to get comfortable with being uncomfortable. Truer words about teaching with technology have not been uttered. My favorite part of Jen's research lesson is that she admits not knowing if her new strategy would work. She got comfortable with discomfort and took a risk to change the way she was exposing students to the Harlem Renaissance, and it worked. But it might not have worked.

I've learned that we have to be willing to fail, and fail boldly. We have to embrace the ambiguity that comes with 1:1 teaching and learning. I love that students are also dealing positively with uncertainty. They are learning how to question their sources and seek consensus among their classmates. In my experience, that deeper engagement just doesn't happen when they are thumbing through the pages of a textbook. Students tend to accept textbook answers as infallible and unchangeable. But when Jen's students found what they thought were answers on the Internet, and noted the often conflicting information available, they looked through a skeptical lens at information that was *possibly* correct but required verification and thought. Now, that's real-world engagement!

Figure 3.6 Embracing Ambiguity: Diana's Response

In the past few years, we have repeatedly created lessons that incorporate images, questions, and online searches to build background knowledge about a subject. Although Jen originally used slides she had already created, today she is able to embed pictures and short videos directly into a Google Form. Many learning management systems support the inclusion of images in their assignments and quizzes and could be adapted to a short research activity this way. Initially, we give students questions that are easily searchable, but over time, we can increase the complexity so that students must use multiple steps to find answers.

Engagement Strategy: Curiosity
Long-Term Research

In our 1:1 classrooms, we have found that students really like doing research. If your previous experience with student research projects involved spending days in the library with encyclopedias followed by a long process of writing research reports, you may not believe us. Consider this: as teachers, we are used to students asking us questions, and we usually answer them. With 1:1 classrooms, we have learned to be less willing to answer students' factual questions, such as "How many moons does Jupiter have?" and "What does Poe mean when he says, 'bust of Pallas'? Who is Pallas?" These are "Google-able" questions, so we encourage our students to search for their own answers. We want them to understand that there is a difference between search and research and a parallel distinction between knowledge and learning.

With an Internet-connected device, students can do quick searches for information daily, but they should also be engaging in long-term research projects. For example, juniors at Jen's school conduct a yearlong research project they call the Expert Project (Burke 2011). Students identify their own topics of interest and develop research questions in September. For the remainder of the school year, they work on their research projects both independently and during English class (see Figure 3.7).

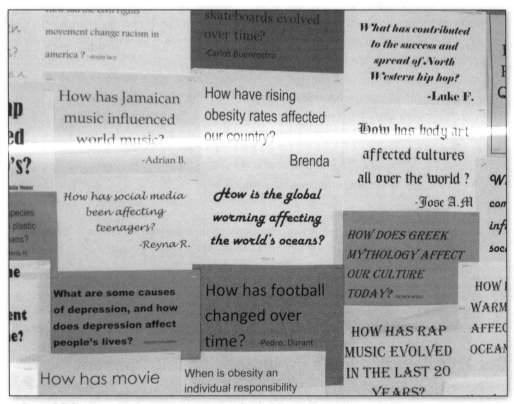

Figure 3.7 Students develop research questions for their Expert Projects.

Although the original plan was to devote one day a week to the research, teachers eventually realized that students needed longer blocks of time to focus on their topics and hone their research skills, such as using the Google News Archive or interviewing experts on their topic. The English teachers revised their pacing guide to devote an entire week to the Expert Project, sandwiched between the other units.

Throughout the year, students created blogs to document the research process, reflect on their findings, and post their next steps. Their blog posts included links to the material they found helpful and their analysis of that material. Each blog became a repository of the most helpful information students could find about that subject. Some blogs have become so well developed that students eventually find their own work in searches about their subject. A student studying the history and art form of body modification was stunned to see his own blog show up as the top result when he did a search in the spring. He showed his teacher and said, "So this work I'm doing putting this together really matters? Other kids are going to find my blog and read this stuff?" Visit pluginpowerup.com for a sample of the Expert Project assignment sheet.

Short- and long-term research projects engage students and prepare them for the demands of finding relevant and accurate information. Whether researching the structure of different types of cells or the history of the cell phone, learning to ask meaningful questions and having the opportunity to investigate their own answers helps students move closer to the authentic work of most academic disciplines. (See Chapter 5 for more about audience.) Research invites students' curiosity, and as all academics know, research almost always leads to more questions for further investigation. (See below for more ideas.)

 **PLUG IN**   Engagement Strategies to Try Now

1. **Do a short research activity** with your students. Start with answers that are easy to find and move to questions that require more advanced search skills.

2. **Convert a reading you normally do on paper** to a digital text. Share it with students through your learning management system (LMS).

3. **Try a collaborative reading activity** with students in small groups or as a class.

Our Five Favorite Tools for Increasing Engagement

The Internet has spawned an ever-expanding group of digital tools we can use to increase student engagement. The specific tools will likely change over time, but the fundamental function and benefits of these strategies will get reimagined and combined into new tools. For us, a big part of the fun of teaching with 1:1 is discovering new tools for engagement and figuring out how to use existing applications in more engaging ways.

Our five favorite types of digital engagement tools are backchanneling, online discussion boards, polling and other forms of data collection, interactive feedback systems, and educational games. Let's take a look at examples of each type of tool.

Backchanneling

Kate Jackson's history class of seventh graders was arranged in two concentric circles. Students in the inner circle were politely debating the factors that contributed to the fall of the Roman Empire. On their tablets, students had a PDF text with their notes jotted in the margins. The texts came from a variety of sources. As students in the inner circle debated the relative importance of political corruption and barbarian invasions to the empire's decline, students in the outer circle stared at their tablets, occasionally looked up to listen closely to a point being made by a student on the inside, and then typed quickly. They appeared to be taking notes, but they were actually engaged in their own discussion through what is often referred to as a backchannel activity.

Using todaysmeet.com, Jackson had created a virtual room where the students in the outer circle could discuss the points being made by students in the inner circle. Through the backchannel, the outer-circle students were connecting with each other and remained engaged in the discussion. Because Jackson configured the virtual room settings to remain open for a week, students were able to go back after the discussion and review the conversation. One of the responsibilities of the outer-circle students was to post questions that were not discussed in depth by students in the inner circle.

"For homework tonight you will go back to the TodaysMeet room and review the discussion there," she said. "I want you to pick a question you wanted to say more about and write your thoughts about it on our Edmodo page." Jackson previously had prepared students for this experience.

As she later told Jen, "With the backchannel, the outer circle of students stays engaged in the process better than they did when they were just taking notes on paper. They really have their own Socratic seminar on the outside at the same time as the inner circle has the discussion face-to-face."

Students having a discussion about the course content are more engaged with that content than they would be listening to a lecture, but we know that often class discussions end up with the teacher doing most of the talking and just a few students actively participating. Diana uses Padlet (www.padlet.com) to allow students to generate discussion questions before the conversation starts. Then, as a class, they organize the questions into topics and decide which ones to discuss. Figure 3.8 shows a screenshot of a Padlet wall that Diana's students created at the start of their immigration literature unit.

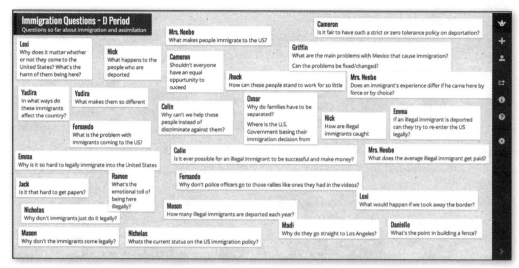

Figure 3.8 Diana's students create a Padlet wall for their class discussion.

Online Discussion Boards

When Jackson's students go home and post their thoughts about the Socratic seminar on the class Edmodo page, they are moving from a backchannel to an online discussion board. Online discussions enable students to connect with peers and see each other's thinking about a topic. This method is a great way to continue class discussions and for students to support one another's learning.

Most discussion boards host "threaded" discussions, which means that each of the posts can be replied to individually. A single prompt can have multiple threads of discussion as students reply to each other. Confused? That's normal. Discussion boards make a lot more sense when you try them for yourself.

Many learning management systems come with built-in discussion features. We encourage you to incorporate them into your class routines. Keep in mind that just as with any new system in your classroom, students will need instruction and practice to make the most of an online discussion.

Suggestions for getting started with online discussions:

1. Post questions that relate to, but also extend, the classroom discussion.

2. Model appropriate responses by showing students what you expect from their answers. We suggest encouraging short but thoughtful responses in the three- to five-sentence range at first.

3. Teach students how to reply to a post appropriately, thoughtfully, and in ways that contribute to the conversation.

4. Be prepared to teach students how to deal with disagreements respectfully and academically. (For more discussion board Dos and Don'ts, see Figure 9.4 in Chapter 9.)

If your students have no experience with online discussions, expect that it will take them weeks or possibly months to develop proficiency with them. Many teachable moments come from online discussions, and the discussions are worth adding to your course for that reason alone, but also consider that the skills needed for online discussion are increasingly necessary for civic engagement. Most college courses now include online discussion forums. The ability to interpret other people's thinking, to ask clarifying questions to build understanding, and to contribute intelligent comments to the conversation are skills that will serve students well long after they leave your class. (See Figure 3.9 for online discussion tools.)

TOOLS FOR ONLINE DISCUSSION BOARDS	
Your Learning Management System	Most LMS have built-in discussion boards ready for you to use with your students.
Collaborize Classroom	www.collaborizeclassroom.com/ This site is focused purely on organizing classroom discussions. Teachers and students log in with free accounts and can reply to threaded discussion topics.
Schoology	https://www.schoology.com Schoology is an LMS that teachers can download for free. It includes a discussion board.
Cel.ly	https://cel.ly Create a cell for your class (or for each class you teach) and host discussions there that can include links and images.

Figure 3.9 Top Tools for Online Discussion Boards and What They Do Best

Polling and Data Collection

When AP economics teacher Roni Habib described what economics class was like "back in the day," it seemed as if we were stepping into a scene from *Ferris Bueller's Day Off*, complete with pin-drop silence and teen eye rolling: "We have the law of supply and we have the law of demand. The law of demand says that as price goes down, the quantity demanded for the good will increase, all else being equal, and vice versa. Thus, we get an inverse relationship if you plot the price on the y-axis and the good quantity on the x-axis . . ." He interrupted himself at this point to say, "Generally, kids die when they hear that." So it comes as no surprise that in Habib's class, kids *don't* hear that.

Instead, Habib now uses polling and data collection to turn his classroom into a lab where students can explore the science of human behavior, as the term *social science* would lead us to believe. Students become the subjects and the researchers, and it is through their process of inquiry that they are able to infer complex concepts such as the law of diminishing marginal utility or the law of demand from the data they help to create.

For this particular lesson, Habib started with a tried-and-true classroom strategy: telling a funny story about himself as a teenager. His students leaned in eagerly. "When I was in college, I told two of my friends that I just *loved* lychee shakes. One of my friends was like, 'How much do you love them? I bet you can't drink ten of them in one sitting.' My response: 'You're on!' What can I say? We were post-adolescent, pre-adult males. We did this kind of thing. So, we went over and I sat in the restaurant, and I was like, 'All right, here we go.'"

Students laughed as he cued up a video re-creating the famous lychee shake dare with a couple of former students. Ten lychee shakes later, he stopped the video and asked his students to describe the satisfaction he had received from the lychee shakes he loved so much.

"The first one looked pretty good, but it went downhill after that," one student remarked.

Another chimed in, "Yeah, by number seven you looked like you were hurting."

"You got that right!" Habib exclaimed. "Take out your devices. We're going to do a little experiment." As students in his BYOD class opened up web browsers on smartphones and laptops, Habib projected a short URL on the screen, linking the class to a Google Form where he had posted some questions, with multiple-choice answers ranging from one to ten. Here are some examples:

- In a period of a month, if lychee shakes were one dollar each, how many would you buy?
- In a period of a month, if lychee shakes were five dollars each, how many would you buy?
- In a period of a month, if lychee shakes were ten dollars each, how many would you buy?

As students responded, the data poured in, populating a graph that Habib had set up in advance with a formula that converts the raw numbers into a histogram. "Our class is the market right now—a group of individuals who are demanding lychee shakes. Let's see what our demand behavior as a market looks like." Students watched as a downward-sloping curve between price and quantity demanded formed on the screen. "Turn to your partner and describe what you see." Habib circulated as students discussed the pattern they had watched unfold.

One girl said, "As things get more expensive, our class is less willing to buy them."

Her partner explained, "Yeah, and when the shakes were really cheap, we all wanted a bunch of them."

Because of access to immediate data and immediate results, Habib turned his classroom into a living textbook that valued every student's voice in the experiment. In the end, they inferred the law of demand from their own data through a process of perplexity and connection in which every child was actively participating.

Habib used a simple Google Form to collect his data, but there are many other tools available to gather and aggregate data, such as SurveyMonkey or Poll Everywhere, which work on any device and accept text messages as responses (see Figure 3.10).

TOOLS FOR POLLING AND DATA COLLECTION	
Your Learning Management System	Polling students may be an option in your LMS.
Poll Everywhere	www.polleverywhere.com Poll Everywhere accepts responses via text message and displays the results in real time as students submit their choices.
SurveyMonkey	www.surveymonkey.com This service lets you create basic surveys for free.
Google Forms	With Google Forms (part of Google Drive) you can create custom data-collection tools and view the results in a spreadsheet or as a summary of responses.

Figure 3.10 Top Tools for Polling and What They Do Best

Interactive Feedback Systems

Student response systems (think, clickers) were gearing up to take over classrooms when they were swept aside by the rollout of 1:1 programs. Being able to gather data from our students in real time while we are teaching and then adjust our lesson as needed creates a huge advantage for teachers and students. Clickers were limited to multiple-choice options. With a laptop or tablet in every student's hands, teachers can still ask multiple-choice questions, but we can also gather short-answer responses as well as have students pick a point on an image to show their understanding.

Our current favorite interactive feedback tools are Socrative and Nearpod. A Google Form can also be used to send students a quick formative assessment or to gather data for classroom discussion. (See Figure 3.11 for ideas and features.)

It usually takes just a few minutes to learn how to use one of these tools. Most have a short video tutorial, and the payoff is easy access to information about what your students understand. Socrative lets us send out individual questions as needed or make up a quiz in advance. Jen loves being able to ask her students a short-answer question and then send the anonymous answers back out for a class vote. The results of the vote become a starting point for class discussion.

TOOLS FOR INTERACTIVE FEEDBACK	
Nearpod	www.nearpod.com Share the content of your lesson directly with students' devices. Add questions and feedback opportunities to make your lesson interactive.
Socrative	http://socrative.com/ Socrative is a multifunction student response system that works with any Internet-connected device.

Figure 3.11 Top Tools for Interactive Feedback and What They Do Best

With tablets, one of the benefits to using an interactive feedback system is the "inking" feature that allows students to handwrite on the tablet with a stylus. Students in Shari Waters's history class use Nearpod to spark debates about regional conflicts and border disputes. After a unit about the Israel-Palestine crisis, Waters projected a slide with a map of the region while students looked at the mini-map displayed on their screens. She asked students to mark the specific area they believed was the root cause of the territorial conflict. As she projected anonymous student answers, the class discussed why each response could be reasonable, what misconceptions might be at play, and what else the student would need to consider. Instead of the teacher holding all the answers, or only a few bold voices being heard, Nearpod made it easy for Waters to give all of her students a voice in the conversation.

Educational Games

No one wants to see students spending all day every day playing games in class, but knowing about a few educational games that relate to your subject area can ensure spare moments aren't wasted. We suggest posting a list of acceptable games students can play when their other work is complete. In some cases, you can make a game a part of your curriculum. For example, Jen found an educational game helpful when she had to cover a colleague's class at the last minute.

Teacher: Jen Roberts (Covering a Colleague's Class)
Class: Advanced Placement English Language

The teacher of this class left early for a doctor's appointment and asked me to cover her last period. The students were supposed to be studying for their upcoming AP test.

"Most of them are reviewing the terms they made into flash cards during the semester," she told me.

When she was gone, I turned on the new interactive whiteboard and used her computer to do a search for [AP Language] on Quizlet. I found many lists of terms. I picked one that seemed reasonable and started a Quizlet game called Scatter. This projected a cluster of terms and their definitions on the board. The object of the game is to match the term to its definition and drag them together. When the term and definition match, they disappear from the board. Players must try to clear the board quickly, because the timer is running.

Because I didn't really know any of the students, I just stood at the board and started playing. A few students noticed what I was doing and began giving me advice. When I had finished playing, several eager students offered to take my place, and other students started giving them advice. Then someone asked, "What's that site?" Soon the whole class had abandoned their flash cards and joined our Scatter game, using lists of AP terms they had found on Quizlet.

"This is so much more fun. I actually like this," one student said.

"Yeah, I would play this at home," said another.

Does playing a matching game on an online vocabulary site help students learn vocabulary better than flash cards? Maybe, especially if the game entices them to spend more time and attention focused on the terms. Quizlet is worth checking out. You can create a teacher account and make your own lists of terms or do a search to see what has already been created. You can use (and assign) lists from other teachers easily.

In addition to the educational games typically found online, there are tools for mobile devices that we can use to create engaging learning experiences. For example, with apps such as Munzee and Klikaklue we can use QR codes to create educational scavenger hunts. (See Figure 3.12 for other ideas.)

What About Disengagement?

Students aren't perfect, and everything we think they need to learn is not always going to be super-interesting to them. Teachers can provide more stimulating learning, but there will still be times when a student is off task. (Have you ever been to a full-day staff training? Were you entirely focused the whole day?) Developing mental stamina and focusing on a challenging task are skills students are learning, whether or not they have a computer in front of them.

The question then is what to do when a student in your class is disengaged or engaged with the wrong task, such as playing an online game when he or she should be reading or writing something. Keep in mind that how you respond says a lot about what you value as an educator, and your students will pick up on that.

The first instinct of many teachers new to 1:1 is to take away the device and hand the student a textbook or paper. We suggest you avoid that tactic. When you take away the device, you implicitly send a message to the distracted student and to the rest of the class that the work he or she was supposed to be doing with the computer or tablet was not meaningful or important. Compare the situation with a student drawing pictures with his pencil instead of writing an essay. You wouldn't take away the pencil. You would redirect the student to the correct activity. Likewise, if a student were on the wrong page of a textbook, you wouldn't take away the book. So, first try redirecting the student back to the correct task and imposing another consequence, as you would for any small discipline matter.

EDUCATIONAL GAMES	
Quizlet	Quizlet.com is a site and app that allows teachers and students to create their own flash-card decks or choose from a bank of cards. Quizlet creates fun learning games from those card decks.
Free Rice	Freerice.com donates rice to the World Food Program for every right answer and is available for a variety of subject areas.
TapQuizMaps	www.rolzor.com TapQuizMaps is an interactive map app designed to help students learn geography.
Code.org	Code.org is a site that makes it easy for students (and adults) to learn basic computer programming skills by playing games.
Kahoot	https://getkahoot.com/ Kahoot is a game-based student response system that works on the web and mobile devices.

Figure 3.12 Educational Games Worth Your Time

If you find that a few students are chronically off task and you have tried a series of consequences, then taking the device might be necessary, but be sure you are ready with some equally rigorous work for them to complete. Also, be aware that some students may adopt tactics of sabotage or deliberate misuse with the intention of having their device taken away to avoid classwork.

There are also some technical solutions that may reduce students' ability to use their devices inappropriately. Depending on the type of devices your students have, you may be able to see their screens remotely. Jen uses LanSchool, which allows her to see her students' laptop screens and sometimes take over the device remotely to close a tab or take a screenshot.

Diana has Reflector software, and she can ask as many as four students to mirror their iPads to her screen so she can be sure they are working in the correct app. But neither solution is ideal, and neither is a good substitute for an engaging project, lesson, or just the teacher's presence moving around the room.

Try these strategies to detect and reduce disengagement and distraction:

- Have students work in pairs. If it takes two of them to get the task done, then it is much harder for one of them to be on the wrong site.
- If you suspect a student is off task, look at the students around him or her. If they seem fascinated by what's on their classmate's screen, chances are it might not be schoolwork.
- Move around the room a lot. Stand in different places. Find the spot that has the best view of the most screens. Our favorite trick is teaching from the back of the room.
- Have students turn the screens of their devices toward you when you are giving directions.
- If you must deliver information verbally for more than a few minutes, use a formative responsive system (see Figure 3.11) to ask students questions about the content as you go.
- If the distraction is a nonacademic app, delete the app. The student will have to download the game later to play it again.

Classroom management is something we all have to think about, with or without student devices in the room. Adding technology to your classroom may feel like a management headache in the beginning, but once you and your students have had some time to adjust to the changes, your classroom management will probably feel about the same. We have noticed one difference, though. Before we had devices in our classrooms, an off-task student tended to be a real distraction to others. With a computer or tablet on their desks, the off-task students tend to get absorbed in the devices. They still might become distracted, but usually they do not interfere with other students' learning.

Overall, we find engagement increases dramatically for our students when we leverage the strategies of curiosity, connection, and perplexity. Having devices in the classroom can make our lessons more interactive, collaborative, and student focused. Adding pedagogies such as shared reading, short- and long-term research, backchanneling, discussion boards, interactive feedback systems, polling, and educational games to our classrooms means our students are less likely to become disengaged with the learning process. We have found over and over in our 1:1 classrooms that the best strategy for classroom management is an engaging learning experience.

POWER UP! Engagement Techniques to Add to Your Classroom

1. **Add a backchannel** to a live classroom discussion, or make a discussion board part of a homework assignment.

2. **Use an interactive feedback system** as part of a lesson or as an exit slip.

3. **Implement a long-term research project** with your students. Give them the choice of their investigation and offer multiple ways for them to document their learning.

CHAPTER 4

Collaboration

Col·lab·o·ra·tion (n): The action of building relationships and working together to produce or create something meaningful.

Teacher: Alison Black
Class: Eighth-Grade English
Observer: Jen Roberts

I was especially excited to visit Alison Black's class at Coronado Middle School. I knew the school had been running a bring-your-own-device (BYOD) program for more than a decade, and I wanted to see how having a variety of devices affected instruction. Before the students arrived, Black told me I had come on a good day because her students would be doing some peer revisions for an essay they had been working on. She planned to have them share papers in Google Docs and then give each other feedback.

After the morning announcements, Black asked students to keep their computers in their backpacks for a few more minutes while she used the class website to explain the directions for the day. "I want you to share your essay with your partner. Then, while you read through each other's essays, highlight the evidence you see that your partner is meeting the expectations for the rubric. Also, help your partner be sure their essay has enough evidence by highlighting quotes from the story in blue and commentary about those quotes in yellow." It was near the end of the school year, and clearly her students had done this routine before. I suspected she was repeating these directions for me as much as for them. "Okay, get to work."

In just a few seconds, every student was reaching into his or her backpack. They pulled out a range of devices so varied that I thought for a moment I had stepped into an electronics store. Every brand of laptop I could think of was represented, running a variety of different operating systems. There were tablets, too, of several sizes and models. All of the students were at ease with their personal devices, and all of them got right to the task of sharing their essays. A few students visited a cart of laptops at the back of the room. Black explained that the school provided extra laptops for students who had forgotten or didn't have their own. Because Coronado has a large US Navy base, the Department of Defense had provided a grant for the extra laptops. Within a few minutes, every student was reading and highlighting a partner's essay.

As students finished reading, they began to have soft conversations about the elements they saw or didn't see in each other's work. "I like the way you used this quote from the story, but then you just stopped," one student said. "I think you need to say more about it. That's why I left you that comment on your doc."

The partner nodded. "Thanks, I see it. I can fix that." Short conversations about what to fix or add were happening all over the room.

Then I came to a young man working alone. I thought he was still working on his draft, because I could see he was doing a lot of typing. His screen, though, told me a different story. He had a chat window open on the Google Doc. He hurriedly explained that his partner was home sick with strep throat, but that they planned to meet online during class because they could still share their papers and even discuss their feedback for each other with the chat window.

Despite different hardware and even different locations, students in Black's class could share their work with each other and collaborate on ways to improve their writing. On the surface, this lesson wasn't much different from the kind of trade-papers peer editing that was common when I was in middle school, but making the trade digitally added several advantages.

First, students were inserting suggested edits and other feedback directly into the working document. From there, the writer could polish the text, but he or she did not have to sit down with a pen and rewrite the whole thing. Second, the collaboration and feedback loop could extend beyond school. In effect, the partners never had to give the paper back. The essays remained shared with each other for as long as they liked, and they could continue to give each other feedback. Third, digital collaboration models the way adults collaborate in higher education and out in the workforce, where projects are completed over time and through multiple revisions. Black noted another advantage: "Digital editing or discussions gives students who are less comfortable with in-person discussions a mode for engaging with peers. Last year, I had a student who was on the autism spectrum. He would shy away from engaging with peers but loved having lively discussions using the chat."

Why Collaborate?

We know entire books have been written about collaboration, and we don't intend to duplicate those efforts (Harvey and Daniels 2009; Buzzeo 2008). What we want to share with you are the possibilities for collaboration that can transform our classroom spaces and our professional spaces when student devices are a part of our daily teaching.

In their *Framework for 21st Century Learning* (2014), the Partnership for 21st Century Skills, or P21 (www.p21.org/), lists collaboration as one of the four most important applied skills for success beyond school. Their "Four Cs" are collaboration, critical thinking, communication, and creativity. Although each of the examples we share in this chapter include all four of the Cs, we will focus our attention, for now, on collaboration. Ken Kaye, cofounder of P21, highlights the value of collaboration in our global workforce. He explains, "There's nothing you work on in the real world that you do by yourself anymore. Work is done in teams. Collaboration is an absolutely essential skill" (Vogel 2009). Educators have long extolled the value of teamwork and cooperative learning, but never has the call from the world beyond school been so loud, begging teachers to prepare students for work that requires *flexible* collaboration—both synchronous (working together at the same time) and asynchronous (working together at different times).

Kevin Cavanaugh (2013), vice president for Smarter Workforce Engineering at IBM, echoes this sentiment in describing the collaborative nature of contemporary employment and the benefits that companies and employees alike can derive from collaborative work:

> This need for interaction doesn't go away when we go to work. As a rule, we don't want to be siloed in our work, toiling away without the benefits that working collaboratively provides. When people work collaboratively, they can easily share their ideas and knowledge. They can tap into the expertise of the workforce so they can get the information they need to do their jobs more efficiently and with better outcomes. We tend to find greater meaning in what we do when we collaborate with others across departments, time zones and countries to resolve issues, innovate or help the company's bottom line.

Our students will need practice working in teams and practice with many forms of collaboration (see Figure 4.1). They will need to intuitively understand how to navigate the dynamics of face-to-face collaboration and remote collaboration. They will need to be adept at building relationships with teammates who sit four desks away as easily as with teammates who live four time zones away. And, if they have a chance to master those skills, they are likely to find real satisfaction from the process and product they collectively create, both during their time in school and beyond.

It is, perhaps, for these very reasons that the International Society for Technology in Education (ISTE) delineates collaboration as one of its six essential standards for students;

Figure 4.1 Students practice teamwork in our classrooms.

beyond Common Core and subject area competencies, students need the soft skills, or applied skills, requisite for life in the twenty-first century. (For more on the ISTE standards, please visit http://www.iste.org/standards.) The collaboration standard clearly incorporates what leaders in business and higher education have come to expect:

> Students use digital media and environments to communicate and work collaboratively, including at a distance, to support individual learning and contribute to the learning of others. [Students] interact, collaborate, and publish with peers, experts, or others employing a variety of digital environments and media. [Students] communicate information and ideas effectively to multiple audiences using a variety of media and formats. [Students] develop cultural understanding and global awareness by engaging with learners of other cultures. [Students] contribute to project teams to produce original works or solve problems. (ISTE 2007)

When they join the workforce, our students will collaborate on projects of ever-increasing complexity and scope, projects we can't even define or imagine yet. Collaboration in school gives students opportunities to practice academic language, social skills, and time management. It enables them to learn from their peers, provides greater autonomy, and lets them prepare for the world of work beyond school. These things are true with or without devices in our classrooms. In a 1:1 classroom environment, collaboration means students have access to the same tools professional adults use to get much of their work done. Now our students can learn to work with shared documents, communicate by e-mail, and practice their digital citizenship. As mentioned in Chapter 2, students are our partners in innovation. When much of their work becomes digital, they will have discussions about which tools are best for their projects, and help teach us along the way.

Teamwork now requires technical skill as team members learn how to merge their separate contributions into a complete project. We are not suggesting that teachers need to know all those technical pieces; working together to overcome technical challenges is a part of group work in our classrooms and in the workplaces outside our classrooms. It is also the part we find students excel at most.

Consider some other reasons for supporting student collaboration:

- Collaboration among students means our teaching style is student centered. This gives us time to check in with the groups, address their concerns, and help struggling students. When students are collaborating, we are facilitating and coaching.
- Collaborative projects often involve more preparation up front but then reduce the amount of time we might have spent preparing lessons on a daily basis.

- Collaborative projects often result in high-quality work and make learning more memorable for students.
- Collaborative projects mean fewer final pieces of work to evaluate.

When Jen was first asked to be part of a 1:1 pilot in 2008, she worried that giving every student a laptop would take away from the collaborative atmosphere in her classroom. She actually suggested a 2:1 model, with only half as many laptops as students. She wanted students to have to work together. What she didn't see coming was the explosion in collaborative production tools now available online.

Diana's experience of moving to 1:1 iPads was very similar. She was worried that having screens between students would diminish the community feeling of her classes. Now all of our students have a laptop or a tablet, but they still sit in groups, discuss their work, and contribute to shared projects. Collaboration is thriving even more with a 1:1 classroom.

Collaborating with Colleagues

If you are reading this book because your whole school is going 1:1, then you are in the same boat with many of your colleagues. To be sure, the transition to digital pedagogy is time consuming, but it is much easier if you work together. Now is the time to gather with teachers in your subject area or grade level and discuss ways you can help each other use the technology in your classrooms. Together you can distribute tasks, share your resources, work with your strengths, and learn from your peers. Teachers who regularly collaborate to share student work develop more reflective practices and are more likely to make instructional changes (Borko 2004).

It took Diana and Fehmeen, her teaching partner, about a year to figure out that they were meeting to plan only to duplicate their efforts at creating documents for their freshman classes. Two slightly different versions of the same graphic organizer existed in isolation on two different laptops. They realized that by streamlining their resources and moving their curriculum to a shared Google folder, they would no longer need to send e-mails with attachments or swap copies during passing periods. The benefit they did not expect was the flexibility of asynchronous collaboration—working together during different prep periods and with different out-of-school schedules. Fehmeen often left comments and suggested edits in their master planning document and handouts in the evening after her kids went to sleep, and Diana, a morning person, would take a look and respond early the next morning. Instead of trying to catch each other for a quick check-in to ask a question about wording or ordering in a set of essay prompts, their collaboration happened seamlessly and on their own terms.

The days of curriculum binders are over. When we have something to give to a colleague, we no longer make a photocopy of it; we send a link. Now is the time to set up a shared folder in Google Drive or Dropbox for your team. Add subfolders to it for the different units in your curriculum and upload the digital resources you each already have. Be selective. Take the time to evaluate and discuss each piece you are adding to the folder. Include only those items the majority of the team can use.

We have another suggestion. When you start to digitally curate and combine your resources, do not put teacher names on any of these folders. Label them by unit. As you work with your team, acknowledge that each person brings strengths to the cause and that having a vast repository of curriculum materials is only one area of strength. When you share openly with your colleagues, all of the students benefit. With digital collaboration, it takes only a few clicks to share a lesson or document that everyone can use.

Regardless of how much curriculum you had on hand before your school went 1:1, you will need to create or adapt materials that take advantage of the devices in your classrooms. This is another great opportunity for collaboration and resource sharing (see Figure 4.2). When Jen created a Google Form to help her students analyze a text, she was able to share it with her whole department. When Diana created a video lesson on writing introductions, it was appropriate for several grade levels. Most of what is in your filing cabinet won't make a seamless transition to digital pedagogy, so work together to change what works and collaboratively create the pieces you want to add.

Figure 4.2 Jen, second from right, is part of an awesome ninth-grade English team made up of (from left) Laura Baker, Jennifer Murphy, Chris Sparta, and preservice teacher Alyssa Black.

The soft skills necessary for collaboration aren't just for students. We strongly encourage you to keep open communications with your colleagues, meet regularly to discuss what is working for you in your transition to digital pedagogy, and manage your collection of digital resources. Keeping digital folders organized by unit helps a lot. You might also find it useful to create a spreadsheet or table that summarizes the materials available for each unit.

This next point is critical: Be sure that everyone included on a shared folder understands how to handle the technical aspects. You may need to explain that making changes to a document means everyone will see those changes. It is common for a tech novice teacher to open a shared resource and customize it for his or her class without realizing that those changes are affecting a shared document. It is worth a few moments to show your colleagues how to use File/Make a copy in Google Drive, or File/Save As in a Word document before they make changes to personalize a shared resource. It is also a good idea to save your own copies of anything you rely on, just in case someone accidentally deletes something from a shared folder.

Figure 4.3 provides some specifics on our preferred collaboration tools. We also suggest visiting pluginpowerup.com for our most current recommendations.

TOOLS FOR COLLEGIAL COLLABORATION	
Google Drive	Shared folders in Google Drive are great for complex collaborations that involve multiple documents, spreadsheets, and so on. You can easily upload existing documents and convert them to Google Docs. Collaborators can edit in real time. Drive offers very generous storage allowances. (Drive also gives you access to Google Forms, which are indispensable in our 1:1 classrooms.)
Dropbox	Shared folders in Dropbox make it easy to share existing files and documents created in Word or Excel. Do not attempt to edit these documents at the same time as your collaborators, however, or you will end up with multiple versions. Storage is less generous but probably adequate for your needs.
Voxer	Voxer is a voice communications app. By creating a Voxer channel, members of your team can have asynchronous conversations, leaving short messages to support your collaboration.

Figure 4.3 Top Tools for Collegial Collaboration and What They Do Best

When digital collaboration becomes the norm for teachers, it breaks down the walls of our classrooms. Imagine for a moment that the curriculum binders on your shelves are enchanted so that any time a colleague adds a paper resource to his or her binder, the same resource magically appears in your binder as well. You would only have to open the binder on your shelf to see everything your colleagues had been adding to theirs. That is exactly what happens when you share folders online. And, if you don't have colleagues to collaborate with at your school because of size or other constraints, then virtual collaboration with distant colleagues is now much easier.

Student Collaboration

Diana's former student Jesse came in at lunch one day looking for a quiet place to work. "I need to do some edits on our script," he said. He was working on a film project for his history class with several other students. They wrote the script for their short film in a Google Doc so they could all edit and comment on it. Although they didn't have much time together in class for writing, Jesse found time on his lunch break to contribute to the project. Diana peered over his shoulder as he read what his team had done so far and couldn't help but see the note from his friend: "Hey Jesse—we need to finish this thing tonight. Google Hangout 8:00?" Given the opportunity, students will collaborate in ways we might never have thought of. This is a wired generation of kids who are already connected to each other inside of class and out; it's about time we give them reasons to use those tools and skills to enrich their learning.

 PLUG IN First Steps in Digital Collaboration

1. **Survey your students about their experiences** with collaboration. Ask them about expectations for digital collaboration. What kinds of things would they like to collaborate on? Which previously individual tasks could they help each other with?

2. **Discuss collaboration possibilities** with a local colleague. Set up a shared folder for resources and subfolders for units. Be sure to discuss the steps for making a copy of anything you are planning to modify.

3. **Reach out to a colleague** at another school, another state, or even in another part of the world. Create a shared folder of resources or even a Voxer channel for sharing ideas. Find out where teachers who teach the same course are posting materials online, and browse what they have already shared.

What Counts as Collaboration?

As the opening definition of this chapter says, collaboration is about working together to produce or create something meaningful, but that is a very broad definition, and there are many gray areas of collaboration. In some sense, your reading of this book is a collaboration as you take our ideas and integrate them into your own teaching practice, but most people would probably agree that collaboration requires more of a back-and-forth exchange of ideas and effort. What does that look like in a 1:1 classroom? We would like to suggest a few models that we use with our own students:

- *Collaborative Preparation*: This type of collaboration means that students contribute to a shared preparation experience. It could be shared brainstorming, shared data collection, shared outlining, conducting an experiment together, or even just talking about their thinking. After a period of shared collaboration, students can create an individual product or continue collaborating on the work.
- *Collaborative Production*: This is the most typical form of collaboration and likely what most of us think of when we plan collaborative work: students working together to produce a shared product. Often this means a presentation, poster, skit, video, or other visual product.

- *Collaborative Feedback*: Sometimes we ask students to collaborate by giving each other feedback and offering revisions after they have done work individually. Students who learn to give their peers specific feedback can offer significant contributions to the final project.
- *Collaborative Presentation*: This form of collaboration often goes hand in hand with collaborative production; students produce work together and then get up together to present it. We advocate additional forms of collaborative presentation: asking students to present each other's work means they have to develop a strong understanding about another student's project. Similarly, asking students to bring together separate projects into a single presentation, website, or video stretches their collaborative skills.

Although collaboration has always been a part of the curriculum, it certainly looks different now that every student has access to technology. The tools we place in students' hands enrich their collaborative experience and make the work they do more closely resemble the work they will continue to do once they leave our schools. What follows is a series of classroom examples highlighting how 1:1 technology transforms each of the four types of collaboration.

Collaborative Preparation
Teacher: Jen Roberts
Class: Ninth-Grade English

My students had been reading, close reading, and storyboarding "The Cask of Amontillado" by Edgar Allan Poe in preparation for an essay that would have them writing about the theme, mood, and irony in the story (see Figure 4.4). I knew my ELL students and my students with IEPs were going to struggle with the essay prompt and the challenge to support their writing with evidence from the text. Actually, I knew all of them were going to struggle with the evidence gathering. I wanted a way to scaffold the process, and I found a method that would let every student contribute.

I created a Google Form with six questions. The first question asked them to find an example of irony from the story, a sentence that they could copy and paste that would work as evidence for the literary device. The second question asked them to explain why that sentence was an example of irony. The third question asked for an example that showed the mood of the story, and so on. I partnered students and set them to work collaboratively as they searched for examples of irony, mood, and theme from the text. They tackled the task, which seemed doable, accessible, and fun. Finding one thing at a time is not so bad. They only had to copy and paste the sentences and say why they chose them. When my students were finished submitting their findings, I had a spreadsheet full of examples of all three elements they would need for their essays. I removed (actually hid) the column of the spreadsheet that had their names and published the spreadsheet as a web page. (To do that in Google Drive, you use File/Publish to the Web.) With a published page, I had a link to their evidence that I could post on my learning management system (LMS).

From the spreadsheet of their findings, I modeled for students how I would choose a piece of evidence—one of the sentences from the story—and use it in the paragraph about mood in my essay. I showed them how I looked at the examples to pick one I liked, and then looked at the explanation next to that example in the spreadsheet to see if I could use it to help me get started with my writing. "Be careful," I warned. "All the examples and explanations on this sheet were chosen and written by ninth graders, and everyone knows you can't trust ninth graders, so you have to make sure the evidence you are choosing really works in *your* essay." My students laughed, but it helped them understand that just copying and pasting off the spreadsheet would not work. They still had to be critical thinkers about the evidence they

Finding Irony, Mood and Theme in "The Cask of Amontillado"

Answer all questions in complete academic sentences. The work you do here will be shared with others. Together we are compiling a collection of quotes from the story that you will be able to draw from as evidence in your future writing.

* Required

Names of your team ·

Period ·
- 4
- 6
- 7

Find a quote from the story that is an example of irony. Include the section number, for example (Poe, 4)

Explain why the quote above is an example of irony.

Find a quote from the story that shows the mood of the story. Include the section number, for example (Poe, 4)

Figure 4.4 Students use online forms to gather evidence from the text.

chose to use in their writing and still had to write their own analyses of that evidence.

As a result, they wrote excellent, individual essays, chock-full of evidence from the text to support their assertions about the way Poe uses mood and irony to create a theme in his story. It was the evidence bank, in the form of the published spreadsheet, that allowed students to enrich their writing with lots of text evidence from the short story. Because of our collaborative preparation, all students were more successful in their writing.

Other Ideas for Collaborative Preparation

- At the beginning of the school year, a chemistry teacher wants her students to create a resource about the periodic table that they can use over the course of the year. She creates a shared online slide deck and asks each student to complete a numbered slide about the assigned element. (There are 118 elements, so she can do this with several classes at once or focus on the elements most crucial for the students at the beginning of the year.) The slide deck becomes a reference for her students.
- A history teacher is starting a unit about the Vietnam War. He sets up a Diigo group, and students add information as they do research about the period. When he asks them to write their research papers at the end of the unit, all of the students can draw from the resources collected and annotated in Diigo.
- A math teacher wants to prepare her students for the upcoming exam but is tired of running her typical review session the day before; she wants students to take the lead and would love for the review to begin earlier than the last minute. She sets up a discussion board on their LMS and assigns pairs of students a concept to explain. As they get to work in class, the partners type their explanations, draw corresponding figures, and upload both their writing and their images to the discussion board. That night for homework she asks the students to comment on two other posts by posing questions or by adding other ways to remember key concepts, other examples, or alternative approaches to solving problems.

Figure 4.5 lists and describes some suggested tools for scaffolding student thinking as you begin a project.

Collaborative Production
Teacher: Steve Martell
Class: Seventh-Grade Social Studies
Observer: Jen Roberts

I spent the first ten years of my teaching career working with seventh graders in English and social studies. In my garage I still have a few boxes of seventh-grade social studies materials I can't bear to part with, so the opportunity to visit a seventh-grade social studies class was a treat. I never had student laptops in my middle school classrooms, and I was excited to see how Steve Martell was leveraging his 1:1 resources. He had told me via e-mail that they were in the middle of their unit on medieval Europe and that the students were working on a castle project in Minecraft, an online creative building space. My own sons are Minecraft fluent, so I thought I knew what to expect.

TOOLS FOR COLLABORATIVE PREPARATION	
Google Forms	Data from forms is collected in a spreadsheet. When you share that spreadsheet with all of your students, everyone will have access to what everyone else submitted. This can be a scaffold, or it can allow students to analyze larger data sets. You can also use the form to collect data from sources outside your classroom by sharing the link online.
Padlet	Padlet lets students add online stickies to a "wall" you create. Students can add their findings or ideas and then group those responses as needed.
Lino	Lino (en.linoit.com) is a collaborative workspace where students can pin and color-code stickies and photos as they gather resources for an ongoing project.
Diigo	Diigo groups allow students to contribute shared bookmarks to a common research collection along with their annotations about each resource.
Scrible	Scrible is a web-based annotation tool that allows students to mark up research texts and share them with each other in group libraries. It has robust tagging and synthesizing capabilities, and ample storage in the student edition.

Figure 4.5 Top Tools for Collaborative Preparation and What They Do Best

When I walked into the room, every student was on a laptop, and every screen was in some stage of castle building (see Figure 4.6). Some students had the skeletal outlines of the castle, and others were busy filling in walls. I sat down near a group and watched as the boy near me began to work on an interior room. He noticed he had a visitor and began to talk about his process.

"This is the lord's bedroom, so it has to have a big bed. I used upside-down anvils and torches to make it look like these torches were sticking out of the walls because they didn't have electricity, and I used red carpet for the floor because the red looks good with the floor. I wanted him to have some comfortable chairs, so I used stairs and then added signs on the sides. Oh, and I gave him stained-glass windows."

"Wow, that's really elaborate. How long did that take you?" I asked.

He glanced at the clock behind me. "What time did the period start? I guess about twenty minutes, but I play Minecraft at home, so I am used to building things."

"Can you show me some of the rest of the castle?" I asked.

"Sure." He began to move his screen around, changing the point of view as we zoomed out of the lord's bedroom and down a long corridor. "I'm going to take you to the dining hall. We finished that yesterday."

Sure enough, we ended up in a large room filled by a long table. He explained why the table was long and

Figure 4.6 Students in Steve Martell's class use Minecraft to design castles representative of those in their unit on medieval Europe.

how a person's rank affected where he or she sat at the table. Then it was back to the tour. "Those doors lead to the kitchens, but let's go up on the roof—I mean, the ramparts." Several staircases later we were looking out over the Minecraft vista toward a virtual horizon where other castles were under construction in the distance. My guide began pointing out the castles of other teams around the room.

"You seem like such an expert," I said. "How has it been, working on a team project this way?"

"Well, these castles are big and elaborate, and we don't have a lot of time to do the project, so having a team is a good thing." He went on to tell me that one of his team members had been new to Minecraft and that he had sent that person starter videos to learn about building.

"Yeah, the hardest part was just getting the hang of the control keys on the keyboard, but once I had those down I was good." This was from a girl sitting on the other side of my guide. She wanted to show me the stables she had been working on. "I looked at pictures of actual stables and pictures of other stables in Minecraft, and then I built my own."

I visited a number of teams around the room that day. I learned about the various jobs people had in the castle, from baker to blacksmith. I toured chapels, kitchens, barracks, great halls, bedrooms, servants' quarters, more stables, and rooftops. Each team explained the defensive measures specific to their castle, and several of them complained that they weren't allowed to use lava as a defense tool. "It wouldn't be historically accurate, but it would be cool."

Their enthusiasm was intense; they were excited to show me their creations. Martell explained that he would be asking them to write expository essays about the construction of their castles, but based on the tours they gave me, I had no doubt the writing would come easily to them. If you let them build it, they will learn.

Other Ideas for Collaborative Production

- Students in a third-year French class are writing dialogues about visiting another country. Together they find images about the country and add them to a shared slide deck. They use the notes section of each slide to write their scripts and then create a screencast of their project while they read their script in French. When they are finished, each team has a short video to share about their trip, which they upload to the LMS for their classmates to see.
- Students in a mixed-grade-level Intro to Computer Science class are approaching the final unit of the year: app design. In teams of four, they apply their newly honed coding skills to design, create, and publish an app for the school that they think their classmates would use and benefit from. Their final projects range from calendar apps that remind students of the rotating block schedule for that day, to homework management apps that allow students to check off a to-do list of assignments.
- Students in an eleventh-grade English class are taking a break from the typical "analytical essay after the book" routine and creating a series of help videos for other readers of *The Great Gatsby*. Groups of three tackle questions about the subtext of the novel ("What's up with the motif of yellow and white?" "What's up with the symbol of the green light?" "What's up with the gray imagery in the Valley of Ashes?"), and produce two-minute creative films that walk novice readers through key passages and provide quick, pithy explanations. Their tutorials take many forms—animations, puppet shows, screencasts, and recorded skits—but ultimately all of them end up on YouTube for fellow readers around the world to watch.

Although sites such as those listed in Figure 4.7 are specifically designed to support collaborative work, and many more will likely offer collaborative features in the near future, other excellent digital production tools are single-user platforms. We have worked around that limitation by encouraging teams of students to create a common log-in that all members can access. We ask our groups to designate one member's e-mail address as the central log-in address, but to make up a unique password for the project that everyone on the team can know. That means that if students want to collaborate to edit a video, trim a podcast, or even build a website, they can.

TOOLS FOR COLLABORATIVE PRODUCTION	
Google Docs	With shared text documents, students can collaborate on scripts, essays, study guides, outlines, plans—the sky's the limit. They can share the document with the teacher for supervision and guidance. Revision history tells us who did what and when for the document. Google Slides work much the same way as Google Docs. Both are part of Google Drive.
Trello.com	Trello is a project management site especially useful for larger, long-term projects that require teams to communicate about the tasks they have accomplished and still need to complete.
Minecraft-Edu	Minecraft is an online virtual building environment that many of your students will already know. The education version provides additional features that make it school friendly. The primary function of Minecraft is three-dimensional building. Students can create models of real or imagined places, design their own structures, and take visitors on a virtual tour.

Figure 4.7 Top Tools for Collaborative Production and What They Do Best

Collaborative Feedback
Teacher: Jan Abrams
Class: Eighth-Grade Humanities
Observer: Diana Neebe

Jan Abrams's eighth graders were working on essays explaining the causes of the Civil War as part of a cross-curricular study for their humanities class. The students had already gotten most of the way through their drafting process when Abrams invited me in to see their writing groups in action. "We've been getting better at this all year," she said. "At first sharing their work took a while, but then the groups made shared folders, and now they just add their essays to the group folder and get going. I can't believe how much time this has saved me. I used to stand over the copy machine for an hour to be sure we had enough copies of their drafts."

She thought I'd be most interested in the technical aspect of their collaborative feedback process, but really, I just wanted to listen to what students were telling each other about the writing. I wandered over to a group in progress where a boy was already reading his essay aloud to his peers. They all had his essay on their screens, and I could read over the shoulder of the girl closest to me as we followed along with the boy's reading. He paused a few times to correct something, but no one in the group spoke or interrupted him. When he was finished, he exhaled hard, and then mimed turning a key over his mouth. I gathered he would not be speaking for a while.

One girl, wearing an incongruous blue bow tie, looked up at me, a stranger in their midst, but then decided to ignore my presence and turned to the group. "Okay, David asked us to see if he did a good job on his introduction and body paragraphs. What do we think?" Silence. The group peered back through the Google Doc.

"I think his introduction's okay," said a small girl with dark hair.

"Really?" This was a new voice, from a lanky boy in a football jersey. "I think he did a great job explaining what the Civil War was, but I don't get that he is talking about the causes."

David, the author in question, silently raised his eyebrows, but said nothing.

"Actually, I think you are right." The girl with the bow tie was peering closely at her screen, rereading the introduction. "He is missing that part where he claims one thing as the most important cause of the war."

David sat up and began to reread the introduction himself. The dark-haired girl, who thought it was "okay," was also rereading. "Oh yeah, he doesn't really have a thesis statement, does he?"

The group talked for several more minutes about elements that needed improvement in David's paper. David did not raise his eyebrows again at any of their advice. I watched him scroll to the parts of his paper they were talking about and make copious comments in his doc to capture their suggestions. Several times, a group member added another comment to a section to put their advice in writing. When the group was finished, it was David's turn to talk.

"Um, okay, so I have some things to fix." Nervous laughter and more glances at the stranger. "Actually this was good. You guys saw things I didn't see, so yeah, thanks. I'm gonna work on it tonight."

I couldn't resist making a suggestion. "You know, David, you can leave your paper shared with your group and ask if any of them would be willing to look at it again tonight when you're finished."

David would go home to revise his paper, using the advice from his peers. Frankly, his essay needed a lot of work, but the group had given him helpful suggestions, and he had listened to all of it. Having the author listen while the group discusses the work is a key aspect of Abrams's collaborative feedback strategy.

Other Ideas for Collaborative Feedback

- In a seventh-grade math class, the teacher takes a picture of a solved problem from one student's homework, being sure to block out the student's name. He posts the picture to VoiceThread. Students log in and view the example. Then, each student adds a voice comment about the way the problem was solved, including suggestions or comments about what they learned from looking at the example.

- Students in an eleventh-grade physics class have built cardboard "houses" with a lightbulb inside for a project about insulation. The objective was to build a house that was the best insulated using only one and a half cardboard boxes provided by their teacher. Each four-person team has its house on display, but all the students are roaming the room with their tablets. At each project, students scan a QR code with their tablets to watch a one-minute video the team made to explain the design of the house. After watching the video, the students click a link in the description to give the team feedback, using a Google Form. The form asks what the team did well and also asks for suggested improvements that would have made the "house" more energy efficient. Teams will review their feedback and get one more day to make changes before the project is officially due.
- Students in a ninth-grade English class are preparing to write novels during National Novel Writing Month, an annual project in November (ywp.nanowrimo.org). Each student posts a synopsis of his or her novel plan to the class discussion board. Classmates review the plans and add suggestions about characters, plot, and setting. The author can consider these suggestions and adapt his or her novel plan before beginning to write in November.

Collaborative feedback tools, such as those in Figure 4.8, will help you and your students provide high-quality, timely feedback for learning.

Collaborative Presentation
Teacher: Diana Neebe
Class: U.S. Literature

Over the course of our unit based on *Adventures of Huckleberry Finn*, my students and I looked into contemporary uses of satire to spark conversation and shape reform, much like Mark Twain did during his time. We studied the way in which masterful contemporary satirists such as Jon Stewart and Stephen Colbert are able to reshape the news through humor, creating an interpretation that makes us think and perhaps also makes us uncomfortable enough to want to change. Then, I presented the challenge: create your own satire that sparks our desire to do things differently.

Our collaborative "satire spark talks" were a riff off of a PechaKucha, which is a timed presentation in which twenty images show for twenty seconds each while the speaker presents to the audience. We decided to confine our satire "spark" talks to ten slides for twenty seconds each. During that time, a mere three minutes and twenty seconds, teams of students presented their critiques of one element in our society that they thought was in need of reform.

TOOLS FOR COLLABORATIVE FEEDBACK	
Google Forms	Forms are flexible enough to be used for individual or group feedback. We like using forms so students can "score" each other's presentations; we then send the presenter the peer comments via e-mail.
Kaizena	Kaizena works with Google Docs to let readers leave voice comments for the writer. Often teachers and peers can more clearly explain their feedback, and provide advice with a more helpful tone, than they can with written comments alone.
VoiceThread	VoiceThread is a paid service that allows you to post an image, video, document, or presentation and have multiple users comment on it by leaving short voice messages or text messages. It works with any web-enabled device.
Discussion Boards	Students can post ideas, plans, and questions to a class discussion board and get answers, suggestions, and ideas from their peers.

Figure 4.8 Top Tools for Collaborative Feedback and What They Do Best

When Camille, Jess, and Lauren took the floor, all eyes were on an image of Barbie, redesigned so that her physical proportions were more in line with the typical woman. The next nine slides were a tour de force, showing pinkified toy aisles and pages of gender-biased children's books. At each step of the way, the girls delivered perfectly timed lines corresponding with their perfectly timed slides. When the image of the Disney princess pageant popped up, Jess quipped, "Growing up in a media-saturated society, we've always known our options: be a princess, or, well, be a princess." And a few slides later, when the image of a "girls' survival guide" book series glowed on the screen, Camille and Lauren took turns reading actual book titles, with a few interjections along the way:

"In the boys' series, they get to learn how to survive in a forest, in a desert, and in a river filled with white-water rapids. And in the girls' series, we get to learn how to survive a BFF fight, a fashion disaster, and a breakout."

"At least the boys will know how to take care of us."

"And at least we have a guide on how to handle becoming rich. You know, in case those boys do a *really* good job surviving the workforce, the promotions, the flip side of the pay gap."

As the satire talk closed, the class burst into applause as well as some spurts of nervous laughter. The girls' presentation had its desired effect, in great part because of their effective collaboration in creating and delivering the presentation. The girls used Dropmark as their collaborative brainstorming space, where they posted news articles, Creative Commons licensed images, and clips of videos from the media, as well as links to their shared Google Doc script and shared Google Slide deck of the finalized presentation. Each of the three students in the group had a voice in creating the work, and more important, each of the three had a voice in delivering the final presentation.

Other Ideas for Collaborative Presentation

- Students in Spanish 3–4 are working in teams to research and present the customs of various Spanish-speaking countries. Students can choose from a range of tools for their class lesson. In addition, they must prepare a five-question Google Form to quiz their classmates about the information they teach.
- Biology students use Prezi to create presentations about animal cells. Because Prezi can zoom in and out of the main picture to reveal new information, they set up the complete cell as the central image, and then zoom into the various organelles to add more details about each microscopic element.
- In a world history class, students are assigned key historical figures early in the year. They must individually research their figures and create a five-slide, image-based presentation about the person and his or her importance in history, leaving plenty of comments in the "presenter notes" section of the slide deck. Then, throughout the course, the teacher schedules the presentations as they fit with the course material. The catch is that the student who made the slides must first explain them to a classmate, and then it is the classmate who presents the material.

Figure 4.9 lists a few of the online collaborative presentation tools available. We expect that there will soon be even more presentation tools that support collaboration. Check out pluginpowerup.com for additional resources.

Managing Student Collaboration

Although we believe that students benefit from collaboration, we also know that designing and managing collaborative projects can create challenges. As teachers, we must make crucial decisions before students begin any collaborative work on a project (see Figure 4.10).

TOOLS FOR COLLABORATIVE PRESENTATION	
Google Slides	Google Slides are just as collaborative as Google Docs. Students can share and edit the same slide deck at the same time. It's great for quick presentation projects and more in-depth, long-term projects. We've used this with small and large groups. It's very flexible and easy. There are fewer fancy features than some presentation software options, but Google Slides is super-functional for collaboration.
Prezi	This zooming presentation tool lets students define their big ideas and then focus on the details. Instead of slides, students work in different areas of a large canvas. Prezi allows for creative collaboration from multiple accounts. Presentations are slick and professional in appearance.

Figure 4.9 Top Tools for Collaborative Presentation and What They Do Best

We have outlined some of these decision points below. It's worth noting that many of these questions are similar to ones we would have had to ask before our classrooms were 1:1.

- How will we structure collaborative groups to best meet our learning objectives?
- What forms of collaboration will we be using, and why?
- What ground rules and scaffolds will groups need? Can students help create them?
- Will we determine students' roles and responsibilities or leave that decision to them?
- Which tools will we suggest students use?
- What technical challenges are they likely to encounter?
- How will students share, publish, or turn in their final products?
- How will we assess the success of their collaborative process?

Grouping Students for Collaboration
A Moment from Jen's Classroom

It was a few weeks into the school year when I met my students at the door and let them know as they entered the room that they had new seats. Projected on the front screen was a spreadsheet with numbered groups, and on the tables were boxes with numbers one through six. Students had to find their name on the screen, find the table with their number, and take a seat. This exercise probably looked like one any secondary teacher might go through when assigning new seats to her students, but there was more to this process.

I had used the data from a recent survey about my students' reading habits to group them, using a spreadsheet I had created. With the spreadsheet, I could sort my students by a score (how well they had done on a quiz), their reading interests, or how much progress they had made on an essay, and then group them accordingly. I could make homogeneous groups based on the criteria, which was most crucial for what we were working on at the moment, or heterogeneous groups for tasks that might be more challenging for some students than for others. There are many digital tools available for grouping students quickly, but they all create random groups. I wanted a way to deliberately group students to help with differentiation in my classroom. (For more on differentiation, see Chapter 6.) I also added pages to my spreadsheet that would group students heterogeneously. I often use the heterogeneous groupings and partners for collaborative work. With a few clicks, I can re-sort my class and assign them to new teams or partners based on any criteria I choose. Re-sorting the sheet often and assigning students to new teams frequently creates the illusion that many of these moves are random. Students get to know a wider variety of their classmates, and I don't get any complaints about partnerships; students seem to think that the computer assigned them to their groups and not the teacher. (For a copy of this group-creator spreadsheet, visit pluginpowerup.com.)

Figure 4.10 Students collaborate on a shared presentation.

Ground Rules for Collaboration

We know that students are more likely to follow rules that they have a hand in creating (Kohn 1993), but we also think it helps if teachers have some ideas in mind to guide students while those rules are being discussed and created. What follows are some suggestions for effective collaboration.

Know the goal: Within the group, students need to spend time discussing and paraphrasing the task they are working toward to get clarity about their ultimate goal. Jumping right into the project without a shared vision about the end game will create problems. Students should first reread the directions, agree on what they want the finished product to look like, create subgoals that will help them get there, and *then* divide up tasks and responsibilities. We know how tempting it is to rush students past this talking part and just get to work, but remember that improving communication skills is probably more crucial than the project itself. Let them plan, but also make planning and discussion an expectation for groups.

Establish an editing protocol: Once students have a plan in place, it is important for them to set some boundaries around editing. We have seen students get their feelings hurt and shed big tears when a teammate deletes work, often with the intention of improving the project but without communicating with the team. Our students often resort to a policy of adding and commenting for asynchronous collaboration, saving major overhauls and edits for synchronous, face-to-face collaboration. Regardless of what your students choose, they will need norms for how they edit.

Respect each other's work: We know that students don't always contribute equally to a project. Assigning roles can help with that, but we still have instances in which certain students think they did all the work. Often they are inflating the importance of their contributions while denigrating the work of their teammates. When discussing collaboration with students, emphasize that everyone contributes as best they can, and anyone who takes over the work of others is disrespecting their teammates' learning process. We teach our students to assume good intentions. This means starting with the assumption that all members of the team are doing their best to make the project turn out well. If something is not turning out well, it is cause for discussion, not accusation.

Say what you think: They need to say it nicely, of course, but we know some students hold back ideas because they fear they will be criticized or offend others by offering constructive feedback. In either case, the project suffers. Good ideas don't get shared and bad ideas don't get improved unless students are willing to speak up and say what they think.

Follow through: As adults, we earn the respect of our colleagues by making sure we get our work done well and on time. Students need to know that. We frame collaborative projects so that students see them as an opportunity to learn with their classmates, but also to earn respect and show that they can do high-quality work. We work with teenagers; we know they are often more concerned about their peers' opinions than they are about a project or a grade.

Evaluating Group Work

Ah, the benefits of group work! Instead of 180 projects to grade, we will have only 90, 60, or fewer. Even so, the projects represent the work of 180 students, and each of those students is expecting feedback and evaluation. Looks like we have work to do.

Sure, we get a say in the final grade of a project, but as often as possible we make the assessment collaborative as well. (See Chapter 7 for more on assessment.) Students can score each other's work in a variety of ways. Google Forms, for example, work really well for presentation scores. Students can also self-assess their work and report on the work of their teammates.

We have a set of go-to questions that we like to ask students to push their reflection on the process of collaborating and help them grow as team members. See Figure 4.11 for suggested questions to include in self-evaluations.

- How well did your group plan your project?
- Did you have to change or adapt your plans at any point? Why?
- What did you contribute to the project?
- How did your contribution help the team?
- Who do you respect more because of this project? What did you find valuable about that person's contribution?
- Did anyone on the team disappoint you or not meet expectations? What advice would you give that person for improving his or her performance on future projects?
- Are you satisfied with the final project? What would you improve if you had more time?

Figure 4.11 Questions for Self-Evaluations

By forcing our students to think beyond *what* they created, and to consider *how* they created it, we expose how much we value high-quality collaboration. Students learn that working effectively with others represents far more than just earning a grade, and that in the end, learning these soft skills will matter as much as learning content material.

Collaboration Across Classrooms and Time Zones

The interconnections of our global society, the speed of the Internet, and the need to know more about how what is happening in faraway places affect our lives and give us opportunities for collaboration far beyond our classroom walls. People worldwide are already contributing to massive shared projects. Consider Wikipedia. On average, it receives ten edits per second from more than twenty-three million contributors. Wikis, like Wikipedia, are web pages that anyone can edit, but there are also smaller wikis that can be limited to specific users.

Dan McDowell and his AP world history students used a wiki to collaborate with three other classes. Teachers assigned topics across the four classes. Each team researched and wrote about their topics, but they were also responsible for validating at least three other articles. Collectively, the classes created their own massive study guide to prepare for the exam.

Blogs, wikis, and Skype calls have replaced the paper pen-pal projects many of us may remember. Today, finding faraway classes to collaborate with is easier than ever (see Figure 4.12). Try searching [global collaboration projects] to access a rich host of resources for connecting.

TOOLS FOR GLOBAL COLLABORATION	
Skype in the Classroom	Skype offers enhanced accounts to educators and provides help finding partners for collaboration, guest speakers, and mystery Skype calls where students have to use clues to guess where the other class is calling from. We have also successfully used Google Hangouts and FaceTime for bringing in virtual guests.
ePALS Classroom Exchange	ePALS connects students through a private e-mail network, including translation services.
Wikispaces	Teacher- and student-friendly wiki pages are useful for a variety of collaborative projects.
Google Sites	Google Sites can be set up to work much like wikis, with multiple contributors, within a classroom or across time zones. Teachers can give students editing privileges on the whole site or just specific pages.
Blogger	Class blogs and individual student blogs let visitors comment on posts. Often teachers set up systems that have students commenting on posts from another classroom on a regular basis. Search [quadblogging] for more information.

Figure 4.12 Top Tools for Global Collaboration and What They Do Best

Does Collaboration Always Involve Devices?

Of course not. Digital tools often remove a lot of the logistical friction that comes with collaboration, but there is a lot of nondigital collaboration happening in our classrooms, too. We have certainly not abandoned the chart paper and markers activities that get students talking, drawing, and creating. Jen still gives her students chalk and takes them outside to draw giant maps of the novels they are reading in groups. Diana is fond of review skits put on by her students, featuring authors whose work they have been reading. It may seem counterintuitive, but we have found that when students take their devices home for independent work and asynchronous collaboration, they can usually spend more time on face-to-face activities in class as a result. (See Chapter 9 for more ideas about rethinking class time.)

POWER UP!   Continue Collaborating

1. Revise your next student project to include some form of **collaborative preparation**. What resource could students produce together that would be helpful to everyone doing their individual work?

2. After your students participate in a form of **collaborative production**, feedback, or presentation, have them reflect on their contributions and experience using the self-evaluation questions in Figure 4.11.

3. Visit pluginpowerup.com and go to the Resources section to get your own copy of the **Group Creator Spreadsheet**. Add your own students' names and a recent assessment score. Then sort the sheet by that score to re-roster or rank your students. Visit the tabs across the bottom to see the groups to which they could be assigned.

4. **Continue your collaborations with colleagues**. How could you share the load of creating collaborative projects for your students? Remember that your adult collaborations provide a model for students about the importance of working together professionally.

Part II

EXTEND

Ex•tend (v): To expand in scope, effect, or meaning

How can technology empower us to kick down the walls of our classrooms so that our learning network is no longer confined by our physical space or the hours we meet?

CHAPTER 5
Audience

Au·di·ence (n): *The readership for printed material; the listening public. Also, a group of ardent admirers or devotees.*

Teacher: Diana Neebe
Class: United States Literature

One Monday toward the end of the year, Karina, an eager sophomore, came in to discuss her personal narrative paper, in which she had imitated the style of the author Tim O'Brien.

"Is it good?" she asked the way most of my students do, giving me all of five seconds to consider the tablet screen before my eyes. "I mean, do you like it?"

Woefully, the first thing I noticed was that every single first-person pronoun was written as a tiny, lowercase *i*. A little short on patience this late in the year, and recalling the countless lessons I had presented on proofreading, my sarcasm crept in.

"Karina, this isn't a text message," I said. "It's, like . . . your final. Why haven't you capitalized your first-person pronouns?"

"My first-person pronouns?" she asked quizzically.

"Yeah. The letter *I*, for example."

"Oh, those! My keyboard doesn't auto-correct anymore. Plus, it's *just you*, Mrs. Neebe."

Right she was. It was *just* me reading her work. I was the only person who would see her writing—sad little lowercase *i*'s and all. I was also the only person who would read a triumphant memoir about dealing positively with social aggression outside the classroom. Karina's quip turned my attention to a bigger pitfall in the assignment: the audience.

The Importance of Audience

We know from experience that when students' work is intended for the teacher's eyes only, the product suffers. But, when provided an authentic and meaningful audience, students rise to the occasion. Grant Wiggins (2009) exposes the importance of audience in relation to the quality of student work:

> Academic writing is notoriously turgid, arguably because the impact of the prose is too often an afterthought, the writing a mere vehicle for offering up new knowledge . . . But the point is to open the mind or heart of a real audience—cause a fuss, achieve a feeling, start some thinking. In other words, what few young writers learn is that there are *consequences* for succeeding or failing as a real writer . . . By introducing a real purpose, a real audience—hence, *consequences*—we get the feed*back* we desperately need to become good writers. (30)

Karina had no *real* audience to write for and, as a result, no consequences for ignoring details such as grammar and mechanics, let alone more significant issues such as building a persuasive argument or developing credibility about the subject. In hindsight and with much more experience with 1:1 under her belt, Diana could have leveraged the technology in her classroom to extend students' audience for this assignment. Instead of writing for *just* the teacher, Karina could have written on a wider stage where they could have "crowd-sourced" her feedback, too.

Often referred to as the Like Generation, Karina and her peers have come to expect the type of responses they receive from their social networks: instant, numerous, and positive. Although teacher feedback is critical (see Chapter 7 for more on feedback), students also benefit from being in immediate conversation with their audience and hearing from a variety of voices with differing opinions. Fortunately, when it comes to engaging with an authentic audience, the opportunities online are limitless. Transformative new ways to communicate with others and find a real audience will continue to surface. In the following section, we offer five approaches for broadening your students' audience, now that you have 1:1 technology at your fingertips.

Five Ways to Extend Audience
Blogging for a Broader Audience

The word *blog* is short for *web log*. Think of it like a journal that is hosted online. We mentioned classroom blogs in Chapter 2. Now let's take a look at them from the student perspective. Blogs fairly instantly enable students to connect with a real-world audience and engage in meaningful dialogue. By opening up to an online audience, language students can practice their nonnative tongue with a native-speaking (writing) peer abroad. Science students can present a working lab report and ask questions to an audience beyond the requisite lab partner. Additionally, students in all disciplines can search for existing blogs and forums where they can join the discourse around topics of interest. Blogging invites conversation.

And, it is through this conversation that students grow. English teacher Bridget Jacobs has her students contribute a piece of their own writing to the class blog. In a senior elective course on creative writing, the most exciting academic moments for her students are when a classmate responds with a thoughtful critique, or when another adult on campus comes up to comment on a favorite scene or turn of phrase.

Through blogs, students can also engage in a virtual exchange with peers in other countries. When Carrie Saunders's juniors began blogging about a novel they were reading—*A Passage to India*—their teacher had established a connection with a colleague in Mumbai, who in turn encouraged her students to write to their American "pen" pals. The response was incredible: Indian students posted interviews with their grandparents about what it was like to live under British colonial rule, filling in the details of the novel's historical context. Blogging can make global collaborations possible. To encourage your students to work for an authentic audience, check out the resources listed in Figure 5.1.

TOOLS FOR BLOGGING WITH STUDENTS	
WordPress	Wordpress.com is a platform used by many professional bloggers. It has a sleek design, an intuitive user interface, and is easy to update from the web as well as from mobile devices.
Blogger	If you are already using Google Apps, then blogger.com is the one for you. It automatically connects with students' single log-in through Google Apps and makes it easy to have multiple students as administrators on the same blog, making it the ideal platform for group blogs.
Tumblr	Students are most likely already familiar with tumblr.com. If you anticipate that your students will post more media than writing—anything from images to audio to reposted news articles—then Tumblr may be a more appropriate platform. That said, it may be blocked at your school or district.
Edublogs	Edublogs is a platform created specifically for education. Teachers can set up their own blog and add student accounts for student blogs.
KidBlog	If you are concerned about privacy, start with kidblog.org, which allows you to limit access with ease. Teachers can set up free classes, provide codes to students, and determine who can and cannot view student work.

Figure 5.1 Top Tools for Blogging and What They Do Best

Practical Considerations About Blogging

We are huge advocates of blogging, but we would be remiss to send you and your students off into the blogosphere without a few words of caution.

- Review the section on digital citizenship in Chapter 2 and access our favorite digital citizenship resources at pluginpowerup.com. If you are looking for more support with teaching and reinforcing digital citizenship, check out the free curriculum that Common Sense Media has developed at commonsensemedia.org.
- Teach students to use only images in their posts that are their own or that are licensed under Creative Commons and cited in the blog.
- Encourage your younger students to select an avatar (cartoon image) for their profile picture instead of uploading an image of themselves.
- Consider grouping students with similar interests and having them contribute to the same blog to reduce the number of blogs going on for your courses.
- Consider the ramifications for students if several teachers ask them to blog for different courses. A blog can be an excellent way of documenting a cross-curricular project.
- Cut down on inbox clutter. Use a Google Form to have students send you their blog URL instead of e-mailing it to you.
- Teach students appropriate etiquette for commenting on each other's posts. Jen shows her high schoolers a video from Linda Yollis's third-grade students about how to leave a high-quality comment on a blog. See pluginpowerup.com for the video.

E-publishing Student Work

Another way to extend a student's readership is through electronic publishing, or ePub. In the midst of their American Studies unit on immigration and assimilation, English and history team teachers Michelle Balmeo and Andrew Sturgill challenged their students to interview and write the story of a relative or friend's experience of coming to America. Their classroom was 1:1, filled with the same computers that the journalism staff used each day after school. They walked their students through the basics of formatting and layout on Adobe's publishing software InDesign, and then set the kids loose (see Figure 5.2 for other software options).

Ultimately, instead of collecting a stack of papers that only Balmeo and Sturgill would read, students submitted their work for inclusion in a collaborative literary magazine. They published the compendium as a PDF that could be read on smartphones, tablets, and computers by students, their families, and the school at large. Other teachers in the English department later based some assignments on the literary magazine, asking students to read, consider, and respond to the experiences of the community members represented.

TOOLS FOR E-PUBLISHING STUDENT WRITING	
Pages and Word	If InDesign is too daunting (and trust us, it's a doozy!), try Apple Pages or Microsoft Word. Both allow you to save documents in PDF format, which you can then post on your learning management system or school website.
Google Docs	Google Docs has a great shortcut for making any document a web page. Students can draft, collaborate, and edit within Docs, and when they are ready to share their work, simply click File/Publish to the Web. Voila: a URL that is ready for prime time.
iBooks Author (Mac only)	For the more "finished" look of a quarterly publication, consider creating an iBook through Apple iBooks Author and publishing to the iBookstore. The only hitch is that iBooks Author lives on one computer instead of in the cloud and thus makes it challenging to collaborate.
Blurb	It is easy to create an electronic book through publishing sites such as blurb.com. Choose from templates for layout, or start with a completely blank slate. Collaborate by sharing a single log-in.

Figure 5.2 Top Tools for E-Publishing and What They Do Best

Practical Considerations for E-Publishing

- Most modern word processing and publishing software programs have templates that will make your students' products look very professional. Trust us: use the templates. It's really not worth futzing around with creating your own margins and spacing when you're just getting started. The templates are there for a good reason.
- Set aside time specifically for students to format their contributions to the final publication. We learned the hard way that this process can be speedy if everyone pitches in but can be overwhelmingly time consuming if the teacher is the only one left to place and polish.
- Most word processing software will give you an option when you print to "print as PDF." This may be your fastest way to create and attach a sleek, readable document.

Connecting with Professionals

What better audience than a workplace professional? Schoolwork gains relevance when students have the opportunity to connect with adults who have expertise and experience in their fields of interest. In *Real Learning, Real Work*, Adria Steinberg (1997) enumerates the questions students might consider in finding a professional mentor:

- Who in our local area might be using such a skill?
- Where can we find local experts?
- Which local institutions could we call?
- What types of tasks or projects require this knowledge?

Learning about the spread of West Nile virus in biology? Connect with the local insect abatement office. Testing out the sturdiness of a structure in physics? Contact an architect or engineer. Prosecuting the protagonist for a novel's mock trial? Run a line of questioning by an actual attorney. It makes sense, sure. But we don't all know engineers and architects and lawyers. The Internet, however, hosts them all. And many very busy adults are perfectly willing to correspond with students who have relevant questions and a desire to learn.

Adults are also often willing to engage with students when they share a passion for the same cause. Students at Jen's school watched *Blackfish* in their video production class and then made a public-service-style video, *Dear Sea World*, recounting their memories of visiting the park and then asking questions about the treatment of marine mammals. The video was spread widely by animal-rights activists. Eventually, the director of *Blackfish*, Gabriela Cowperthwaite, visited the school and spoke to students, encouraging them to do their own research about the treatment of animals and to keep speaking up about what they believe is right.

When we encourage our students to appeal to a *real* audience for their concerns, the research they conduct becomes more meaningful and potentially transformative. The students at Jen's school saw that they had a voice and that adults actually cared what they had to say.

We have also both been on the receiving end of such requests. A week after Diana's school posted an opening in the English department, an unusual e-mail application appeared:

> *Hello. My name is Carly. I am 12 years old and I would like to "apply for the English teaching job." Yes, I know it sounds weird, but I have a valid reason why. For my history class, we have to pretend we are adults and take on the role of an adult. My person is a woman with a Masters Degree and a Bachelors degree. I need to find an English teaching job. I have a couple of questions about the job. What is the salary (hourly, daily, monthly, yearly)? How many hours would "I" work? Does this job come with health benefits? Thanks again for your time and I hope that you can answer all of my questions soon.*
>
> Best Regards,
> Carly

Carly's e-mail illustrates the power of the Internet to widen a child's world. Faculty members in the English department were delighted (once they stopped trying to calculate their hourly rate). They responded with gusto—sent her the application, a salary schedule, an explanation of the interviewing protocol, and a line about how their school is an Equal Opportunity Employer and does not discriminate based on age. A few minutes of online research can connect students with a community of supporters who never knew they were needed until they were asked. Our students have found tremendous success looking up contact information for employees of local nonprofits, community colleges, and nearby universities. (See Figure 5.3 for more ideas.)

TOOLS FOR CONNECTING WITH PROFESSIONALS	
YellowPages.com	Just like the good old phone book, yellowpages.com makes it easy to search by location and type of work. Students in Jen's class looking to connect with environmental professionals for their research project started by typing in the city and job: [San Diego, Environmental Consultant].
LinkedIn.com	LinkedIn is a professional networking platform. Students can search by occupation, location, or degree, and find local businesspeople who have added their profiles (and often, résumés) to the site.

Figure 5.3 Top Tools for Making Professional Connections and What They Do Best

Practical Considerations for Connecting with Professionals

- Teach students how to find professionals relevant to their inquiry by modeling the practice in class. It is useful to demonstrate how to search by field and is certainly worth reviewing e-mail etiquette with students before encouraging them to send off their requests. We often ask students to first submit a draft of their e-mails.
- Require students to reach out to more than one person at a time. Many times students will contact only one person and then wait days for a response. We typically ask students to send e-mails to three different professionals.
- Unless the professional contact is a friend or family member, ask students to limit their contact to the web or the phone. Often, working folks prefer a lunch-hour conference, which works nicely for school hours. During project time, we regularly have students on Google Hangouts or Skype Chats in our classrooms during lunch. This enables us to monitor student–adult communication and ensure student safety.

- On rare occasions, we allow students to meet their professional contact face-to-face. In those situations, we require parent permission and that students go in groups of three or more to a public place. For example, Diana has had a group of students meet a local college professor at the university's student union.

Face-to-Face Audience

Using 1:1 devices gives students access to VoIP services, or Voice over Internet Protocol. If you have used Skype or FaceTime before, you were using VoIP. In the same way that the Internet can connect students to a readership half a world away, VoIP can provide face-to-face correspondence. Instead of (or in addition to) blogging back and forth with students in Mumbai, for example, Saunders's eleventh graders could have met online for a videoconference.

There is also something egocentrically magical about online videoconferencing. Diana's student Andrew provides a great example. Andrew, one of her earnest and totally rule-abiding freshmen, was scheduled to miss the big trial for Jack in *Lord of the Flies* because of a family wedding out of town. "I'll Skype in," he said. "Class is at eleven, and the wedding doesn't start until later that day. No problemo!" At the start of the trial, the class dialed the absent juror and positioned an iPad, showing his smiling face, on a music stand in the corner of the room. Andrew was dressed up for court in his suit and tie, and at the end of the trial when he helped deliver the verdict, he added, "I feel famous!" Video does that to a person.

Sometimes the allure of the silver screen is what hooks a student, and what ensues far exceeds a teacher's plans. In an article for *Edutopia*, science teacher Shawn Cornally (2012) explains the power of expanding students' audience beyond the walls of the classroom through VoIP technology:

> I once watched a room full of chemistry students furiously fermenting an exotic species of switchgrass. The fervor in the room was contagious, and I jumped in to help. I asked the students why they were so excited, and one turned to me and said, "This is for a town in the Philippines. We Skyped with them last week, and we found some of the same grass they have. We want to help them make ethanol. Regular gasoline is a really high cost of farming for them, and they have *a lot* of switchgrass." I almost tripped over what seemed too contrived to be true, but I realized that these kids were actually doing what people claim to want to do: they found a problem, and they were fixing it.

Cornally's experience attests to the power of connecting students to an audience other than the teacher alone. When the four walls of the classroom begin to stifle the "bigger picture" conversation, it might be time to invite a bigger audience in. (See Figure 5.4 for ideas.)

TOOLS FOR VIDEOCONFERENCING	
Google Hangouts	Free, reliable, and easy to set up, Google Hangouts has one feature that puts it at the top of the list, in our book: you can record and archive your videoconference. With permission from everyone on the call, Google will automatically store the conference to YouTube video, which you can then set as private, unlisted, or public. Additionally, it is simple to screen-share during a Google Hangout. Check out https://plus.google.com/hangouts for more information.
Skype	Skype has options for paid and free accounts and is a familiar service to many people living outside the United States; this is useful to know, depending on whom you are connecting with. Skype's paid account also allows you to screen-share.
FaceTime	FaceTime is the native video calling software for every Apple device. It is free to use and comes built in to iPads, iPhones, and Macs. Schools with 1:1 iPads may find that FaceTime is the easiest to set up for student use.

Figure 5.4 Top Tools for Videoconferencing and What They Do Best

Practical Considerations for Videoconferencing

- Schedule a test call, if you can, to make sure the equipment is all working before you call as a class. This also ensures that you and your guest will be familiar with the process.
- A wired Internet connection will give you better results, so if at all possible, plug your computer in with an Ethernet cable.
- Consider investing in a webcam that will give your audience a better view of your students than the camera built into your computer. (Some modern document cameras can do this well.) And plan to project the caller onto a larger screen.
- Discuss the protocol for the call with your students ahead of time. Will they be asking questions or just listening? Consider arranging hand signals to help things run smoothly. This is a great time to use a backchannel (see Chapter 3) to manage student questions.
- If a student is asking a question or giving an answer, ask him or her to move closer to the camera so he or she can be seen by the caller.

- Consider using screencasting software or a recorded Google Hangout to record the session for later review or to show to your other class sections that have missed it live. (Make sure everyone knows it is being recorded.)
- Schedule the call with clear start and end times to respect the busy schedule of the person you are calling as well as your class time.

Submitting Work to Professional Sites

Diana's US literature students were at the end of a unit on race, prejudice, and the power of language. She wanted them to write about their experience—to name and own what they had learned. Yet, every prompt she came up with felt contrived and inauthentic: "Describe a time when you were hurt by language." Describe for whom? For what purpose?

Discouraged and needing a solution, she began her daily brainstorming ritual on the drive to work, soothed by the familiar sounds of NPR's *Morning Edition*. Steve Inskeep murmured softly in the background: "Let's hear another installment of the *Race Card Project*. That's a project curated by NPR's own Michele Norris. It invites people to send in six-word stories about race and identity."

Not an hour later, her students were plugged into their iPads, listening to the NPR podcast of their choice from the *Race Card Project* and starting to consider their own six-word stories. That night for homework, they submitted their thoughts to NPR, for a real audience online and on the air. Just a few of the students' stories were published and featured online, but that wasn't the point. "The world" knew their ideas; feeling heard was both powerful and compelling.

The web offers endless ways to extend the audience for student writing, thinking, and questioning, well beyond the classroom alone. Whether submitting a story to an online competition or responding publicly to news reports or product reviews, students have agency when they write for a broader readership. Both of us start class each day with free reading. For each book that students finish, we ask them to write a brief review on goodreads.com to help other readers in the next book decision-making process. Our students love the satisfaction of publicly rating their novels and the excitement of knowing that other readers are looking to their reviews for advice. On a handful of occasions, Jen's students have even received comments back from the authors—via Goodreads and Twitter—thanking them for their feedback and encouraging them to keep reading. Below are a few more ideas for submitting student work to professional sites. Being heard by the "listening public" has never been so easy!

- Literature students can rate and post critiques of the novel they recently completed on sites such as amazon.com or goodreads.com.
- Budding social studies scholars can reply in the "comments" section at the

bottom of a current events article on news sites such as nytimes.com, npr.com, economist.com, or your area's local online paper.

- World language students could do the same thing, but for non-English online papers such as lemonde.fr, elpais.com, or even bbc.co.uk/chinese.

 PLUG IN Get Familiar with the Technology in Your Hands

1. **Jump online to your favorite news source.** Find a compelling article that interests you. Read it! Think about it. Then, pose a few questions or respond in the "comments" section that typically lives below the article. Wait with bated breath for others to reply.

2. **Test out your device's VoIP capabilities!** Give a faraway friend a free call. Or play around with the face-to-face video stream with someone in the next room. The more comfortable you become, the more likely you are to see possibilities for integrating this tool into your classroom. Jen was happy to have VoIP when the flu starting taking out her students one at a time.

3. **Set up a personal blog or website** to journal about—well, anything! No matter what you write about, you are sure to find some like-minded readers and an interesting conversation space. It's a great place to practice what you'll teach.

Classroom Case Study: Audience

Teacher: Diana Neebe
Class: Sophomore World Literature

Authentic audiences, without a doubt, improve student products. There are multiple ways of reaching an audience for student work, as demonstrated in the first half of the chapter. What follows is a case study of e-publishing in a tenth-grade English class.

During the typical "second-semester slump," my students had turned into little machines: focused but not interested. As a result, our classes had become very transactional. I assigned, they completed, I graded, they haggled: wash, rinse, repeat. To add insult to injury, we hit this slump right in time for our department's requisite sophomore research unit—inevitably ending with an eight- to ten-page research paper synthesizing informational texts that my eighty-seven sophomores would churn out, and I would miraculously grade before summer.

By the end of the year, within the four walls of C210, we had ceased to serve as a "real" audience for each other. My students had written countless papers, reflections, journals, and reading responses for me. They had shared their thoughts, daily, with peers. We had collectively provided feedback, scribbled comments in margins, and posed questions on sticky notes. This was good work, but it felt artificial. It was my job, and their assignment, to provide feedback. There was no choice to opt out. I wanted my students to have an audience engaged out of enjoyment or interest rather than duty. One simple fact remained: no one outside our classroom would know about, or come to care about, the research my students would soon undertake.

This is the generation of kids who have come of age in social networks and who live for connection to others. If it isn't documented online in a status update, tweet, or photograph, it didn't happen. So how could I possibly expect a paper that ends its life cycle on the teacher's desk to carry any significance or power for my students?

With the standards firmly fixed in the back of my mind, I began to redesign the unit, looking for alternative ways to teach inquiry, investigation, synthesis, and writing about informational texts. Taking a cue from James Moffett's *Teaching the Universe of Discourse* (1968), in which he argues that school is one of the only places where we ask individuals to participate in the inauthentic task of writing for an audience more informed than the author, I decided to put students in the position where they could become the experts and write for a less-informed audience: first graders.

I placed students in publishing teams, each responsible for researching a different contemporary human rights violation from anywhere in the world. With some guidance, they selected a core text (novel-length nonfiction) from our school library to read and discuss in conjunction with their digital database research. Ultimately, each group would electronically create and publish their own children's book on an online platform that was searchable, public, and permanent. Through their books, my students would teach a message (read: theme!) to the next generation about their human rights issue. If the research was about the unethical treatment of women, the children's book might be about how boys and girls are equally capable and strong. If students read about racism and genocide, they might write about learning to appreciate and respect differences. Using the online store of our selected e-publisher, students would be able to sell their finished products and donate the proceeds to the charity of their choice.

The chart on the following page (Figure 5.5) explains the progression of student tasks as they engaged in the children's book research project. Notice that the technology used in the right-hand column progresses in alignment with Bloom's revised taxonomy (Anderson and Krathwohl 2001). For more on curriculum design with Bloom's revised taxonomy, see Chapter 9.

	STUDENT TASKS	TECHNOLOGY USED
Weeks 1–2	**Initial Learning on Human Rights Topic** • Preview texts available on this topic and select novel-length nonfiction to read over the next four weeks. • Conduct an initial search on the topic to narrow down field for research and get a sense of context.	**Explore** • Read amazon.com text previews and goodreads.com book reviews. • Google the topic and read for ways that it is in the news lately. • Test-drive blurb.com. Get comfortable!
	Conduct Research; Discuss Reading • Gather multiple sources that provide historical overview and root causes. • Discuss findings and progress in longer text with group. Look for gaps in data.	**Understand and Evaluate** • Examine articles, podcasts, and newscasts on Gale's Global Issues in Context. • Refine search based on gaps in the data; consider keywords and Boolean search terms.
Weeks 3–4	**Synthesize Findings; Checkpoint Interview** • Connect group research findings and determine similarities and differences. • Explain historical context, root causes, and possible solutions. • Consider metaphorical ways to explain group's solution to first graders.	**Analyze and Synthesize** • Keep track of research in an annotated bibliography on Google Docs. Share with teacher and research team. • Brainstorm and outline together using Google Docs, Poplet, or Padlet.
	Construct a Genre Definition and Rubric • Read at least five children's books as a group and look for commonalities. • Define what a children's book *must* have, *may* have, and *must not* have.	**Apply** • Create and share a spreadsheet in Google Drive to categorize student findings. Then, as a class, edit the spreadsheet and turn the "must-have" section into the rubric.
Weeks 5–6	**Create Storyboard and Manuscript** • Write story manuscript, following Freytag's Pyramid for plot sequence. • Consider the layout of the book and how to match words and illustrations.	**Create** • Type manuscript on Google Docs and allow for multiple contributors/editors. • Design illustrations manually or electronically using an app such as SketchBook Pro.
	Upload Illustrations, Words, and Submit! • Proofread content, have copy editor reread manuscript for mechanical errors. • Read and consider comments and reviews as they come in!	**Publish** • Scan any hard-copy drawings and save as JPEG files. Upload illustrations. • Upload text to blurb.com. Tag book as *Blurb for Good*. Add it to class bookshelf.

Figure 5.5 Children's Books Research Project Progression

Thinking Through a 1:1 Solution

Using 1:1 devices changes the game when it comes to *audience*. We instantly have access to a world outside the classroom and have tools to connect us to our "listening public." For years, educational researchers (Slagle 1997; Wiggins 2009) have touted the benefits of writing for an authentic audience—a readership that, because of its realness, compels the writer to take ownership of content, interest in editing and proofreading, and pride in the final product. In starting her unit redesign, Diana's initial question was, How can I leverage the technology in my classroom so that students will be excited about research and writing?

The answer was more obvious than she could have anticipated. When she gave students access to tools and technology that put polish on their product in a way no word processor ever could, their research energy rocketed from disinterested to excited and creative. There would be multiple "end users" for their hours of thinking and laboring.

Along the way, as with any major 1:1 project, we have to reconsider and negotiate the traditional format and flow of class time. What follows are some of the questions we ask whenever we extend our students' audience, and the answers that Diana discovered through her project.

How do I select the right web tool for publishing online?

Diana stumbled upon blurb.com after perusing a colleague's online work with digital portfolios at High Tech High School. She was so impressed with the Blurb electronic store, and the option to preview an entire text, that she immediately signed up for a free account. Often, this is how we find our next best tool—by looking to others in the education field, or in other professions, for ideas. It's amazing what gems we can find in 140 characters and a link on Twitter. Regardless, you will still need to test the resource to make sure it meets your needs. Here are some of the questions we ask when considering web tools such as Blurb:

- How much does it cost to sign up? What does the signup process expect of me?
- Do I need to download software to use it, or does it exist only online? Does the software cost extra?
- How intuitive is the user interface? Can I understand the basics after watching the tutorial video? Are there tutorial videos available on the website or on YouTube?
- Can students easily collaborate? For example, can students access the book-in-progress from multiple devices, or does the work have to live on one computer?
- For publication: Is there an option for free previews online, or will we be required to purchase a hard copy product? Will it publish to tablets, too? Can we buy e-books if we want to?
- Are there any other surprising reasons to use this tool?

The answer to the final question is what sealed blurb.com as Diana's web tool for this project. Her students were able to sell their children's books through the Blurb for Good program and elect to send the profit to a charity that works in the same field as their research.

Truth be told, she could have selected any number of web tools, and they all could have been awesome for different reasons. She could have circumvented the physical publishing step by encouraging e-publishing and reading electronically. Her students could have used different software with ePub capabilities. But at some point, she had to make a decision so they'd have something to do *tomorrow*.

What will the final product look like?

This is one of the more important details to firm up early on. We tend to think in terms of content, audience, and purpose, and let the specifics of the final form remain flexible. For the children's book project, Diana knew she wanted students to respond to their research in a way that could teach a solution to the problem. This required them to consider multiple perspectives in their research, to discuss and grapple with the challenges of complex human issues, and finally, to work toward a creative output in the form of a children's book. What the book looked like would be up to them. They had to decide whether their illustrations would be digital or "old school" with colored pencils, if the words of the text should be black or another color, if the size and placement of the text should change on each page.

Given the quality of the tools we can access, we always try to hold our students to high standards when it comes to their finished products. We find it helpful to start with real-world models and work backward from there. In the case of the children's book project, Diana started the unit by reading from a class collection of children's stories as models. Drawing from Heather Lattimer's *Thinking Through Genre* (2003), they studied the models of successful children's books to help determine what a good book must have, may have, and must not have. We use this technique often and with great success. (See Chapter 8, "Creativity and Innovation," for more examples.) Figure 5.6 shows the list that Diana's students came up with when constructing their genre definition, which later became the foundation for building their final products.

How will I maintain the rigor of a research project when the teacher is no longer the audience?

Writing for an outside audience—whether for peers or preschoolers—means that students are donning the mantle of the expert. That is, if they plan to teach others, they must first become scholars in their subject matter. Framed in this light, where research is the responsibility of being an author, the expectations for quality and careful work actually increase. Although the teacher is not the ultimate audience, she is the one reminding students how high the bar has been set, because the audience is truly depending on the work that students produce.

Story *(Plot, Character)*	• Original, interesting, and quickly developing. Story gets to the conflict quickly. • Polished: follows Freytag's Pyramid, no plot holes, logical "flow" between story parts. Relevant plot with situations children would encounter in their own lives. • Clearly leads children to the theme or moral. • Characters are round, dynamic, and relatable for kids. May be made up, but are always interesting.
Language *(Diction, Syntax, Vocabulary)*	• Level: simple enough words that children can understand on their own; complex enough to "push" kids. • Vocabulary: new/stretch words are introduced in context and repeated later. Clear and descriptive. • Syntax is varied by length, but most sentences are simple in structure. • Flawless grammar and punctuation. • Catchy title!
Illustrations	• Big pictures, some taking up full pages or two-page spreads. • Ratio: more of the page is taken up by pictures than by words. • Illustrations should enhance the story and provide more context for the plot and vocabulary. • Consistent with other pictures and with the tone of the text. • Vivid color, portraying emotion through detail. • Cover is catchy and aesthetically pleasing. Screams, "Pick me off the shelf!"
Appeal *(Moral, Relevance, "Pop")*	• Clear moral / theme that is relevant to and appropriate for children. • Unique presentation of theme that is clear (not undetectable) but not "in your face" (or cheesy!). • Memorable.

Figure 5.6 Children's Books "Must-Have" List

In Diana's project, with collaborative research as a requirement for completion, independent library time was no longer the most productive way to spend sixty minutes with all of the students assembled. In the department's traditional research model, students would scour sources during class time in the library or computer lab, and consider what they read at home. They would submit note cards and outlines to their audience of one—the teacher—and await feedback before continuing their research and writing.

Instead, after an introductory lesson on using the library databases and vetting sources, Diana sent students to conduct their reading and research at home. When it came to their hour of English class the next day, students were ready to confer with classmates, ask questions, make connections, synthesize, and consider their needs for follow-up research. Because students would be writing for a real audience, the stakes for real research were high, and time to collaborate was precious.

Diana wanted to ensure that they would be prepared to write for the first graders, so while teams of researchers and writers worked feverishly, she interviewed each student individually to ask about what he or she had learned so far. Verbally, students synthesized their research and "defended" their ideas for the book. They walked through their annotated bibliographies, summarizing the studies they had read, rationalizing how they knew their sources were credible and reliable, and illustrating how their research informed their pitch for the children's book. Eventually, every sophomore passed the "checkpoint interview," the litmus test for the privilege of writing for children. They were able to maintain the rigor of the research process despite their juvenile readership.

Diana's Reflection on the Process

Ten days after clicking the "submit" button on blurb.com to order fifteen original books, I lumbered into C210, lugging a heavy cardboard box. My thirty young authors in first period ran to greet me at the door like small children awaiting a birthday surprise. They tore into that box with an agenda:

"How do we look?"

"Where's *our* book?"

"Did my illustrations turn out?"

"When do we get to read to the first graders?"

Every time I pulled a book from the box, the author's were right there, ready to take it from me. Then, silence. I looked across my room at teams hovered over tables, flipping through weeks of inquiry, investigation, synthesis, and eventually, writing they could be proud of. (Figures 5.7 and 5.8 display some of the children's book covers and interiors they created.)

Figure 5.7 Students love creating books for a real audience.

Figure 5.8 The interior of one book shows the narrative, dialogue, and illustrations reflected in the students' creative stories.

The next day, I gathered my students for our field trip across the parking lot. As we walked, I overheard what could only be described as excitement bubbling up: "I hope they like it!" "How should I do the Panda voice?" "Who's going to hold up the book and show the pictures?" "Wait—we should all say the farmer lines together!"

The first graders at Lincoln Elementary ended up being the best possible audience: ardent admirers and devotees. They sat dutifully in circles on the playground with their high school buddies, giggling at the voices the "big kids" made and pointing at their favorite pictures. We had a couple of renegade third graders who got permission to leave their classes to come and hear the stories that their big brothers and big sisters had been working on for so long.

Far beyond the comments I wrote for students, they learned what was successful in their books (and what wasn't) through the reactions of their elementary audience. Delighted squeals at well-planned jokes, gasps when big mysteries were revealed, and even bored-looking faces when books became "too preachy" were all forms of constructive critique. We learned that authentic feedback to student work multiplies when we expand the audience.

After our morning at the elementary school, we noticed a surge in the number of hits we had online for our digital store. Parents at our partner school had read—and commented on—the digital "view-only" versions of our books online. Another teacher at the school ordered a copy for use in her second-grade class and wrote, "Wonderful story! I loved the message that school is important. I would read it to my students. The ending is good because it will teach them inferencing."

When I asked my students for their feedback, they insisted that this was the most memorable, most influential assignment they had done all year. Part of the excitement in writing for their younger counterparts, they explained, came from the joy of creating a product that looked professional. They were proud. I couldn't help but think of the saying I heard from my colleague Rushton Hurley: "Work for an audience has to be good. Work for my teacher only has to be good enough." Their work was *really* good.

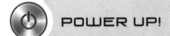

POWER UP! Put Your Tech Tools to the Test, and Extend Your Students' Audience

1. **Team up with another class, grade level, or school as blog buddies.** Or, find an existing **blog** about your content area, and encourage your students to join in.

2. **Collect students' "personal best" work of the semester or year, and e-publish it** for the school community. This year's students could even create a guide for next year's students and share it as a PDF or e-book.

3. **Get online and start looking up local experts.** Consider assignments in which your students would benefit from connecting with professionals, and bring the outside in!

4. **Listen for real-world opportunities.** Perhaps you already know an expert in your field—a Shakespearean actor in another state, an environmental biologist researching in a rain forest, a historian working for the Smithsonian. Arrange for your guest audience to "attend" student presentations, project planning meetings, or Socratic seminars face-to-face via Skype, FaceTime, or Google Hangouts.

5. **Invite virtual visitors.** Keep your ear to the ground for opportunities for your students to submit their work to competitions or open calls for opinion pieces on professional sites.

CHAPTER 6

Differentiation

Dif·fer·en·ti·a·tion (n): The act of recognizing and giving expression to a difference; development from the one to the many, the simple to the complex, or the homogeneous to the heterogeneous.

Teacher: Diana Neebe
Class: Sophomore World Literature

A few days before the start of my first year teaching, I received a thick envelope in my school mailbox. I pulled out the contents piece by piece: the school calendar and bell schedule, five class rosters (*How will I remember 148 names?*), and a purple folder with information about seventeen special education students who qualified for an Individualized Education Plan (IEP) and six students with 504 plans. During orientation, I learned that I would have regular meetings to discuss the accommodations and progress of my special needs students, as well as training about how to use an EpiPen, determine the correct turning radius for one student's wheelchair, and spot the physical signs of cutting and eating disorders.

I was overwhelmed but also determined to serve my students well. I remember one day, a few months into the job, when the school district support specialist asked me to present a writing review lesson with differentiation strategies. I designed a lesson that I thought would be a slam dunk, including setting up three centers where students could review and revise their essays, working alone, with partners, or in a small group with me.

When class started, nothing went according to plan. My super-eager students scurried up front for more instruction with me. The socialites surged to the back of the room to hang out with their friends. And the students who needed the most attention sat quietly on the sidelines, staring at a handout that highlighted their missteps but provided little support for improvement. After the lesson, my district support provider shared a "selective scripting" that she had captured during the class. Most of the partner conversations were about homecoming and the next day's science test. I was horrified. Would I ever be able to reach all learners?

Accessibility for All

Effective differentiation requires a tremendous amount of flexibility. As Carol Ann Tomlinson notes in *The Differentiated Classroom: Responding to the Needs of All Learners* (2014), "Today's teachers still contend with the essential challenge of the one-room schoolhouse: how to reach out effectively to students who span the spectrum of learning readiness, personal interests, culturally shaped ways of seeing and speaking of the world, and experiences in that world" (1).

Over the years, researchers have lauded the effectiveness of many kinds of differentiation, targeting students according to their varied learning styles, multiple intelligences, gender, language, ability or readiness, experience, and interest, to name just a few. Although those are all valid considerations in determining the best match of strategy to student, it may be simpler to think of differentiation as the "teacher moves" we use to create appropriate learning experiences. Tomlinson (2014) breaks the moves into three categories:

- **Content:** the material the teacher wants students to learn, and how that material is delivered
- **Process:** the activities that help students learn content, use key skills, and make sense of essential ideas and information
- **Product:** the vehicle through which students demonstrate and extend what they have learned

In all cases, 1:1 technology in our classrooms makes differentiation much more manageable. It enables us to both remediate and accelerate, transforming how and what we can reasonably do in a class period (or outside of it). For example, we can e-mail handouts, made to order, to students in the middle of class. We can post a link to a website in real time so students can use it for a test review. We can compile class notes in a shared document to ensure access for all.

Moreover, differentiation in a 1:1 classroom is differentiation with dignity. In the days before 1:1, if a student needed extra instruction or a modified curriculum, it was darn near impossible to supply that support discreetly. Students hesitated to ask for help if it meant sitting with the teacher at the little round table at the front of the class during workshop time. But, with technology in our classrooms and in front of our students, our support can become invisible, pervasive, and targeted. When the rest of the class is oblivious to the extra feedback a student receives, such as the guided notes the teacher e-mailed before class, kids retain their dignity.

I didn't understand all the complexities of differentiation when I was a new teacher. When I think back on the catastrophe of my writing review lesson from the days before my 1:1 classroom, I can't help but chuckle. I want to take my new teacher self by the hand and lead her to a computer lab or laptop cart, or better yet, give her a true 1:1 classroom to facilitate the learning stations she spent so long planning and had so much trouble executing. So much has changed since those days! Five years after my foray into differentiated stations, at a new school and working with a different grade level, I got my courage up to try the lesson again, but this time with iPads and hindsight.

The day before our review and correction activity, I returned a batch of graded essays and asked the kids to start thinking about what they'd like help with for their revision. That night, their homework was to reread their essays with my comments and complete a Google survey (see Figure 6.1), answering four simple questions: their name, class period, what they wanted to spend their class time reviewing, and how they'd like to learn.

When students walked through the door the next day, I projected a spreadsheet listing the groups and asked them to grab their things and move into their new teams. Once they were situated, I gave them the plan for the day: "Good morning! Go ahead and log in to Schoology and click on the link for your group. It should take you to a shared document with your objectives for the day. Each group will be working on something different, but you will all leave class with strategies to improve your paper for the revision due next week. If you have questions during the period, put them on our backchannel. The room URL is on the board."

And with that, students got to work. The teams that wanted to revise their own work spent the first part of class reading a

Figure 6.1 We ask students to use Google surveys for formative self-assessment.

model paragraph or paper together, and discussing the annotations I had left for them to consider. Once they were primed, they each shared a Google Doc containing the part of their paper they wanted help with. Peers edited simultaneously through comment boxes in the margins.

The teams that needed more instruction started the period by watching a screencast reviewing how to write an introduction, or a thesis, or whatever the subject was for that group. Then, the group read the same sample paragraph as their editing peers, but instead of comments, I left questions for them to discuss as a team. Finally, the review group read a not-so-stellar model that I wrote and talked about how they would fix it.

As students worked, I walked around. But instead of my usual, "How are you guys doing?" line of questioning, I targeted my visits (see Figure 6.2). I answered specific questions based on what was in the backchannel. This gave groups the space to work together without my interruptions but also the hands-on support they needed to surmount any hurdles they faced along the way.

Because my class was actively engaged in activities that spoke to their individual needs, I was free to check in on a couple of students who were working below grade level and needed extra scaffolding. Knowing that Sharon, a recent South Korean immigrant, and Mira, a student with dyslexia, would be hesitant to broadcast their questions on the backchannel, I strategically planned my approach for their support. The night before, after seeing what Sharon and Mira requested for help, I added a series of voice comments to both girls' papers, essentially creating a virtual writing conference before class even began.

Figure 6.2 Diana watches for student questions in the backchannel.

(See Chapter 7 for more on using voice comments for feedback.) Between answering other students' questions from the backchannel, I stopped at Sharon's and Mira's desks for a brief discussion: "Did you listen to the comments I left for you?" I asked. Once I saw the obligatory "yes" nod, I asked each girl to explain what she thought I meant in each of my comments, and what she could do in her revision in response. In the middle of a differentiated class lesson, I was afforded the space to offer remedial support and one-on-one instruction.

In the days that followed, I noticed that the number of visits to each page of resources we used during the differentiated lesson went up significantly. When I asked my students what was going on, they affirmed what I had hoped would be true:

"I only got to do the thesis group in class. I wanted to see what you said to the Introductions team."

"I didn't totally remember everything from the evidence video, so I went back and watched it again."

"I was looking at the sample topic sentences to help me revise mine."

In addition to providing class time for students to process challenging concepts with the support of peers and their teacher, making the stations "virtual" meant they became permanent sources for remediation and acceleration. Not surprisingly, the revisions I collected the following week were some of the best I had seen.

Differentiating with Dignity

As educators, we have choices about how and when we decide to differentiate a learning experience, and the point at which we need to remove the scaffolding. One of the key considerations is how to form groups for differentiated learning. Here again, technology can be a game changer.

Our students are in constant contact via social media, and this constant social communication might affect student self-perception inside and outside of the classroom. Regardless of what we'd like to believe, our students talk about us (and our homework) behind our backs—and, usually, online. When a teacher differentiates assignments, provides varying content, or encourages multiple methods of mastery, students talk. They tend to know who received which reading assignment, and are aware if they are always in the "low group" that just gets videos instead of challenging articles. They know, just as they did in elementary school, which students are "bluebirds" and which are "turtles."

Accordingly, we must be aware of how and when we group students and what types of materials we provide as examples of differentiated content. Our strongest students may be great critical readers but need practice listening to a challenging college-level lecture and discerning key points. Perhaps the "challenge" assignment is the video, and the remediated, scaffolded assignment becomes an accessible article. It's important for us to challenge the assertion that more media is easier and less is harder. With a few thoughtful considerations about grouping and assignment types, differentiation has tremendous possibilities *because* of technology. Let's take a look at some new options that enable us to differentiate according to content, process, and product.

Content, Process, and Product

Differentiation by Content: What Students Learn and How It's Delivered

Jon Chang was getting his students ready for the big "stock market crash simulation" in his senior economics course. He needed every student to come into class the next day with a basic understanding of Black Thursday and the history around the moment that signaled the Great Depression. His class comprised a wide range of students, some of whom had been AP history students in the past and others who had struggled to keep up in the mainstream track. As he handed out the graphic organizer for students to synthesize their reading, he told them to check their inboxes for the text itself. That afternoon, instead of assigning one chapter to everyone, Chang sent out e-mails linking students at varying reading levels to different articles and sites. He used the "bcc" function on his e-mail to keep the names of students on each list private (see Figure 6.3), and simply said, "Click here for your reading assignment."

Group One, the students who were ready for the challenge, received an academic journal article from JSTOR similar to what they might read the following year in college. Students in Group Three, needing more support, were sent to an interactive page on worldhistoryproject.org, which is full of shorter chunks of text, images, interviews, and clickable time lines. Students in the middle, in Group Two, received both links, and their e-mail said "start here" next to the interactive page link and "once you feel you get it, try reading this" before the journal article. The next day, all students had enough information to respond to the takeaways outlined in the graphic organizer that they would turn in, and every student had reading geared to his or her level.

At the core of Chang's homework assignment is the practice of tiering, which Tomlinson (2014) describes as fundamental to differentiating content. The students with less-developed reading readiness found support; at the same time, students who needed less support found a ladder up. Using 1:1 technology makes this type of invisible tiering possible. If Chang was confident that his students would self-select into appropriate reading levels, he could have posted a few links on his learning management system (LMS) and directed students to select the challenge that best suited their skill and readiness. Regardless of the assignment selected, once in class, everyone was back on the same page, ready for the simulation.

Let's be clear: sending an individual e-mail to every student seems completely crazy. Except, that's not what Chang did. Here was his step-by-step work-around:

1. In the fall, Chang collected all of his students' names and e-mail addresses in a Google Form and saved the spreadsheet for the rest of the year, adding to it when new students joined his class.

2. For this assignment, he created a new column in his spreadsheet to code the students: One, Two, or Three. Chang's students never knew which group they were in, or what number they were assigned; the spreadsheet was for his organizational purposes only.

3. He sorted the spreadsheet by those numbers (regardless of class period).

4. He copy and pasted the e-mail addresses for students in Group One into the bcc line of the e-mail, and sent the first assignment to Group One.

5. He repeated the process for Group Two and Group Three.

Figure 6.3 Work Flow Work-Around: How to Not Send 150 Separate E-mails

Just like Chang, we like to think of the tablets and laptops as behind-the-scenes waiters, serving up content matched to the taste of our customers. Here are some more ideas for using 1:1 tools to differentiate by content:

- In the days before 1:1, it was a real challenge when a student entered a grade level or course without the requisite foundational skills to make the year worthwhile. But, when Ian Cooper realized that Chrissy was struggling with the multivariable slope formula because of a deficit in single-variable algebraic equations, he quickly turned to his tablet and started sleuthing for **remedial support.** By pairing Chrissy with a set of Khan Academy video lessons, and following up with her after school to fill in the gaps, Cooper could continue teaching the students who were ready for the next step while simultaneously bringing Chrissy up to a level where class was meaningful and accessible for her.

- Because of the diverse range of **learning styles** in our classes, we try to select novels in the beginning of the school year that we know have audiobooks available online. Every fall, we send out an e-mail to students outlining the best sources on the web for audio support (our usual list includes Overdrive—the public library's lending system, and LibriVox—a free collection of audiobooks for texts in the public domain, as well as paid options from Audible.com and iTunes). We typically play the first chapter in class while students read along so that everyone has a chance to hear a great narrator.

- To gauge **student interest** in the choices for her novel study unit, Diana's classroom roommate, Fehmeen Picetti, sets up an online survey based on the topics and style of each book. Gone are the days when her students would collude to pick the same book as their best friends. Now she is able to match her students to a book she knows they'll love based on the results of their interest survey. For sample interest surveys, visit pluginpowerup.com.

- In an effort to develop students' **processing skills** and push them beyond relying on their preferred learning modes, Miguel Santiago posts a set of links to his learning management system for homework in his environmental science class. The reading for the week, focusing on the truth behind plastic recycling, includes a brief TED Talk video, a *Time* magazine photo essay, an article from the *New York Times,* and an infographic. Santiago encourages students to start with the resource that is easiest for them to understand, and then to use it to support their understanding as they access the remaining resources throughout the week. He asks them to respond by writing a paragraph making connections and explaining how the four "texts" tell the same story in different ways.

Differentiation by Process: How Students Make Sense of New Information

Beyond adjusting what we teach and how we teach it, 1:1 tools give us a great deal of flexibility in how we ask our students to interact with content and process new information. Laptops and tablets can liberate us from the doldrums of standard note taking and handout making, if we let them.

- If **note taking** is core to your class, switch up how students approach the task. At the start of a direct instruction lesson, post the slides for your presentation. Students with tablets can ink (digitally write) on the slides, as well as record audio to correspond with the lecture, using programs such as Notability. When we know that students will have our slides, we tend to pare down what we include; a title and a key image will suffice to trigger their visual memory as they note the key concepts they pick up by listening. By supporting one modality (visual), we can stretch another (auditory).
- Encourage high levels of **discussion** participation from all types of discussants. Consider using a backchannel (see Chapter 3) such as todaysmeet.com or padlet.com to activate simultaneous forms of academic conversation. Some students are strong verbal and auditory processors and can easily manage new information in a dialogue. Others need the space to gather their ideas and write them down. Backchanneling is a way to honor both kinds of conversation and processing.
- After students finish making review posters for an upcoming quiz, Diana has them snap a picture for the class and send it to her. She then uploads the JPEGs to a shared deck of **flash cards** on Quizlet.com where students log in to study. They love that they can see the same images inside the classroom and out. Added bonus: sites such as Quizlet have the option to speak words aloud—even in foreign languages! And, they catalog decks of flash cards from other teachers and schools, sorted by subject and text (see Figures 6.4a and 6.4b).
- When we document learning on the whiteboard, Diana likes to save a minute before the final bell for students to make use of the camera on their devices. By digitally stitching together (using Notability) their writing from class and the pictures of the whiteboard, students gain **visual cues** to help them remember the essentials from class. In Diana's classroom, students jokingly call this photo break a "paparazzi pause."
- Similar to Chang's tiered reading assignment model for differentiating content, **tiered activities** work well for differentiating how students will make sense of the content. Instead of presenting the same activity to every student, the LMS

Nostos

homecoming. Go out, adventure, gain fame/honor, come home. Dangerous, often unsuccessful. Related to concepts of Oikos, Kleos, Time.

Figure 6.4a (left) and 6.4b (right) Diana uses Quizlet to create flash cards with students

makes it easy to offer multiple "routes of access" to practice a new skill or review a new concept. Through 1:1 technology, we can instantly and invisibly provide simultaneous experiences that vary by complexity, abstractness, and open-endedness (Tomlinson 2014). A math teacher, for example, might offer three different links after a whole-class lesson: (1) more instruction on a two-column PDF, with steps explained on one side and the problems for the student to solve on the other; (2) guided practice with one model problem and a set of review problems; (3) a challenge set that pushes students to test their learning on a handful of tough questions. Students can then select their own option based on their comfort level.

- **Scaffold reading** assignments by literally placing yourself in the middle of the text. Add questions at key junctures, make clarifying comments, and respond to student questions—all in the middle of a novel, article, or PDF. For example, all of Diana's sophomores read her annotated iBook version of *The Scarlet Letter,* complete with preview questions to focus student reading, pop-up vocabulary for instant clarification, student artwork from previous years, and chapter check-in boxes to guide student annotations (see Figure 6.5). The reading experience was a hit! Alternatively, online tools such as Actively Learn infuse reading with the very best that social networking has to offer. Students can see each other's questions and comments while reading a class text. Collaboration *and* differentiation! What's not to like?

No matter how we scaffold learning experiences to help students process new content—whether through reading guides, writing tutorial videos, or illustrated flash cards—we post all of the links on the LMS as a menu of choices; we let students learn how they learn best by giving them access to a variety of support materials. (See Figure 6.6 for ideas about collaborating with your colleagues to expand differentiation options.)

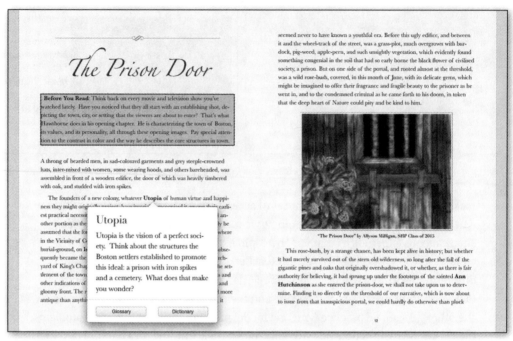

Figure 6.5 Students love reading Diana's *Scarlet Letter* iBook, which includes preview questions, pop-up vocabulary, student artwork from previous years, and chapter check-in boxes.

As we mentioned in Chapter 4, we can collaborate with colleagues to efficiently create multiple iterations of one assignment. If one of our colleagues makes a differentiated assignment that isn't quite right for our students, we can still modify it quickly because it is shared digitally (instead of as a hard copy). There's no reason to reinvent the wheel, and there's no reason to go it alone.

Figure 6.6 Collaboration for Differentiation

Differentiation by Product: How Students Show They've Learned

At the core of differentiating by product is the belief that there are many ways for students to demonstrate learning and that assessments do not have to be identical for each learner. We both use a "mastery menu" for our assessments, drawing upon the RAFT acronym for guidance (changing the student's <u>R</u>ole, the assignment's <u>A</u>udience or <u>F</u>ormat, and either the <u>T</u>opic or <u>T</u>echnology). We can't help but laugh when students tell us that one of the options looks *really easy*, only to hear moments later from another student that the same exact option seems impossible. That's differentiation! Diana has adapted this model for writing prompts by using the "spicy chili" notation system we often see at restaurants in California: one chili, two chilies, three chilies (see Figures 6.7a and 6.7b). Students select whether they need a mild "one chili" prompt or are ready to light their learning ablaze.

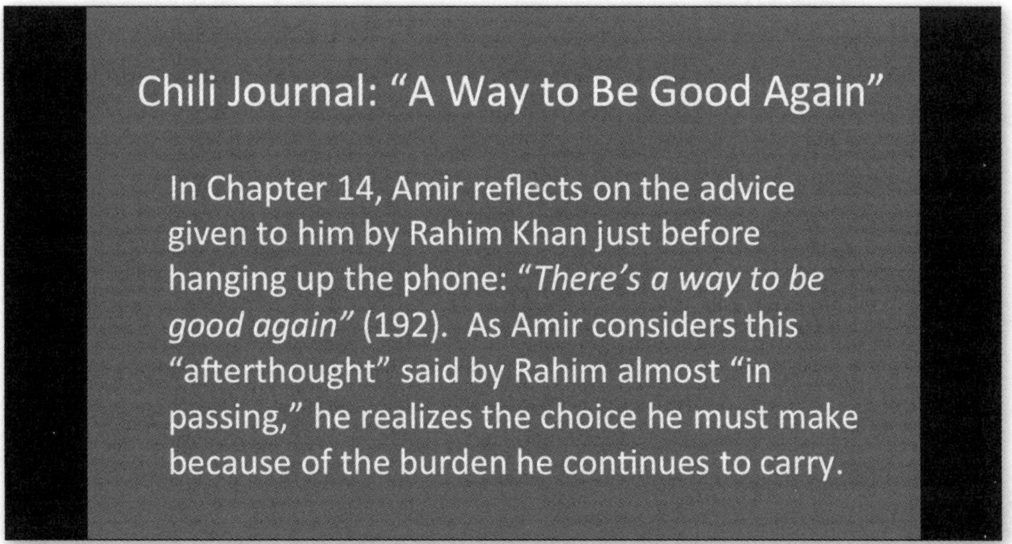

Chili Journal: "A Way to Be Good Again"

In Chapter 14, Amir reflects on the advice given to him by Rahim Khan just before hanging up the phone: *"There's a way to be good again"* (192). As Amir considers this "afterthought" said by Rahim almost "in passing," he realizes the choice he must make because of the burden he continues to carry.

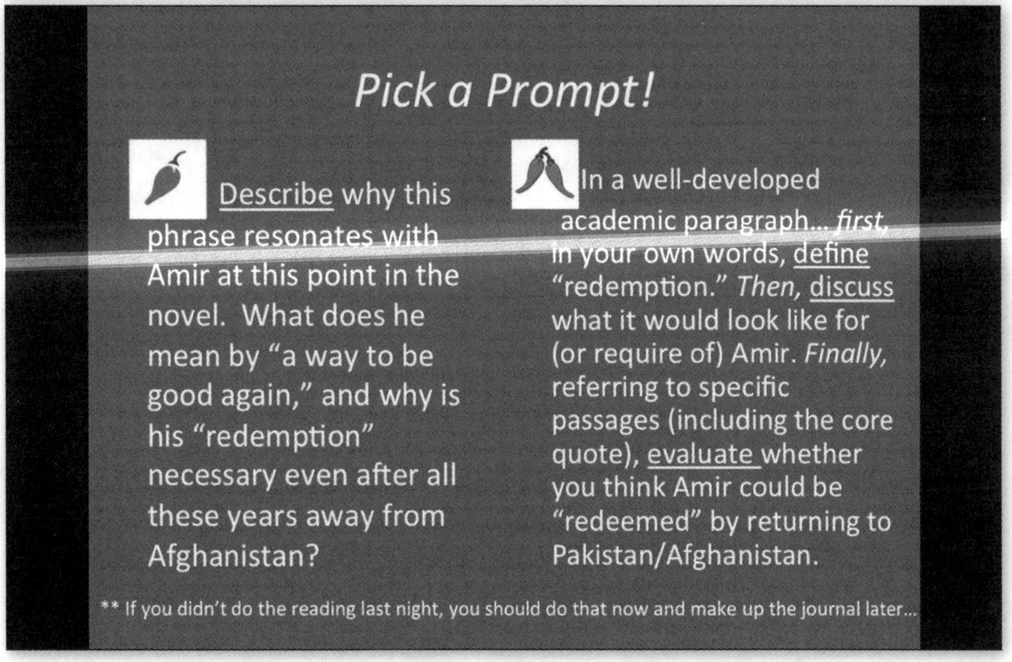

Pick a Prompt!

Describe why this phrase resonates with Amir at this point in the novel. What does he mean by "a way to be good again," and why is his "redemption" necessary even after all these years away from Afghanistan?

In a well-developed academic paragraph... *first,* in your own words, define "redemption." *Then,* discuss what it would look like for (or require of) Amir. *Finally,* referring to specific passages (including the core quote), evaluate whether you think Amir could be "redeemed" by returning to Pakistan/Afghanistan.

** If you didn't do the reading last night, you should do that now and make up the journal later...

Figure 6.7a (above) and 6.7b (below) Students choose their own level of spice for the *Kite Runner* assignment.

In Figure 6.8, we show some strategies for tiering student assessments in the traditional classroom (Wormeli 2013) as well as some ideas for what those strategies might look like in the 1:1 classroom.

Traditional Classroom	1:1 Classroom	Principle in Practice
Manipulate information instead of echoing it.	Create an online infographic about the content.	Rather than write an explanation or report a current trend, ask students to portray that same data visually using Piktochart or easel.ly.
Increase the number of variables to be considered.	Augment traditional teacher input with the professional content and sophisticated tools available online.	Challenge students to use a specific type of interactive technology in their assignments, even if they have no experience with the tool. Check out thinglink.com or tildee.com for places to start.
Add an unexpected element to the product.	Manipulate technology to simulate real-world scenarios.	Replicate the demands of the modern workforce by requiring students to collaborate online with a peer in another state or country. Or, change the intended audience (and with it, the final digital format of the assignment).
Work independently.	Have students create a website, wiki, blog, or video that features the subject being studied.	Have students document their independent research or project online so you (and others) can observe their progress and process.
Work with abstract concepts and models.	Redesign a traditional assignment in a nonstandard way.	Turn a debate for civics class into a graph that illustrates the relationships among ideas and arguments using DebateGraph.
Respond to more open-ended situations.	Use the Internet as a source for igniting open-ended discussions and debates.	Post a YouTube video as a writing prompt or a Flickr image for a discussion starter in a foreign language class. Play footage of a science experiment gone awry, and ask students to analyze the blunder.

Figure 6.8 Increasing Challenge in Student Products—Tiering Tasks in the 1:1 Classroom

Students don't have to create a podcast or a video for their final products; they can choose the best way to demonstrate mastery. In Chapter 7, we delve into ways to enhance assessment practices and feedback, and in Chapter 8, we explore ways to boost creativity in student work. Many of those ideas transfer to differentiation.

Content, Process, and Product in Review

A tailor-made education, fit to measure, seems to be the way of the future. Our students "live in a moment when personalizing the learning experience is not just a possibility—it's almost an expectation. We personalize our playlists through Rhapsody and iTunes, our reading through Amazon and Twitter, and our search results on Google and Bing" (Richardson 2012). Students live and breathe in a "culture of customization." We know this worldview trickles into the classroom, and we think that's a good thing! Our flexibility in the classroom helps us meet students where they are and stretch them beyond where they could go without us. The best part is that with 1:1 technology, we can provide these scaffolds to *all* students, creating an environment that individualizes instead of standardizes the education of every single learner (Bellow 2013).

 PLUG IN   Get Acquainted with the Diverse Possibilities on Your Device

1. **Content:** Consider a hobby that you'd like to learn more about (painting, cooking, hiking, skiing . . .). Now Google it. What kind of resources are available on the Internet? Consider YouTube videos, online forums, photographs, TED Talks, audiobooks, apps, games, and so on. Check out the body of information available to support your own learning, and the different learning modes that are supported with a quick Internet search.

2. **Process:** Push yourself to take in the news of the day in a different way. If you are accustomed to watching the nightly broadcast on television, read about the world's affairs on Twitter instead. Sold on reading the newspaper? Listen to a podcast. Devoted to your paperback? Try an audiobook or interactive e-book. Get comfortable with the different learning modalities supported by your personal devices.

3. **Product:** Think about the ways that you deliver information to others (through e-mail, verbal instructions, recipe cards, written directions, and so on). Now play around with a new way to deliver the same message. Instead of sending a list of driving directions, try annotating a Google Map online. Instead of sending a recipe, create a step-by-step clickable photo guide using Tildee.com. Practice reenvisioning what it means to communicate "mastery."

Differentiating for Special Populations
Supporting English Language Learners

English Language Learners (ELLs) are a unique population within our classrooms. Although we believe that strategies for ELLs can help all students, we sometimes need to find targeted approaches to accommodate nonnative speakers.

One of Diana's sophomores immigrated to the United States in the intermediate grades. Although she soared with verbal communication and auditory processing, she stumbled with writing. Diana discovered that the student could catch her mistakes if she could hear them aloud, so she encouraged her to download a text-to-speech app, turning her iPad into a reader that would patiently recite her writing. The editing process quickly changed from the frustrating experience of looking with confusion at a screen riddled with red underlines and awkward auto-corrections to a practice session that delivered results. Best of all, she felt confident in her work! (See Figures 6.9a and 6.9b for more reflections about speech-to-text supports for students.)

I have witnessed the power that apps such as Dragon Dictation have to more fully and equitably include students with special needs in my classroom. One student struggled with severe dysgraphia, and had endured years of hearing his classmates complain that they couldn't read his illegible handwriting or jesting that he wrote like a young child. My teacher-heart broke every time I asked students to write the answers to their reading quizzes or exchange work for peer editing, because I knew it meant social isolation for one child. That same year, we were piloting iPads at the freshman level, and our special-education director managed to get iPads in the hands of all of our students with learning differences. The transition from paper and pen to dictate and type was glorious. My student could e-mail me his quizzes or speak his responses into the iPad if his joint pain was particularly bad on a given day.

Figure 6.9a Point-Counterpoint: Diana's Experience with Speech to Text

A word of caution: dictation apps are not a panacea for students who struggle with writing. Organizing thoughts in speech is difficult, especially for those who have little experience organizing their thoughts for writing. When we write, we naturally pause to think about the next sentence; however, students may think they must speak in one fluid line of thought when using a dictation app. I have had to teach students using dictation apps to speak an outline first, and then go back and speak into the parts of that outline. Many students spend just as much time fixing the mistakes of the dictation program as they would typing words in the first place. We can't assume that just because a student can dictate an essay that his or her writing will be as polished as other students' writing. A student using a dictation app will likely still need teacher support.

Figure 6.9b Point-Counterpoint: Jen's Experience with Speech to Text

Some students freeze when they start writing. Jen helped her student Juan with language frames by pasting sentence starters in his Google Doc. In the days before 1:1 classes, Jen might have had to provide assistance to Juan by stopping at his desk throughout the class period. Or, Juan might have had an aide at his side and suffered the social stigma of too much adult attention. Now when Juan needs a way in to introduce a research article or story, Jen can provide a cue such as,

"In her essay, _____, [author] explains that _____."

Or, when Juan is writing a reflection about how his opinion has changed, Jen might prompt,

"At one point I believed _____, but now I believe _____ because _____."

This form of support is invisible to the class, but it gives Juan vital models for completing assignments. For more sentence frames like the ones above, check out *They Say, I Say: The Moves That Matter in Academic Writing* (Graff and Birkenstein 2009).

Depending on your students' English language needs and whether they have recently arrived to the United States, have had formal schooling, or are long-term English learners (Freeman and Freeman 2007), some of the strategies listed below will be more or less applicable.

- For newly arrived students with limited previous schooling, many districts have found success using Rosetta Stone's K–12 language proficiency program. Additionally, Imagine Learning has an online program for English language support.
- Help students make connections in their vocabulary using websites such as vocabulary.com or an online visual dictionary such as visuwords.com or freerice.com.
- Develop context for classroom content through online schema builders such as Instagrok or OmniGraffle.
- Equip students with tools to show comprehension. Check out free drawing apps such as Explain Everything or Doodle Buddy.

- Draw upon photography to elicit (or explain) an emotional response to content. As one of the teachers we follow on Twitter wrote, students don't "have to speak the same language to appreciate or react to a photo" (@MrsJudyNguyen).
- Support developing readers by inserting yourself in the text with sites such as Actively Learn. For students who need more reading comprehension practice, consider paid services such as Reading Assistant from Scientific Learning, and My Reading Coach from Mind Play.
- Empower developing writers by teaching them to use tools such as paperrater.com and hemingwayapp.com, which will "grade" their papers and give advice about word choice, grammar, and so on.

Supporting Students with Special Needs

The director of the special-education program at Diana's school often refers to technology as "the great equalizer," giving students with disabilities the accommodations they need to fully participate in the least restrictive environment possible. Once, at a faculty development day, she drew a parallel between an iPad and a pair of glasses: If a person has imperfect vision, he wears glasses. If a student has learning differences, give him access to apps and tools that allow him to see class more clearly.

There are many apps and websites available to support students with all kinds of learning needs. Here are a few of our favorites (and the favorites of those we know and trust in special education):

- **Vision Impairment:** We have been amazed at the possibilities for customizing the devices in our classrooms. Through the accessibility feature, students with vision impairment can increase text size, zoom, enable speaking text, and invert the color palate, all with the swipe of a toggle button. Beyond these features, teachers can support students with vision impairment by screen sharing. Before launching a PowerPoint presentation or starting class directions on the projector, create a screen share from the teacher computer to the student device so students who need to can zoom in and look more closely from the comfort of their desks. Sites such as join.me offer this service for free. Alternatively, you can use screen sharing through Google+ Hangout or use interactive presentation apps like Nearpod.

- **Hearing Impairment:** Depending on the students' proximity to the teacher, dictation apps and sites can work to create real-time captioning of a lesson on a tablet or laptop, turning the teacher's spoken words into typed text. More expensive, subscription-based products are also available for captioning.

- **Fine-Motor Challenges:** For students with fine-motor-control difficulties, a ten-dollar fix may do the trick! By adding an external mouse or giving students a chubby stylus to point and click, we can lessen the difficulty of navigating the highly sensitive responses of an interactive screen. If typing or tapping is too cumbersome, consider a dictation program such as Dragon Dictation.

- **Attention and Focus Challenges:** Using 1:1 technology can offer tremendous benefits to students but can also make for a distracting work experience for students with attention deficit disorder (ADD) or attention deficit hyperactivity disorder (ADHD). Many special-education departments use the PC-based Kurzweil system to highlight words as students read, speak while they type, and support reading with annotation and brainstorming templates as well as the option to block surrounding text to direct student focus. This program is also effective with ELL students.

- **Organizational Challenges:** By the time students reach middle school, they typically have up to seven classes to juggle, with different due dates, homework assignments, and parameters for punctuality. Managing the load can be overwhelming for any kid, but especially for students with learning disabilities. User-friendly phone and tablet apps such as Clear, Wunderlist, and Reminders help students prioritize deadlines and keep track of completed work.

- **Autism:** In October 2011, *60 Minutes* aired a show called "Apps for Autism," highlighting the incredible experiences of families in which children with autism have greatly benefited from using tablets and smartphones for communication. In the years since the creation of the tablet, scores of apps have been written specifically with the autism community in mind. For a comprehensive (and frequently updated) list of apps, go to http://www.autism speaks.org/autism-apps.

It is because of these technological breakthroughs, and the others that are sure to occur in the coming years, that educational researchers such as Michael Behrmann (1998) predict that "assistive technology will certainly mainstream more and more children in wheelchairs, children who cannot physically speak, see, or hear, and children who need computers to write, organize, think, and function educationally." That's an exciting development in differentiation!

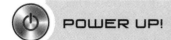

POWER UP! Put Your Tech Skills to the Test to Extend How You Differentiate Instruction

1. **Set up a spreadsheet** with your students' names, e-mail addresses, and class period to facilitate grouping and sending tailored assignments. Be sure to save a master and edit only copies of the spreadsheet so that you can keep reusing the same document over and over. You may be able to pull this data directly from your school's student information system or use a Google Form to have students submit their names and e-mails.

2. Take a closer look at your students' interests and readiness levels by creating an **online survey to collect and organize their data**. Consider the skills students will need to be successful in the upcoming unit, and the areas in which you have the flexibility to offer them choice. Visit pluginpowerup.com for digital surveys you can use.

3. **Sit down with your stack of IEPs** and home in on the section that describes the student's challenges and accommodations required. For each student, brainstorm a few 1:1 tools that you would like to try to help make class time more engaging and productive, and support outside of class more ubiquitous. Maybe you test a shared Google Doc between you and the student for a question-and-answer log, or perhaps you make a plan to share your presentation slide deck before class for the student to mark during a lecture. Consider sitting down with each student and talking about strategies that he or she would find helpful, and what tools would best deliver the support needed.

CHAPTER 7
Feedback and Assessment

Feed·back (n): Information about how we are doing in our efforts to reach a goal. (Wiggins 2012)

Teacher: Diana Neebe
Class: Tenth-Grade English

It was a Tuesday about 9:00 p.m. The house was quiet, my mug of tea was hot, and I had finally carved out some time to take a look at those explication paragraphs that would be coming in over the next few days. I had promised my students that I would be available via e-mail that night for last-minute help, but between e-mails, I figured I would pop in and out of our shared docs on Google Drive to see the progress for myself.

I left a few comments for a few students before I got to Emily. When I clicked in, my name icon appeared at the top of the screen, and I saw that Emily was also in the document, typing away. I started a chat window by clicking the icon next to our pictures. What follows is a transcript of our conversation, which I had open in one window while simultaneously checking on other students' paragraphs as I waited for Emily's responses.

Me:	Hey Emily—just checking on your paper. How's it coming?
Emily:	Hi Mrs. Neebe! Ummm, I am trying to figure out how to word my thesis and I'm not really sure what to say.
Me:	What do you think the passage shows about Janie's character? Or about her dreams?
Emily:	I think it's trying to show that she can't pursue her dreams as long as she's with Jody because he treats her like a mule who carries his heavy load and won't let her do or have what she wants for herself.

Me: awesome

Emily: and she wants to walk away from the relationship but decides to keep to herself about it and just put on a happy coverup

Me: let's refine it

Emily: ok

Me: how do you know those things? What evidence supports it?

Emily: well theres all the talk of "no more blossomy openings dusting pollen over her man" and just talking about how its not natural anymore and there is the dinner disaster that shows he's restricting her by dehumanizing her to the role of a mule. plus the whole broken image extended metaphor thing where she just straight out admits that she doesn't really want anything to do with him anymore and just wants to walk away from his broken image

Me: exactly . . . so what do those things have in common?

Emily: spring imagery, her broken ideal of marriage?

Me: and where does Jody fit into all of that?

Emily: he doesn't live up to janie's dream of the ideal marriage (the pear tree scene)

Me: okay, so in order for Janie to be true to her dream, what does she have to do?

Emily: hmmm . . .

Me: what do you think? will Jody be in that picture?

Emily: No. not unless she gains the courage to express herself in the community she is in. I guess she either has to get a voice or get out.

Me: so, let's go back to that thesis of yours . . .

Emily: ok. through the motif of spring and the extended metaphor of the broken image of Jody, Hurston illustrates that the only way Janie can pursue her dream of a perfect marriage is to leave Jody and express her own voice.

Me: Ready to write now?

Emily: for sure!

Me: Go get 'em! Can't wait to see what you write!

Emily: Alright! Thanks for the help. oh and this google drives chat thing is awesome :)

Needless to say, this is a conversation I never would have had in the days before 1:1. Although it isn't feasible for me to hold "virtual office hours" for every paper or every big exam, I can use digital tools to provide meaningful feedback to my students, often at just the right time. Technology makes us present to our students and their needs in ways that just weren't possible in the past. And despite the sometimes-overwhelming feeling we get because technology never seems to take a rest, we can learn how to leverage it selectively for the good of our students and our own workloads.

The Challenge of Giving Effective Feedback

Inevitably, the challenge of feedback comes up somewhere around the beginning of November. We have long since broken with the sweet, slow place of summer, and gotten into the rhythm of school. We have moved through a couple of units, and have given substantive feedback on a number of assignments. November is the time in the school year when we start to wonder if our students have internalized *any* of the things we have said, written, marked, or highlighted on rubrics. It's the month when we sincerely wonder if we'll make it to Thanksgiving in one piece. If we could capture all the grumblings about grading that we hear over lunch and over copy machines around this time of year, it would sound something like this:

- "I'm so tired. I just can't seem to get through this stack of essays without falling asleep."
- "I wouldn't mind giving them feedback if they'd actually read it and think about it."
- "I can't believe I've had these tests for three weeks already. I've barely gotten started."
- "I think I have written the same thing over and over about fifty times."
- "I wish they had told me they were all confused with the same concept *before* I gave the test."
- "I don't know why I bother to write so many comments. My students only care about the grade."

Sound familiar? We know, because we have felt these same sentiments, too. Providing effective feedback is challenging. And spending precious time giving feedback, only to see a room full of students jam their marked-up assignments into the caverns of their backpacks, never to see the light of day again, is nothing shy of soul crushing.

And yet, we acknowledge the incredible importance of feedback in the process of learning. The oft-cited educational researcher John Hattie (2012) reports from his meta-analysis of more than 900 studies that among the many moderating factors in student achievement, "feedback has one of the highest effects on student learning" and is the "common denominator in many of the top influences" on learning. Moreover, when we focus on feedback *for* learning instead of feedback on what has already been learned, students get a "clear picture of their progress on learning goals and how they might improve" and receive the encouragement they need to work toward improvement (Marzano 2006).

Given the value of feedback for student growth, it is imperative that we define from the start what feedback *is* and what it *isn't*.

Feedback is . . .

- *Informative.* High-quality feedback is aimed at "reduc[ing] the gap between where students are and where they should be" (Hattie 2012). Effective feedback helps students see clearly what the objective is, where they are in relation to mastering that objective, and what their next steps ought to be.
- *Timely.* This is the "strike while the iron is hot" principle. The longer the gap between when students complete a task and when they receive feedback, the less valuable that feedback becomes (Wiggins 2012).
- *Useful.* This one seems like a no-brainer but is perhaps the least followed in practice. Providing useful feedback means giving our students specific comments and concepts they can apply right away to their work that is in progress. When feedback comes with a summative assessment instead of midstream with a formative assessment, it is often too late for students to make use of our advice.
- *Mutually beneficial.* Teachers need feedback just as much as our students. When we can identify patterns in student errors and misconceptions, we have the opportunity to make adjustments to our instruction and target our support of students to specific areas of need (Fisher and Frey 2012).

Feedback isn't . . .

- *A grade.* In fact, despite the incredibly common practice of pairing feedback with a numerical score, and despite the myths around letter grades as effective motivators (Kohn 1999), we know that when students see feedback and a grade in the same sitting, they ignore the feedback and focus on the grade. What's perhaps more alarming is that they hunt and peck through the feedback, and read only the evidence that confirms the score: praise for higher-than-expected grades, and mistakes for lower-than-expected grades (Belanger and Allingham 2002).

- *Praise.* "Great job!" and "Well done!" fail to provide students with the information they need to understand where they excelled and where they should go next with their learning. To foster a growth mind-set (Dweck 2007) around learning, in which students attribute their successes and failures to effort and actions rather than to whether they think the teacher likes them, or whether they think they are smart, we must push ourselves away from the "atta boys" and toward more substantive remarks.

This generation of students is programmed for digesting rapid, continuous feedback. Just consider their participation in computer and video games; they innately understand what it means to learn through the feedback loop. Grant Wiggins (2012) notes that "if you play Angry Birds, Halo, Guitar Hero, or Tetris, you know that the key to substantial improvement is that the feedback is both timely and ongoing. When you fail, you can immediately start over—sometimes even right where you left off—to get another opportunity to receive and learn from the feedback" (15). Our students are ready for a kind of immediate feedback that is rare in most classrooms.

The challenges of providing effective feedback are many. The good news is that 1:1 technology gives us a tremendous advantage by offering innovative approaches to problem solving our way through obstacles. With 1:1 technology, we can provide more feedback, more efficiently, and in many more forms than we could before. We can turn around a set of quizzes or checks for understanding in a matter of seconds. We can easily collect the data we need to make informed decisions about our instruction. We can shortcut the task of giving the same comment over and over again. We can easily add follow-up instruction to help students fix common errors. We can separate feedback from grades to encourage students to focus on growth and learning. We can monitor student writing during the drafting phase without having to wait for a paper to be turned in. What follows are six classroom-tested strategies for providing stronger formative feedback.

Six Strategies for Stronger Feedback
Instant Feedback

Our challenge is clear: researchers are calling on us to give "efficient and timely feedback" so that our students can think about their learning in the moment and reflect on their mistakes without waiting the day or two (or week) that it takes most of us to turn their work around (Magaña and Marzano 2014). Challenge accepted. How much more efficient and timely can we get than providing feedback *instantly*? The technology is ready.

The first time Jen used Google Forms and Flubaroo to auto-grade one of her vocabulary quizzes, she thought it was like someone from *The Jetsons* buzzing into her classroom in a self-flying car. It seemed crazy. And wonderful. With a little setup before students walked through the door, she was able to check their understanding and quickly e-mail the results to them with a few clicks. Immediate data can drive instruction while showing students what they individually need to work on improving.

Geometry teacher Gary Ashanti uses instant feedback at the start of class each day. The bell rings and students take out their tablets, opened to the app for the learning management system. They click on the quiz, and the five-minute timer starts counting down. When students submit their quizzes, their score reports pop up: green check marks for the questions they got right, and red X marks for the ones they got wrong. The correct response is always highlighted, so students know what they missed before class really gets going. Ashanti's daily quizzes give him a clear picture in the first few minutes of the period of what students understood from the homework and what they still need to review before he moves forward. More important, the quizzes help students recognize where they need support and help them select their review or extension activity for class that day. Ashanti encourages students to choose their own path in class: review the basics, work through a couple of comparable problems, or apply the concept to an advanced problem. The feedback equips them to make good decisions about their learning needs. (See Figure 7.1 for more ideas.)

Some educators have taken to "gamification" as a form of providing instant feedback, in which students earn badges for mastering content and can progress through learning stages, or "level up," in their learning objectives based on recent assessments or assignments, much like they would in a video game (Klopfer, Osterweil, and Salen 2009). Although neither of us has really done much with gamification, many educators love it. As a pedagogical practice, it tends to be more popular among elementary grades than upper grades. If gamification is a concept that interests you or that you think would help your students, we encourage you to learn more about it and then proceed thoughtfully.

Peer Feedback

We know intuitively that students care what their classmates have to say about their work. Research into assessment models confirms and extends our classroom observations: feedback from multiple peers is more effective than feedback from one expert, such as a teacher (Cho 2004). When we design opportunities for students to hear from their classmates, everyone benefits. One of our favorite questions to ask students after they provide peer feedback is "How many of you, in the process of reading/watching/listening to your partner's work, thought of something you'd like to revise in your own work?" When all the hands in the room fly up, we know the task has been worthwhile.

TOOLS FOR INSTANT FEEDBACK	
LMS Quiz	There is a really good chance that the learning management system you are already encouraged to use has some form of quiz or assessment system built into it. To find out, search for the name of your specific LMS and the word quiz. If your LMS will handle assessments, you will find articles and tutorials about how to use that feature.
Socrative	Socrative lets you send students single questions or create full quizzes. When you create the quiz, you can add custom text to explain the correct answer, giving students immediate feedback about their choices. See Socrative.com.
Nearpod	Nearpod is a website and corresponding app that takes a simple slide deck and makes it interactive for students with quizzes and checks for understanding. The teacher can access, or push, that feedback during the lesson. You can see what all of your students have typed, selected, or scribbled in presenter view. For multiple-choice questions, you will also see a graph of the percentage of the class who selected each response. Go to nearpod.com.
Poll Every-where	Poll Everywhere is a polling or surveying website that accepts responses via web or text message, and displays the anonymous results in real time on a graph or word cloud as students submit their responses. Visit polleverywhere.com.
Flubaroo	Flubaroo is an "add-on" that works with Google Sheets. If you used a Google Form to create a multiple-choice quiz, you can use Flubaroo to grade that quiz based on your answer key. If you asked for students' e-mail addresses when they took the quiz, you can have Flubaroo e-mail them their scores. Go to flubaroo.com for quick tutorials.
Hemingway App	The Hemingway App lets students paste in their writing and get instant feedback about which sentences are hard to read and which word choices they can improve. Though absolutely not a substitute for an experienced writing mentor, Hemingway App can give students some instantly action-able feedback about their writing. See hemingwayapp.com.

Figure 7.1 Top Tools for Instant Feedback and What They Do Best

Cori McPherson's seniors were in the final stages of creating public service announcements for their nutrition and sports science elective. Each student in the class tackled a different health concern in the school community, ranging from the effects of sugar on the body, to the effect of alcohol on the brain, to the upsides and downsides of teen weight lifting to build muscle mass. McPherson knew that if the PSAs were going to be ready for prime time on the campus television monitors and in the school announcements, students would need substantive feedback before they got to the recording step of the process. She certainly didn't have time to turn around thirty-two PSAs in a matter of days. Instead, she decided to have students "road test" their projects on fellow classmates.

A few days before the project deadline, she planned a "last ditch pitch" day for her students, during which they met in teams of four to review project pitches before recording their final screencasts. Students arrived in class with completed slide decks in Google Slides and with their scripts typed out as presenter notes. In a sixty-minute period, each student got fifteen minutes to be in the hot seat, sharing his or her slide deck with the rest of the group, reading through the presentation, and waiting patiently for feedback. Once the student finished reading his or her script and progressing through the slides, group-mates had five minutes to silently add comments to the shared deck. Some of the comments were about the quality of the images selected; others were about the script and how the student delivered his or her lines. At the end of the period, everyone went home with targeted, actionable feedback that would lead to more refined PSAs. When the videos finally went live on campus, they were polished, and students were confident that they had done their best work. See Figure 7.2 for more ideas.

Global Feedback

Contrary to how it may sound, global feedback is not a way to get people from around the world to do our jobs for us (although that would be nice). It is a method for giving high-level feedback to the whole class at the same time (see Figure 7.3 for more). Providing substantive feedback in a timely manner is the albatross of assessment. Usually, there's a trade-off. Either students receive brief notes fairly quickly, or longer, more in-depth commentary a while after submitting their work. It's time to give targeted global feedback to the entire class instead of specific feedback to individual students (Fisher and Frey 2012).

In Phil Follet's US government class, students were studying the origins of social reform through nonviolent peaceful resistance and were in the process of analyzing Henry David Thoreau's "On the Duty of Civil Disobedience." For homework one weekend, Follet assigned his students a discussion board, asking them to post once and reply twice, explaining when it would be justified to break the laws of government according to Thoreau and according to their own sense of justice. As the initial posts started trickling in, Follet made a point of jumping in, not so much to moderate the discussion as to provide early feedback to all his students at once.

TOOLS FOR PEER FEEDBACK	
Google Comments	With shared documents and presentations in Google Drive it is easy for students to insert comments and suggest edits to their peers. To add a comment, students simply highlight the item they want to comment on and click Insert/Comment, and then type what they want to say in the side box.
Blog Comments	Most blogging platforms allow readers to comment on each post on the blog. Usually, it is as simple as clicking the word *comment* at the bottom of the post, typing an appropriate message, and hitting Submit.
Google Forms	Google Forms are a great way to collect information, feedback included. These surveys collect data in many different formats: multiple choice, select from a list, text fill-in, graph, and scale, to name a few. A student can set up his or her own Google Form and send it to classmates to solicit feedback about a project, or a teacher can create a form and ask students to submit comments that will then be shared with the student(s) who created the work. Jen uses Google Forms for peer feedback about presentations. Then she e-mails the comments to the presenter the same day.
PeerMark from Turnitin	If your school subscribes to the plagiarism checker service from turnitin.com, you may also already have access to PeerMark, which allows the teacher to digitally swap papers and assign them to students for peer editing and reviewing. It is easy to add questions for students to answer about the paper and for both classmates and teacher to view the remarks.

Figure 7.2 Top Tools for Peer Feedback and What They Do Best

After one student's post that glossed over the argument without providing any reasoning for support, Follet wrote, "I'm interested in this line of thinking. Could you develop it more with evidence from the text? Just add on below in this thread . . ." And, after a one-line reply to a classmate that simply nodded in agreement at the original post, Follet added, "It's okay to agree with each other, but the goal here is to build a conversation with lots of ideas. If you want to agree, give us a *yes . . . and* statement that furthers our understanding. Go ahead and add your extended argument below!" Instead of waiting until he had assessed the posts and comments to provide course corrections, Follet made notes for all to see, to help students self-correct while they were still in the process of thinking and learning.

We have used recorded think-alouds for similar reasons, drawing on one model or example to anchor our feedback. For example, when Jen's ninth graders were working on their novels for NaNoWriMo (National Novel Writing Month), she noticed that many of them struggled with writing believable dialogue. She ended class one day asking students, "Who is really brave and really wants to improve the dialogue in his or her novel?" Five or six hands popped up, and after carefully scanning her options, Jen selected an excited girl from the back of the room whom she knew needed some help but could also handle the spotlight of sharing her learning with the whole class. That afternoon, Jen recorded a video think-aloud, reading the student's dialogue and providing feedback as she went. She paused, highlighted text, and noted elements that made both of the characters sound the same, as well as places where the author had started to develop really distinct voices. She asked questions that would help her student dig into the characters' quirks and personalities and ultimately lead to more genuine-sounding dialogue. The next day, Jen posted the video on the class blog for students to come back to review as they wrote.

TOOLS FOR GLOBAL FEEDBACK	
Discussion Board	Early replies from you to a few students will be seen by, and shape, the responses of other students. Your learning management system (LMS) probably has a discussions section already that you can probably use.
Course Announcements	Your LMS probably has a way to let you send a message to all of your students. This can be a great way to let them know you are enjoying their work or seeing a similar problem repeatedly.
Video Think-Aloud	A screencast you make of feedback to one student can become a lesson for all of your students. Or, if you see many of your students making a similar technical error, you can make a screencast to show them the right way to do the task. Jen's students sometimes post the wrong link to their work, giving her the editing link instead of the finished product. She made a screencast showing them how to get the correct link and submit it to her Google Form. Try QuickTime, ScreenChomp, Jing, Camtasia, or Screenr.

Figure 7.3 Top Tools for Global Feedback and What They Do Best

Frequent Feedback

This form of feedback addresses the common frustration of writing the same comment over and over again on multiple assignments, and it addresses the need for providing students with a clear path to improvement. We know of many thoughtful English and history teachers who, in an attempt to save time on frequently made comments, have devised a coding system for the marks they place on students' essays. Students get a copy of the key, and upon receiving their graded work (we hope), spend some time deciphering the code. (See Figure 7.4 for examples.) A student might see N/PN in his paper and could go to the key to figure out that N/PN stands for noun-pronoun disagreement error. But, what happens when students still don't understand why the error is wrong, or how to fix it? Imagine instead an interactive key built right into their essays.

Noun-Pronoun Disagreement	Oops! Your noun and pronoun don't match in this sentence. Remember that nouns (the subject) and pronouns (the little words referring to the subject) need to match up by number, gender, and case. So, if your sentence is making a claim about "a person," the correct pronoun would NOT be *their*, but rather, *his* or *her*. This is a tricky concept because we don't have a plural gender-neutral pronoun in the English language. If you feel like you could use more review, check out this brief tutorial: (This is where I would paste in a link to Kevin Brookhouser's Writing Felonies video for students to watch. You can find this link and others in the Chapter Resources section of our website, pluginpowerup.com.)
Revisit Conclusion	I'd like you to take a second pass at your conclusion paragraph. Remember that the goal of the conclusion is to powerfully synthesize important ideas in the paper and extend them to the broader implications of your argument. If the introduction was the funnel, the conclusion is the reverse-funnel. I have put together a brief, six-minute tutorial for you to review that goes along with the conclusion overview handout you have in your writing handbook, pages 27–28. Here's the link: (This is where I would paste in a link to my writing tutorial video on conclusions.)
Evidence Quality?	I'm wondering about the quality of your evidence here. Remember, GOOD quotations offer opportunities to analyze specific words, phrases, literary devices, character development, thematic development, important changes, and/or conflict, in order to support argument. They also can be broken down into small (one- to four-word) chunks that you can explain, explore, and connect back to your topic sentence. BAD quotations tend to have one or more of the following flaws: they restate your thesis or topic sentence, are simply plot summary, and/or lack opportunities for analysis (nothing deeper than surface level to explain, explore, or connect back to the topic sentence). If you feel as if you are repeating yourself over and over, or are just restating the quote, you might start by reevaluating your evidence. If you need a refresher on selecting high-quality evidence, check out this quick video tutorial: (this is where I would paste in a link to my writing tutorial video on evidence).

Figure 7.4 Frequent Comments

Because our students submit their work electronically and we provide feedback directly on their documents, we can make the coding system work both for the students and for ourselves. We each have a bank of frequently used comments that we drop into student assignments as we go. Jen uses a Google spreadsheet from which she copies and pastes her feedback directly into the students' Google Docs. Diana uses GradeMark, a paid service through Turnitin.com. (Many teachers at schools that already pay for Turnitin.com as a plagiarism checker have access to GradeMark. It's worth checking with your tech department.) Because our comments are saved, we don't worry about how long it takes to write a few sentences explaining the error and providing a path to improvement.

It's safe to say that we would *never, ever* have written that much in a margin note on a draft of an essay. But when our frequent feedback is saved and ready to reuse, it feels sensible to invest some time up front to write out complete explanations and provide links for further instruction. See Figure 7.5 for tools to use for frequent feedback.

TOOLS FOR FREQUENT FEEDBACK	
GradeMark	What we love most about GradeMark is the ease with which it lets us drag and drop feedback and instruction into students' written work. Once you set up your bank of "custom comments," you can quickly add them to student work by clicking *one button*. It is crazy-fast: highlight the sentence you want to comment on, and voila, feedback and instruction is embedded. GradeMark is a paid service and, depending on your LMS, may mean students have to turn in their work twice—once to your LMS and then to GradeMark.
Google Docs	Adding comments to student work, whether in a document, spreadsheet, or slide deck, is a cinch (Insert/Comment). It's just as easy to save a master document in your own Google Drive to refer to and build on. And of course, it's free. The biggest downside is that you have to click back and forth between the student's document and your master comment document.
Kaizena	Kaizena is known for letting you leave voice feedback on student writing, and we love it for that. We can often say more than we can type, but you can also create tags for comments you make often and link to resources students could use for additional information. This is an even easier workflow than copying and pasting from a Google spreadsheet. See kaizena.com.

Figure 7.5 Top Tools for Frequent Feedback and What They Do Best

Audio Feedback

Our students are most responsive to feedback when our comments are personalized and the tone is clear and kind. Sometimes, despite our best intentions, written comments lack that conversational feeling and serve only to distance the teacher from the student. We have found that when we give students verbal feedback, whether in a one-on-one conference or as an audio memo in a document, students listen.

We remember reading an example from Carol Jago's *Papers, Papers, Papers* (2005), in which she asked her students to submit their essays with a blank tape cassette so she could record an audio narrative of their writing; she read their work aloud, providing feedback along the way. We love this idea, but we really love that we no longer need to collect 150 blank cassette tapes. When Diana's students finished with the final drafts of their *Scarlet Letter* essays, she opted to try Jago's narrative audio feedback model instead of her usual methods. She recorded her feedback think-alouds using the built-in recording software on her computer (QuickTime) and uploaded the audio files to SoundCloud. She then e-mailed students the private link to their feedback, with a set of directions. Figure 7.6 shows the e-mail she sent to her student Ben.

Dear Ben: I have finished reading and commenting on your *Scarlet Letter* paper. Here's how this is going to work . . .

1. I have recorded an audio think-aloud of your paper in which I provide you with my feedback while reading your paper out loud to you. Here's the link for your feedback: (this is where I would paste in a link to his SoundCloud file).

2. Your job is to sit down and listen to the feedback **while following along on your own copy of the paper**. It's super-important that you take notes and jot down my comments as you listen (you can do this either on a paper copy or as Insert --> Comment in Google Drive). Most recordings are around fifteen minutes long, so make sure you set aside ample time.

3. Then, I want you to assess yourself using the rubric that is attached to this e-mail. Check the boxes you think best describe your paper.

4. Once you've done all those things listed above, come in and see me during office hours or lunch. We will determine your paper grade together and talk about options for revision if you are interested. I have purposely not assigned a letter grade to your paper. I want you to focus on the feedback, not the score. Tricky, right?

You have **one week** from the date of this e-mail to come and meet with me. Looking forward to our conversation!

Mrs. Neebe

Figure 7.6 Student Audio Narrative E-mail

The very next day, Ben showed up at the start of office hours, marked-up paper cued up on his iPad, ready to talk.

"That was really cool, Mrs. Neebe!" he started.

"What about it was cool?" she prodded.

"It felt like we were having a conversation . . . and you gave me a *ton* more feedback."

"You know, Ben, what's funny is that it took me about the same amount of time as when I normally grade your papers. It's just that you were the one writing, not me."

"I actually liked that part of it. I had to really pay attention."

"You mean you weren't paying attention before?" she asked with a grin.

"Well, sometimes I'd skim your notes, or I wouldn't really understand them but I wouldn't ask about them."

"Why not?"

"I didn't have to."

Ben's final response summed up all of Diana's worst fears about the hours she had spent dutifully writing margin notes in the past. This writing conference felt different. Ben had ownership. They talked and compared notes for five or ten minutes, moving systematically, category by category, through the rubric. As the conversation came to a close, Diana asked Ben to give himself the grade. To Diana's delight, Ben (and almost every single other student in her classes) gave himself the same grade that Diana had in the back of her mind. But instead of focusing on the score and ignoring the feedback, he had to focus on the feedback to help determine an appropriate score (see Figures 7.7a and 7.7b).

Whereas Diana tends to use audio feedback for lengthier assignments, Jen uses it more frequently for quick comments and ideas. She adds her memos right into students' Google Docs, using an add-on called Kaizena. Instead of inserting a written comment in a document, you highlight the text and click Record. There are added benefits to using audio comments, beyond the student experience. First, recording feedback often takes less time than writing personalized feedback, because most of us speak faster than we can write or type. Second, recording feedback has the effect of a conversation without requiring us to find time to meet with every student. Because it's asynchronous, it is more flexible and more manageable. (See Figure 7.8 for a list of recommended audio tools.)

Reflecting on Feedback

For feedback to transfer to future work, students need regular opportunities to reflect. Marzano (2006) suggests that "one of the most powerful and straightforward ways a teacher can provide feedback that encourages learning is to have students keep track of their own progress" and to "reflect on their learning" (89). Reflection can take many forms, including writing about areas of strength and areas for growth, considering the most useful piece of feedback for a revision, tracing patterns in errors and successes, and reviewing previous feedback before starting a new assignment. Fortunately, with technology in the hands of our students, we have a myriad of tools for empowering them to take charge of their feedback and apply it to future learning.

Evidence	High-quality, relevant examples that build on each other, and contain important literary devices. Examples *show* rather than *tell*.	Relevant examples that support each part of ts, but may be too "surface level." May be a repetition of quotes discussed in class.	Redundant examples that *tell* rather than *show* the argument. Examples may be too long, or include too much plot.	Examples unclear, irrelevant, or missing.
Analysis	Demonstrates the writer's ability to read and interpret a text deeply and perceptively, and write with a high degree of clarity and sophistication. Insightful!	Enough discussion of evidence to support reasonable assertions. However, may not demonstrate a full awareness or understanding of topic.	Superficial. Tends to scratch the surface by being too general or simplistic. Analysis may be redundant or simply repeat the argument in new words, or read like a "laundry list" of ideas.	Summarizes the text without actually conveying its message. Observations may be presented without textual support.
Conclusion	Fluidly and clearly revisits main points, and smoothly leads reader to the broader implications of the paper by provoking thought about larger issues. Kicker brings paper "full circle."	Conclusion revisits main points, but may re-use language from earlier in the paper. Clearly leads reader to the broader implications of the paper, but kicker seems forced or trite.	Conclusion is stale and generic. Author revisits main points, but does not does not extend to the broader implications. Most pieces are present, but nothing is fresh.	Format of the conclusion is not followed or is missing entirely.
Sentence Fluency & Grace of Writing	Exhibits a clear voice through varied syntax and accurate diction while avoiding prevarication ("bs") and verbosity (wordiness). Well-focused, articulate, & consistently coherent.	Most sentences sound natural. Writer chooses words accurately, and transitions smoothly between ideas. May attempt sentence variety.	When read aloud, many sentences are awkward or are difficult to understand. Writer attempts to include transitions, but they are too forced. Contains some inaccurate diction.	Many sentences are fragmented or run on. Transitions between ideas are missing. Simplistic or inaccurate word choice.
Grammar, Writing, & Conventions*	Practically flawless!	A few errors that are minor enough that they do not distract the reader.	Several errors that distract the reader but do not detract from the argument	Contains multiple flaws that seriously confuse the reader.

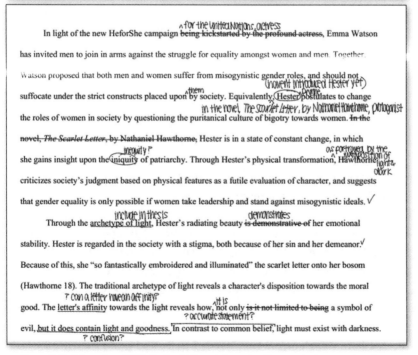

Figure 7.7a (above) and 7.7b (below) The rubric and self-corrected essay show how audio feedback can help teachers address students' diverse learning needs.

TOOLS FOR AUDIO FEEDBACK	
Kaizena	Kaizena is an add-on for Google Drive. With Kaizena, you highlight sections of text and then record your comments about that section. Students must also have the Kaizena add-on to be able to hear your feedback. Kaizena's motto is "Give Great Feedback," and they offer many resources to help you do that.
QuickTime	QuickTime Player is built into every Mac and allows for easy audio recording in addition to its screencasting function. Small audio files can be attached to e-mail or posted in your LMS.
SoundCloud	SoundCloud is the YouTube of audio. It is a website that hosts sound files and makes linking to these files, or embedding them in an LMS or class blog, very easy. It also has an audio-recording option in addition to just uploading, which means you can work directly through SoundCloud instead of recording elsewhere and uploading.
LMS	Some learning management systems build support for audio feedback into your teacher tools. Schoology, for example, has a button at the bottom of every announcement and assignment for teachers (and students) to record voice instructions or feedback. The audio button is also available for quizzes and tests, which is especially wonderful for language teachers.

Figure 7.8 Top Tools for Audio Feedback and What They Do Best

By the second semester in John Grey's chemistry class, students have accumulated data from their feedback on twelve lab reports. At the beginning of the year, Grey posted a list of questions for students to copy into a Google Form in their own Google Drives. The form consisted of six questions—one for each section of the lab report, and one final reflection prompt. The first five were multiple-choice questions, asking for the student's rubric score for that section of the report: introduction and purpose, hypothesis, procedures and materials, data, and discussion. The reflection was a fill-in question, asking students to summarize the feedback they had received in their own words, starting with the phrase "Next time, I need to . . ." Grey pushed his students to add their own ideas to the fill-in reflection, asking them to include both the elements they needed to fix and those they needed to repeat because they had been successful.

Before assigning each new lab report, Grey asked students to pull up the spreadsheet that contained their reflective feedback data. "Let's start with the summary of results. How have you been scoring in each section, and where do you need to focus your effort for this report?" Students looked at pie charts that synthesized the data and graphically represented their highest and lowest scoring sections. Then he asked them to reread their written notes. At the top of the new lab report, students wrote a learning objective for themselves, which ranged from "I need to double-check my data tables!" to "Go in and meet with Mr. Grey at lunch to talk through my hypothesis."

Grey's students could have easily done this type of reflection in an ongoing Google Doc, but by using a Google Form instead, they were able to see the data visually instead of through text alone. (See Figure 7.9 for more information about using feedback tools.)

TOOLS FOR REFLECTING ON FEEDBACK	
Google Form	As we mentioned earlier in the chapter, Google Forms collect data in many different formats: multiple choice, select from a list, text fill-in, graph, and scale, to name a few. If students regularly enter their own reflective data on a form, they can track their growth over time.
Google Voice	Teachers can set up a free Google Voice number to have students leave voice-mail messages. Jen encourages her students to leave a message about their revision plans. They like the opportunity to process their ideas aloud, and Jen likes the process because it requires students to read their own work before they submit a final draft.

Figure 7.9 Top Tools for Reflecting on Feedback and What They Do Best

With a 1:1 classroom and the digital tools available to us today, we can offer our students personalized and prompt feedback in a variety of ways. By layering these strategies together—combining peer response with whole-class feedback and teacher audio feedback—we surround our students in a feedback cocoon in which they can grow their wings. When we can see student work in process through Google Drive and assess understanding on the spot with classroom feedback tools such as Socrative, we are armed with the information we need to make sound pedagogical decisions. We are no longer guessing about the lessons our students need.

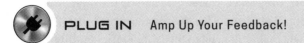

PLUG IN Amp Up Your Feedback!

1. **Try out one of the feedback tools** from this chapter with three or four students. Based on that experiment, try it again with the whole class.

2. **Experiment with an instant feedback tool.** For your first try, consider using the tool as an "exit slip" so you can review the student data at your leisure and work through any tech challenges you may encounter.

3. **Ask students to reflect on feedback** you have given them or feedback from their peers in a survey or form.

Assessing Unconventional Assignments

Think back to Chapter 1 in which we first presented the TECH model for teaching and learning with 1:1 technology. Consider for a moment the section about "handoff" to students, where they own the learning and the product is ready for the real world. Our assessment of that work also has to shift when student products become less traditional. We love that teaching in a 1:1 environment presents opportunities to give more unconventional assignments (see Chapter 8, "Creativity and Innovation," for ideas). Our students thrive when we ask them to publish their work in an authentic form for an authentic audience. But when the audience changes from teacher to some other entity, and the format moves from a standard essay or test to a creative project, assessing becomes incrementally harder. The set standards we have used time and time again may no longer seem appropriate, and it is really easy to get swept away by the glitz and glamour of digitally enhanced student work.

Diana recalls the first time she collected documentary films as an assessment instead of a traditional research paper. When she sat down to grade the finished products, nearly everyone got an A because she was so darned impressed with what students could *do* on such a tiny machine. She wanted to grade the films based on what she thought was reasonable for someone like herself to produce. But the students were trying to create something that looked professional enough to share with the audience at the school's film festival, an audience who would pick up on (and care about) technical components such as asynchrony between audio and video or scrolling text that scrolls too fast. Diana was too busy wondering how they had made the text move to notice that she couldn't actually read what it said.

What she had overlooked is that when students engage an authentic audience in their work, their work should look authentically like what we see in the real world. We have both moved to a model where we now co-create and co-assess student work, using professional examples to craft the rubric. If the objective is for students to write for a specific readership, then we need to grade them based on what those readers have come to expect. If the final product simply *exhibits effort* (one of our former rubric categories), it does not meet the higher standard that the professional world demands. It must exude purpose, awareness of audience, and command of content.

When it comes to unconventional assignments, we tend to assess each student in two ways: The first focuses on *process*, with a rubric tailored to assessing the individual action steps students were supposed to take along the way, such as meeting interim deadlines, bringing in research, completing storyboards, and actively participating in group brainstorming. The second emphasizes *product*, which is a score we holistically determine together—teacher and student—for the finished product. For this latter score, we meet with each student or team of students (depending on the nature of the project) and discuss the successes and shortcomings of their work in relation to the co-created rubric, based on real-world models. When co-assessing with students isn't possible, or the assignment is small enough that it isn't necessary, we still divide student grades into process and product to reinforce that how they got to the goal is just as important as having reached the goal itself.

Although we consider a range of criteria when assessing any piece of student work, we must factor in a few additional considerations when we fold technology into the mix. We always ask ourselves these questions:

- What is the learning curve like for the software and/or hardware students are using for this project?
- What should students reasonably be able to teach themselves about this technological tool or technique over the course of the project?
- How many other times have students done this type of project? (If it's the fifth time students have used screencasting software in our class, our expectations will be higher than they were the first time.)

Since moving to a 1:1 model, our students have created videos, podcasts, websites, blogs, digital portfolios, and a variety of multimedia presentations. Over time and in the process of figuring out how to assess these projects, we have come to learn that although the finished results look and feel quite different from one another, they share a number of common traits. For each of the finished products, we care about content mastery, presentation, and deliberate use of tools. To address this overlap, and save ourselves time reinventing rubrics for every project, we created a common rubric. Then, for each individual project, we add a row or two that speaks to the unique elements for that form of media. The master rubric is shown in Figure 7.10. You may notice that the rubric doesn't look like a traditional grid with all the boxes filled in with text. We have moved to using a single-column rubric for our creative projects (Fluckiger 2010). Our students like that the expectations for excellence are clearly laid out, and we like that our feedback tool doesn't send them into cognitive overload as they try to tease out what they did well and where they need to improve. The columns on either side of the "expectations" column are blank so that we can write in individualized feedback for each student or group.

Exceeds Expectations	Expectations	Needs Work
	Content Mastery: Illustrates a sophisticated, comprehensive understanding of the topic; demonstrates student's ability to think deeply and perceptively about complex issues.	
	Presentation: Professionally presents a cohesive and thoughtful final product. Creatively edits work, and makes purposeful artistic choices, demonstrating an awareness of the target audience and how to engage that audience.	
	Use of Tools: Product demonstrates that student evaluated and deliberately selected digital tools based on the appropriateness to the task. Online content is used legally and responsibly.	

Figure 7.10 Common Rubric for Uncommon Work

For each of the project types that follow—video, podcast, websites and blogs, digital portfolios, and multimedia presentations—we have included the project-specific rubric categories that supplement the master rubric. We have also included the *process* steps that fold into our consideration of the student's *process* grade. You know your content objectives; we made those intentionally broad and recommend adapting and clarifying that section to meet your needs for each project.

Assessing Video

Diana and her history partner, David Smock, were in the middle of teaching an interdisciplinary lesson on slave narratives as students read *Narrative of the Life of Frederick Douglass* in their English class. Interested in engaging students in cross-curricular thinking about abolition, the power of language, and oral histories, Diana and David designed a mini-documentary assignment that students would have three class days to produce. Before launching the assignment, the class watched the HBO documentary *Unchained Memories: Readings from the Slave Narratives*, in which contemporary African-American actors dramatize the interviews and stories of former slaves that were recorded by the Federal Writers' Project of the Works Progress Administration in the 1930s. Drawing on this real-world example as a model, the class brainstormed a list of the characteristics describing a professional documentary film. The students determined that documentaries

- include expert opinions. Students would address this objective by bringing in direct quotations from the articles, speeches, and interviews in their history reader.
- showcase poignant images. This characteristic provided the opportunity for students to include pieces from the primary source documents they researched in history class.
- select and reenact powerful scenes. As the bulk of the assignment, students were charged with choosing what they believed were the most critical scenes in Douglass's *Narrative,* and re-creating those scenes in a tasteful, historically accurate way. Many groups elected to film without sound and to add a voice-over of narration from the text. Because this was the second film assignment of the year, Diana and David did a brief review of film angles and shots to help the students make deliberate choices about their videos.

Over the course of the next three classes, Diana and David's students met in small groups, addressing the central ideas in Douglass's narrative: treatment of slaves by their owners, education and intellectual awakening, the effect of slavery on the slaveholder, forms of rebellion, and escaping the dehumanizing effects of slavery. They worked on the following *process* steps leading up to the final production:

- Determine one or two key scenes that illustrate your group's angle. Trim those scenes in a shared Google Doc if they are quite long.
- Gather at least three possible excerpts for the expert interview, and three possible primary source images that your group could use as supplementary materials.
- Draft the storyboard of the mini-documentary, focusing on the order of your film and how you plan to sequence the scene dramatizations, interviews, and images.

- Write your script and film your scenes.
- Edit, upload to YouTube, and submit the link to the LMS.

Figure 7.11 shows the two additional rows we add to the master rubric for video assignments.

Exceeds Expectations	Expectations	Needs Work
	Images and Video are thoughtfully selected to support the overall message of the project. Images and video are used legally and responsibly. Student-created video demonstrates an awareness and deliberate use of camera angles, shots, set, and transitions between scenes.	
	Audio is clear and at a consistent level. Sound effects, words, and music are used to support the overall message of the project. All audio material, including songs, is used legally and responsibly.	

Figure 7.11 Video-Specific Rubric Categories

Assessing Podcasts

Diana's tenth graders were nearing the final project of the year: a podcast speaking to one of the course's essential questions. As the bell rang to start class, Diana began with the instructions for the assignment:

The US literature course you are about to complete is ripped from the headlines of the newspaper. A few years back, I spent a summer combing through the news to find the major topics that emerged. I looked for the social issues that have sparked debate on the national stage and devised a way to bring that dialogue into the classroom and frame a discussion within the context of great literature. News anchors—whether online, on television, on the radio, or in print—are talking about the economy, income differences, poverty, gender equality, racism, immigration, gay rights, conflict abroad, privacy, individual liberty, and the ideal of the American dream. In our major units of study this year, we considered essential questions targeted at understanding those issues.

To demonstrate your ability to practice radical listening and deliberate, thoughtful speaking, you will create a feature story podcast that explores one of the core questions of our course by interviewing people who experience that issue or are experts in that field. Your podcast must frame the course question in a current conversation about something that matters to you in American life. This might be a social or political issue, current event, statistic—something that makes you think, wonder, and want to know more.

Drawing on the feature stories produced by NPR as a real-world guideline, Diana required her students to include the following:

- An introduction to their topic and question
- An angle that was clearly established and defined for the audience
- An interview of one person who experienced the issue under discussion or was an expert in that field (or interviews of two people to provide a counterpoint or alternate perspective)
- A connection to something significant they had learned in English that year, weaving in a direct quotation, and properly citing and integrating it into their speaking
- A final sign-off that touched back on the opening statement, concluded the story, restated their name, and thanked the listener.

Before submitting the final draft, students worked through check-in steps that were folded into their *process* grade:

- Decide on essential question, core issue, angle, and interviewee. Submit these to the Google Form on the LMS.
- Draft ten interview questions. Make sure these questions are open ended and will invite the interviewee into conversation and personal storytelling.
- Complete the interview and bring in raw footage to class for an editing day.
- Write the narrative script that you will record to supplement the interview.
- Record narrative and make final edits to the podcast.
- Upload the final podcast to SoundCloud, and submit the link to the LMS.

In Figure 7.12, we show the two additional rows we added to the master rubric for podcast assignments. (Thanks to journalism teacher Michelle Balmeo for sharing her expertise in crafting this project and rubric.)

Exceeds Expectations	Expectations	Needs Work
	Style: Podcast is presented in a journalistic style, smoothly weaving together expert interviews with narrative explanation. Narrator avoids "telling" instead of "showing" by drawing upon sensory detail to bring the story to life.	
	Audio: Sound is clear and at a consistent level. Sound effects, words, and music are used to support the overall message of the podcast and contextualize the final production with a sense of place and voice. All audio material is used legally and responsibly.	

Figure 7.12 Podcast-Specific Rubric Categories

Assessing Websites and Blogs

Middle school science teacher Eric Cross uses websites to have students document and explain their learning in a selected area of investigation. His students post pictures from their experiments, reflections on their learning, and videos they make to explain science concepts. As Cross says, "Essentially what I want is to teach my students how to have a digital presence with a purpose." He and his students looked at other science websites, and though they lacked the resources of an on-site programmer to make the really fancy things happen, they decided they wanted their sites to include the key elements listed on the following page. (See the rubric in Figure 7.13 for more details.)

- A description of their research project, including a hypothesis and a plan for investigation
- Links to related projects, sites, and information: a digital version of a literature review
- A blog about their research process, data collection, and reflections on class activities
- Photos related to their subject, with captions

The *process* blends the elements of a typical science project with the elements of website development.

- Select a website platform suitable to the needs of the project. Google Sites and Weebly were some of their top choices.
- Identify the subject and research questions of the project. Cross had his students do this in blog posts on their sites, so that he and other students could comment on the questions students were posing. He noted that "helping students understand which questions were too broad and which were too narrow was a big part of this process."
- Find out what research had already been done on the subject and add a section to the site for links to research, creating an annotated and linked bibliography.
- Continue adding blog entries on a regular basis as the project progresses.
- Add pages for summarized data, including charts and graphs if appropriate to the project.
- Add a page for findings and conclusions when the project is complete.

The concept is authentic to what scientists have to do to compete for grants and publish their findings. At the high school level, students who compete in the Google Science Fair and other national science competitions have to produce websites like this as part of their application process. Having early access to this experience in middle school gives Cross's students an edge. It also gives him an online window into their learning.

Exceeds Expectations	Expectations	Needs Work
	Subject Matter of the blog/site is relevant, current, correctly cited, and used legally and responsibly. The content includes text and images that engage the reader and add value through the information provided.	
	Design/Layout/Navigation The elements of the blog/site are thoughtfully arranged so the information is clear, easy to find, and easy to navigate. Crucial information is never more than two clicks from the landing page.	

Figure 7.13 Website and Blog-Specific Rubric Categories

Assessing Digital Portfolios

We read a lot about teenagers (and adults) needing to be careful about their "digital foot-print." Our friend Adina Sullivan says it is more like a digital tattoo because it is hard to re-move. We think of it as a digital foundation. The work our students put online will represent them now, and we want them to be able to build on it in the future. A digital portfolio (DP) is an organized online space where a student posts his or her best work. A DP can be built from a variety of tools, but most are based off a website or a blog. Our go-to platforms are Google Sites, Weebly, Wix, WordPress, and Blogger.

At Jen's school, students in the digital photography course post their assignments to a blog. Each student has his or her own blog, and each assignment is accompanied by a reflec-tion and the image the student created for the assignment. Over time the blog becomes a digital portfolio of the student's photographic work. For a class where all of the work is cre-ated in a digital format, online collection makes sense, but it also mimics the expectations of professional photographers who host examples of their work on sites such as 500Px.com or build their own sites to display and sell their work. All professionals, especially those in "creative" fields, are expected to have an online presence, résumé, or portfolio of their work.

Asking our students to create digital portfolios helps them showcase their creativity and prepares them for the technical demands of their potential future careers.

Diana asks her students to create a digital portfolio as an-end-of-course exercise. Her objective is to have students build a site that they can add to over time, with space for their learning and thinking in the humanities, STEM, fine arts, and service learning. After looking at digital portfolios from other schools and a few professional portfolios, Diana and her students determined that a digital portfolio should include the following elements:

- A range of exemplary work samples that highlight student interest and engagement in learning
- A reflection about each of those pieces, including a description of the assignment, any difficulties the student encountered with the assignment, and lessons learned from doing the work
- An "About the Author" section. The balance here is to help students provide a description of their interests, strengths, and goals without providing specific identifying information.

Figure 7.14 details the way in which these categories translate into a rubric for grading the final product. The process of creating digital portfolios includes these items:

- Identifying which work samples to include and, if necessary, converting them to a digital format
- Selecting a platform for the portfolio from an available range of blogging and website hosting options
- Creating the skeleton of the site structure, and/or using a template provided
- Adding the work examples and reflections
- Adding images and other design elements to make the site aesthetically pleasing
- Testing site navigation. (Do all the links work the way they should?)
- Checking site organization. (Is all the work in the right place?)

Exceeds Expectations	Expectations	Needs Work
	Exemplary Work Samples: This digital portfolio includes a variety of exemplary work samples as well as descriptions of those assignments and a reflection on what was learned from the project.	
	Site Design and Navigation: The site is organized in a logical way that makes it easy to navigate. Links have specific and helpful names and go to the content expected.	

Figure 7.14 Digital Portfolio Rubric Categories

Assessing Multimedia Presentations

It was three hours before senior exhibitions were about to begin when Albert arrived in Jen's room and asked her to help him practice for his presentation. He had been a student in her class several years before, as a freshman. He pulled up his slides and began to read through his bullet points . . . his many, many bullet points. He summarized how he had been born on the East Coast and then moved to California. He covered the sports he had played in school and the importance of his friendships and then talked about where he was going for college, all with bullet points. Jen stopped him. She printed out his slides, handed them to him, and said, "These are your notes." Then she made him delete all of his bullets and fill every slide with images that matched his story. Although it meant pulling pictures off his phone, his Facebook page, and even the website of the college he was planning to attend, he redid all of his slides in less than an hour. At the end of the afternoon, he was back. "That was so much better," Albert said. "Thank you so much for making me change my slides."

We've all experienced death by PowerPoint. (They are called bullet points for a reason, right?) Let's do our part as educators and teach the world about effective presentation design. Few of our students are going to match the polish or hours of practice that professional speakers achieve, but they can still understand the basics of choosing thoughtful images and not filling their slides with text. Before students present, we like to watch TED Talks given by children and teenagers. From that we determined with our students that an effective talk should have these characteristics:

- A clear message, though it's not always obvious in the beginning
- A story arc told in an interesting narrative style
- A clear voice, appropriate pace, and strategic pauses
- Simple, uncluttered, thoughtful slides that use an anchoring image or word to ground the story. When text is present, it is usually just a word or two, for emphasis.

Figure 7.15 illustrates these *product* elements in rubric form. When developing presentation projects with our students we generally use these *process* steps:

- Concept Development. Often, we ask our students to set up a new Google Slide deck and use the first slide to type notes, brainstorm, and consider the narrative story that will bind the presentation together.
- Storyboard. On the subsequent slides, students break their stories into small, manageable chunks. Just like the thumbnails in traditional storyboards, the individual slides provide an isolated space for students to deal with just one idea at a time.
- Script Writing. In the presenter notes section below each slide, students write their scripts. For timed presentations, such as those delivering PechaKucha and Ignite Talks, we remind students that most people speak an average of 150 words per minute and that (with pauses) a twenty-second slide should have about forty-five words. These are helpful parameters.
- Image Collection and Editing. Once students know the language they will use in presenting and have a solid grasp of their story arc, they look for images. We encourage them to always start by taking or creating their own images, and to look to the web to fill in whatever they can't create. If they do go to the web, we require students to use Creative Commons licensed images, or images in the public domain, and to cite each image appropriately (see Appendix A for more about Creative Commons and citations).
- Practice, Practice, Practice. The slides are ready, and the script is finished. Now it's time to practice. This is a crucial step to help our students avoid standing up in front of the class and reading their scripts verbatim. We like to build practice time into class and give students a partner to practice with. Feedback *before* the presentation is always better than feedback after.

Exceeds Expectations	Expectations	Needs Work
	Images are thoughtfully selected to support the overall message of the project. Image quality is excellent. Slides are simple, clear, and contain an anchoring image to ground the story. Presenter keeps words on the slides to a minimum, and effectively uses font and text for emphasis.	
	Delivery: The speaker's pace is natural and is varied for effect. Words are said clearly. Voice is animated and lively. Deliberate gestures are included for emphasis. Speaker makes consistent eye contact with the audience, and rarely glances at notes for prompting.	

Figure 7.15 Multimedia Presentation-Specific Rubric Categories

We have entered a brave new world of multimedia production. The digital tools and the audience they give us access to can motivate students to dive deeply into content material and create professional representations of their learning. First and foremost, we must still assess the understandings, critical-thinking skills, and content mastery critical to our subject areas. A slick presentation without synthesis of content information should not score well in our courses. As the initial novelty of technological production wears off and students become more comfortable with the tools, their focus—and ours—returns again and again to learning. Our assessment criteria has been augmented by new forms of communication, but teaching our students to master content, present it well, and choose the tools appropriate to their intention are the core values to which we must always return.

POWER UP!   Real-World Assessment

1. **Start by tuning in to real-world examples** that surround you every day. Listening to a feature story on NPR while you drive to work? Think about what you've come to expect in such broadcasts. What are the qualities and characteristics that make it a professional radio podcast? Watching an online tutorial that is really effective? Ask yourself what makes it effective. Start making mental notes to add to your future rubrics.

2. When you are ready to jump into creative assessments, **enlist the help of your students**. It's always easiest to start with the end in mind. Before you launch the assignment, get your students on board with helping to design the rubric by which they will be assessed.

Part III

TRANSFORM

Trans•form (v): *To make a thorough or dramatic change in character, condition, or form.*

How can technology ignite a creative disturbance in our teaching routines so that students are free to own the learning?

CHAPTER 8

Creativity and Innovation

Cre·a·tiv·i·ty (n): *The process of developing original ideas that have value.*

—Sir Ken Robinson

NaNoWriMo Interview
Jen and Calvin

NaNoWriMo stands for National Novel Writing Month. It started small in 1999 and has been growing every year since. Nearly every ninth grader at my school has participated in NaNoWriMo since 2011. Though we do surveys about the way students react to the experience, I wanted to know more, so in 2014 I conducted some interviews with my students about the process. Calvin's answers were very helpful.

Jen: Calvin, we just finished NaNoWriMo. Can you tell me in your own words what that was?

Calvin: NaNoWriMo is basically a month to express yourself in words. You have a month to write a given amount of words about a story that you want to create, so you are creating something that's your own. [Students set their own word count goals for NaNoWriMo. That's what Calvin means by "a given amount of words."]

Jen: So, what did you create? What's your novel about?

Calvin: My novel is about an East Coast rapper who is frustrated because the rap industry is taken over by the West Coast. They're pretty close to having, like, a war about it. When my character, Casey, goes to L.A., he goes with his three main recording artist friends. They fund-raise and sell their albums, and they try to start a movement. They run into a bit of trouble when somebody gets shot at a sporting event.

Jen:	That's intense. How did you get the idea for that story line?
Calvin:	Ever since NaNoWriMo started, I've been wanting to write a book. Well, I wanted to write a book before, but I didn't know what to do with that. So then I thought about what I liked and it was music and football, but I decided to write about music. Also, I read this other book about a rapper and I thought I could write like that, too, but make it the way I wanted it.
Jen:	NaNoWriMo is short—only thirty days. How did having such a short time affect you as a writer or as a creative person?
Calvin:	Okay, I swear I'm not just telling you what you want to hear, but I was thinking about this last night. NaNoWriMo made me have to think of ideas really fast, and I think I got better at that. I also relaxed about making my story perfect, so if I thought of something crazy, I just put it in there, and those are some of my favorite parts now. I didn't worry about the month time because I was just thinking about writing enough words every day.
Jen:	Would you do NaNoWriMo again?
Calvin:	Well, I think I'd like to write another novel, maybe a sequel. But I'd want more time—like, maybe two months. I might not do it on my own, but if it was a school thing again and everybody was doing it, then, yeah, that'd be fun.

I was surprised by how many students said they had been thinking of writing a book or had made previous attempts to start a novel. All of the students I interviewed cited their own interests and other books as inspiration for their writing. Often they said that their novel was a mix of ideas from several other books that they had combined and changed to suit their preferences. Tanya was writing about vampires, but she didn't want to deal with blood, so her vampires ate only red food. Wyatt had created a steampunk apocalyptic version of history after World War I, in which humanity's only refuge was a giant airship floating over the desert wasteland of France and Spain. Every year I find that there are fantastic other worlds, desperate story lines, and charming rapscallions floating around in the heads of my students. NaNoWriMo is their chance to learn the skills that could help them bring their ideas into reality.

From Imagination to Creativity

Imagination and creativity are not fixed traits. We can develop and encourage them within our students and ourselves. Imagination, as defined by Sir Ken Robinson (2011), is "the process of bringing to mind things that are not present to our senses"(2). Imagination, by its nature, is a private endeavor. It lets us envision and explore the worlds we read about in books. It invites us to consider a myriad of perspectives and investigate challenges from new angles. It conjures images and scents and sounds when we ask ourselves, *What if . . . ?*

Creativity is the process of bringing those imaginings to reality; it requires a degree of artistic or technical skill. Often we can create what we imagine within the range of abilities we already have, but sometimes we have to learn something new to be able to create what we see in our imaginative vision.

Think of a fabulous meal, one full of dishes you've never actually cooked before. You could probably make that meal, given the recipes, because you probably already have general cooking skills. Now imagine a beautiful landscape painting. Could you paint that? You could try, but chances are, you lack the training of a classical painter. Your landscape would likely not live up to the image in your mind, but if you made the attempt to paint, you would learn a lot about painting in the process. Your next painting would be better. This is where practice and skill come in. In our classrooms we give students room to imagine, time to create, and support to help them match their creations to their imaginations.

Creativity is also an iterative process. A couple of years back, Diana set out to publish a free, interactive iBook of *The Scarlet Letter* to help scaffold her students' reading of the most challenging text in her US literature curriculum. When she pitched the plan to her students, they started coming up with ideas to help— including a fully searchable text to help with vocabulary, prereading questions to give readers a sense of what to look for, and video footnotes explaining allusions. At the end of the period, one of Diana's most artistic students came up to chat. Ally offered to create a set of illustrations

Figure 8.1 Ally drew a portrait of Pearl in *The Scarlet Letter.*

to help bring the text to life, and during the next few weeks, she met with Diana several times to plan the passages she thought needed the most visual support for novice readers of the novel (see Figure 8.1 for an example). During the summer, Ally sent her digital renderings of the passages, which are now featured in the iBook.

Fast-forward two years. Diana's current sophomores were reading *The Scarlet Letter* and discussing Hester's transformation after the community excludes and isolates her. Later that afternoon, Diana received an e-mail from another artsy student, Ciara, with a one-word subject line: "Picture." Attached to the e-mail was a spectacular sketch of Hester and Pearl, years after their initial banishment to the outskirts of town (see Figure 8.2). In class the following day, Diana pulled Ciara aside and whispered, "I got your e-mail. The picture is beautiful. What made you draw it?"

Figure 8.2 Ciara's depiction of Hester and Pearl, years after their banishment in the story, reveals the different ways in which students can respond to text when we tap into their creativity.

"You didn't have an image for this chapter. I thought the book needed one. So I drew it."

Ciara's response underscores two key principles of creativity as an iterative process. First, when we create in a digital format, such as the iBook, the product rarely feels "finished" or static. Ciara knew that Diana could add her image and republish an updated version of the book. Digital creation draws more people into the creative process. Second, when we open the door to creativity, we invite collaboration. Diana's interest in publishing the iBook led to Ally's art, which led to Ciara's. Creativity inspires more creativity.

Can Creativity Be Taught?

Where do imagination and creativity come from? Why does the process of growing up seem to sap the creativity from our students? Can imagination and creativity actually be taught? These are some of the questions that today's neuroscientists and researchers are trying to answer. Although many agree that our understanding of the brain, and its creative functions, is still cloudy (Limb 2010), there are a few things we know for sure.

First, humans by nature are creative beings. In his 2010 TEDx Talk on creativity and the brain, Dr. Charles Limb, a surgeon and neuroscientist at Johns Hopkins University, explained that "artistic creativity is a neurological product." Based on his studies, he concluded that creativity is not some mythical talent doled out to a handful of artsy types at birth but rather, a normal function of the brain. Ken Robinson (2011) reiterates this finding, suggesting that "there are many misconceptions about creativity: that it's wrongly thought to be solely the domain of special people or special activities; that you're either creative or not; or that it's all about cutting loose and being uninhibited" (3). Rather, Robinson explains, imagination—and, by extension, creativity—is "the primary gift of human consciousness" (141).

Second, creativity involves both convergent and divergent thinking. Sadly, convergent thinking is the bulk of what students do in school. It is the type of thinking that gives "correct" answers to narrow questions, fills in blanks, follows prescribed steps, and focuses on knowing and retaining discrete facts. Divergent thinking, on the other hand, is the cognitive process of generating ideas—sensible ones, barely plausible ones, and totally absurd ones—in hopes of landing on a creative solution that works.

These two modes of thinking are increasingly considered to be the work of the two different hemispheres of the brain. In a TED talk on "The Divided Brain," psychiatrist and author Iain McGilchrist (2011) notes that "the right hemisphere gives sustained, broad, open vigilance [and] alertness, where the left hemisphere gives narrow, sharply focused attention to detail." Humans share our bilateral brain construction with mammals and birds, who rely on the left hemisphere for focusing on very specific tasks and familiar problems—such as picking out a seed in the grass—and simultaneously rely on the right hemisphere for observing bigger patterns—such as listening for predators. Just as animals need both hemispheres of the brain to work in concert, so too do students benefit from batting an idea back-and-forth between the hemispheres of their brains. But how does a process that used to be important for our survival become the process needed for our creativity?

In 2010, *Newsweek* published a feature on creativity and the brain called "The Creativity Crisis" that led to flurries of discussion around how creative thinking occurs and why it matters. Bronson and Merryman, the lead authors, explain how this back-and-forth process of convergent and divergent thinking leads to creativity: "Creativity requires constant shifting, blender pulses of both divergent thinking and convergent thinking, to combine new information with old and forgotten ideas. Highly creative people are very good at marshaling their brains into bilateral mode" (Bronson and Merryman 2010).

Pushing students from convergent thinking to a combination of convergent and divergent thinking requires that we ask students to engage in open-ended tasks that reward a multiplicity of solutions. When we pose these types of challenges, our students will inevitably start by looking for the narrow, convergent, left-hemisphere answers. When that exercise proves insufficient, the right hemisphere kicks in, posing broad, novel, divergent possibilities. As McGilchrist, Bronson, and Merryman all assert, the creative process requires both types of thinking but, more important, requires the brain to be able to quickly switch gears between divergent and convergent thinking. We absolutely can teach this skill and encourage creative thinking in our students; it simply requires an awareness of the types of learning experiences we design.

Third, creativity means learning to shut off the filter. In a 2014 interview on NPR, author Elizabeth Gilbert shared her thoughts about moving from fear of failure into a creative endeavor: "I think the thing that stops people from doing [something creative] is always exactly the same thing, which is fear. And what I've discovered over the years is not that you have to be fearless . . . I think instead what you have to do is recognize that fear and creativity are conjoined twins . . . Creativity is going into the uncertain, and the uncertain is always scary" (Gilbert 2014).

Science supports Gilbert's experience. In an fMRI study of how creativity affects different regions of the brain, neuroscientists found that when individuals are engaged in a creative activity, such as improvising music, the medial prefrontal cortex, responsible for self-expression, lights up, whereas the lateral prefrontal cortex, responsible for self-monitoring, shuts off (Limb 2010). It would seem, then, that creativity requires a certain degree of separation from filtering and self-critique. In our classrooms, this means more than just celebrating the "no wrong answers" mantra; rather, it means actually pushing our students to embrace all of their ideas, including the ones they know aren't feasible.

From Creativity to Critical Thinking

Young children ask hundreds of questions each day, as anyone who has taken a road trip with a three-year-old can attest. We know that children start off as innately imaginative, curious, and creative. They play make-believe at recess and, at home, can entertain themselves in magical, alternative realities with nothing more than a few bedsheets for a fort.

Then, something shifts. In school, as students move up the grade levels, the free space for creative thinking and play diminishes until they must digest a steady diet of content objectives and test-prep exercises. And yet, parents and politicians alike wonder why our students are ill prepared for the creative, critical-thinking tasks that are requisite skills for success in the twenty-first century (Casner-Lotto et al. 2006).

Most educators feel the crunch of state and district mandates, the push to effectively and efficiently implement standards, and the vocational call to avoid stifling students' natural love of learning. In this environment of accountability, how do we rationalize spending time on something as fluffy as creativity? The first step is to stop thinking of creativity as an add-on or as synonymous with "arts and crafts."

It's true that weaving creative work into the curriculum takes time, as surely it takes more time for students to think up five solutions rather than one. But creative thinking doesn't mean a lack of critical thinking. In fact, creativity begets critical thinking. In *Creating Significant Learning Experiences* (2013), Dee Fink explains how we ask our students to do three types of thinking: practical thinking, creative thinking, and critical thinking. Each one leads to the next: practical thinking leads to creative thinking, and creative thinking leads to critical thinking. Asking students to engage in meaningful, creative work sharpens their ability to conceptualize, apply, analyze, and synthesize—essential skills for critical thinking.

For this reason, the Partnership for 21st Century Skills lists creativity (right next to critical thinking, collaboration, and communication) as one of its "Four Cs," the four pillars that constitute the framework for necessary twenty-first-century learning and innovation skills. Similarly, the International Society for Technology in Education (ISTE) places creativity at the very top of its list of student standards, citing a need for students to "demonstrate creative thinking, construct knowledge, and develop innovative products and processes using technology." This means that our students must be able to "apply existing knowledge to generate new ideas, products, or processes; create original works as a means of personal or group expression; use models and simulations to explore complex systems and issues; and identify trends and forecast possibilities" (ISTE 2007). Visit http://www.iste.org/standards for more information.

Creativity in the Classroom

Creativity *can* and *must* be taught; encouraging imaginative thinking in our classrooms is the first step. Teacher leader Rushton Hurley spoke on this topic to a group of teachers in Coronado, California, in 2014. He showed them a small piece of a picture and asked them to imagine what it could be. He said they needed to work with a partner and come up with at least five possibilities. Notice that he did not ask, "What is it?" He asked what it *could* be. Those are very different questions. The teachers talked and laughed. One woman said, "I'm glad we did this. I realized that, like my students, I stop thinking of possibilities once I think I know the 'right' answer."

When Hurley stopped their conversations he asked, "Which was your favorite possibility?" He had prompted them to imagine and reflect on a range of possible choices, and then pointed out that their favorite answer was surely more interesting and thought-provoking than the right answer. Bringing imaginative thinking to our classrooms means asking about what could be possible, moving our students to abstract thinking, and focusing less on questions to which the answer is already known.

We add creative projects to our classrooms the same way we integrate technology: consistently and as part of our normal expectations. We don't say, "Oh, it's a creative project day" just as we don't say, "Today is a technology day." Creativity and technology integration have become ingrained into our classroom culture. Our students know we expect them to be able to use their laptops and tablets to accomplish a range of tasks, and they know we expect them to be creative about the way they solve problems, complete their work, and work with one another. Implicitly and explicitly, we show students that we value their creativity.

Although creativity is often used as an ambiguous umbrella term for a range of imaginative and outside-the-box thinking, we find it helpful to consider the conditions that allow creativity to thrive in our classrooms. When we are thinking about how to work more creative thinking into our unit plans, we review these elements and often find that one or more aspects inspire an idea we can put to use with our students.

Original Work

When creativity is a valued skill in our classrooms, our students have more ownership of their learning and their demonstrations of that knowledge. This means ceding some control over exactly how things are done to allow for students to imagine creative solutions. As Chris

Lehman, principal of the Science Leadership Academy, tells us, if we assign our students a creative project and get back mostly identical products, then we didn't assign a project; we gave them a recipe. And yet, creativity often thrives within some very formulaic constraints such as a sonnet, a PechaKucha, a six-word memoir, or a geometric proof. When crafting projects to cultivate creativity, we recommend constraints that will challenge students in one direction but allow them limitless possibilities in another direction.

Figure 8.3 The six-word memoir wall is one of the ways Jen encourages community building in her classroom.

As part of the process of building community in her classroom every fall, Jen asks her students to write six-word memoirs (see Figure 8.3). They watch some videos of examples and then dive in. The only constraint is that they must use six words. Students craft their memoirs in a Google Doc; for some of them it is their first experience with online word processing or using a computer in class. Jen lets them have free rein with fonts and layout. (She does ask them to make their work large enough to fill the page.) She fills the printer with different colors of paper and lets them print. Eventually, these terse but evocative phrases will cover a bulletin board in the hallway, but each student first gets to share his or her memoir and explain its meaning. With this simple project, Jen shows her students that creativity, technology, and personal reflection are all important aspects of their learning experience.

Occasionally, a student will do an Internet search for six-word memoirs and use someone else's words as their own. Plagiarism does seem to come more readily to students when copy and paste is an easy shortcut. Fortunately, the same search that students used to steal work can usually help us trace the source. The better solution, though, as our friend Jon Corippo is fond of saying, is to assign projects that have never been assigned before. This requires some creativity on our part, but it can also be fun to ask students to reimagine a character from the novel they are reading as a student or teacher at our school. Or, what happens when students create a podcast of a talk show host interviewing two characters from a Shirley Jackson short story?

During a unit on Transcendentalist writers, Diana asked her students to create aphorism posters featuring the short, pithy sayings from the essays they were reading, paired with a coordinating image. She pitched the assignment as "memes with meaning." To avoid the crummy results and total irony of allowing students to search keywords such as *marching to beat of own drummer* and *great, misunderstood people*, Diana added, "Remember, the Transcendentalists were all about having an original relationship with the universe. Please don't just search for someone else's interpretation of the aphorisms. I care about yours. All images in your aphorism poster must be *original*, as in, you have to create them yourselves." What could have been just another copy-paste-print task quickly turned into something that required metaphorical thinking, a creative eye, and the willingness to see ordinary objects in unique ways. One student went home and photographed four miniature pumpkins that her family had set on the dining table for Halloween and applied a filter to make one of the pumpkins stand out in a different color (see Figure 8.4). In white handwriting, she inked over the PDF, "To be great is to be misunderstood."

Originality in our assignments will lead to originality in student projects. We can and should give constraints, sometimes in unique ways, while giving students the choice to imagine the solution and produce a result that shows their learning.

Figure 8.4 Students create aphorism posters as part of Diana's unit on the Transcendentalist writers.

Authentic Tasks

When students put thought and time into creating something, they naturally want to share it with an audience. Authentic products, things that the world actually needs produced, already have an audience waiting for them. Asking students to create authentic work is one of the core tenets of project-based learning (Steinberg 1997). When we provide students with the opportunity to engage in meaningful work, we move them away from step-by-step recipes and a teacher-only audience toward student-owned learning that draws upon real-world connections for its context.

We know that finding an audience for everything your students create won't always be possible, but considering how you can make a task more authentic, helpful, or shareable is always worth thinking about as you and your students plan projects. Contests, community service projects, video tutorials, and self-publications are just a few ways to give authenticity to creative endeavors. Here are some other ideas:

- Students in a business communications class could reach out to local businesses and offer to redesign logos, menus, or websites.
- Students in a graphic design class at Jen's school annually compete to design the cover of the student planner and yearbook.
- Many of our English teacher friends ask their students to create and publish video book trailers to preview and advertise their favorite free reading texts from the year.
- Eric Marcos and his middle school math students create video tutorials on all aspects of middle school math and share them at mathtrain.com.
- Diana's tenth graders create short instructional videos explaining symbols and motifs in their class novels.

It is also helpful to consider the purpose for students' creative projects. Although learning and the pleasure of creating are always our implicit goals, we usually also have a set of explicit instructions that include a specific purpose. Of course, many of the things we list here fit into more than one purpose. These are just some ideas. We ask our students to

- create to **instruct** when we have them create video tutorials, stop motion animations, infographics, presentations, Gooru collections, and feature articles.
- create to **entertain** when they create song parodies, satire spark talks, Docs Stories, NaNoWriMo novels, digital stories, original music, podcasts, and more.
- create to **innovate** when they remix, invent, reimagine, and build things people need. (More about innovation in the second half of this chapter.)
- create for **pleasure** when they blog, create graphic designs, make memes, edit photos, write stories, create films, and design what brings them joy.

Abstract Thinking

Asking students to engage in a task that requires abstract thinking fosters imagination and creativity. Jen asks her students to create visual metaphors when they study civil disobedience. Her students draw or find images of waves, trains, trees, and soccer matches and then label the parts of the image to represent the contributions of Emerson, Thoreau, Gandhi, and

King. By placing the ideas of these leaders into a visual metaphor, students have to think about how their ideas influenced each other and the world. When Jen asks her students to explain their visual metaphor in writing, it becomes clear that they now understand much more about how the thinking about civil disobedience evolved. Through the act of abstract creation, students develop a stronger concrete understanding of the material.

Studying the Constitutional Convention is an expected part of a senior government class, and probably not something you'd normally expect to find in a chapter about creativity . . . unless memes are involved. LeeAnn Rupley challenged her students to create a meme that showed their understanding of the US Constitution, much like a contemporary political cartoon. They used a meme-generator app to pull in images and add text. Memes have room for only a few lines of text, so images and words need to work together closely. Memes also should be funny, or express irony. With an image and a few words, Rupley's students were able to make critical commentary about contradictions in our society and government. After creating a "draft" of their memes, the students went through a peer review process. Rupley asked her students to look at their partners' memes and then explain in writing the kind of background knowledge someone would need to have about the Constitution to get the point of the meme. Student writing reflected that they had knowledge of the Constitution that they could apply to understanding the memes. In reflection, Rupley noted, "I am proud of [my students] for participating so fully in this lesson and am overjoyed that some of my most reluctant students found their voices, at least temporarily, during this project." And as we so often find, her students enjoyed making memes so much that they went on to make more, continued to share them with her, and made memes about the content of their other classes, too.

Abstract thinking means moving beyond the silos of subject areas to acknowledge that creativity is inherently interdisciplinary and multimodal. Divergent thinking requires students to blur the lines between the discrete bits of information they have stored in their brains and to consider alternative ways to express their ideas. When we challenge students to explain content knowledge with incongruous tools, such as the memes about the Constitution, we stretch their imaginative muscles, access *all* of their learning, and honor the flexibility required for true creativity.

Workflow Flexibility

Creativity often involves combining things in new ways, just like we might add an unexpected ingredient to a familiar dish and improve it in the process. In a 1:1 classroom, creativity might encourage us to use ordinary tools in unexpected ways or combine them differently. What if I make a Google presentation to show what I learned and then embed it in my blog instead of presenting it to the class? What if I use remind.com to send my students different images, and then tell them to partner with someone who has the opposite image? What if I take a screenshot of this document, send it to a tablet, and then have students use an app to write on it while we record our voices talking about the revisions?

Once our students begin to understand what each tool does, they can combine them in new ways. A common term for that kind of combining is *app-smashing*. Our tech-savvy students will think nothing of taking a photo with their phone, editing it with an app, e-mailing it to a friend to add to a presentation, and then posting that presentation on their websites. Our less tech-savvy students will need supportive peers who can show them how those technical elements come together. We see our high school students building their knowledge of apps and web tools the way younger students build their sight-word vocabulary. As the first graders learn new words, they can combine them in new ways to read and say new things. As our older students learn new tools, they combine them in new ways to create new ways of communicating a message (see Figure 8.5).

Having a range of devices available facilitates creativity with digital tools. We often allow students to combine the capabilities of their personal devices, usually phones, with the complementary capabilities of our school-issued devices. Diana's students were making a movie and wanted to show characters sending and receiving text messages. They wanted, but did not know of, a way to make a recording of what was on the phone. Without seeking Diana's help they started searching online for options. Then they asked her if she had the Reflector app on her laptop. Reflector lets you project the screen of an iPhone or iPad to the laptop screen. The students reflected the phone to the laptop and then used screencasting software to record the text messages as they sent them. Next, they used video-editing software to speed up the exchange of the text messages to make the transfer seem faster. Along the way, the students hit several technical challenges that stood in the way of their vision, but each time, they were able to find a solution through a search and a video tutorial. When we encourage our students to find a better way, combine tools in new ways, and search for answers that will help them execute their vision, we are showing them that imaginative thinking and creativity are valued in our classrooms.

Handoff

Once again, we refer you to the TECH model in Chapter 1 (see Figure 1.5). When we hand off learning experiences to students, we give them the ownership and responsibility to craft their own understanding and then apply their knowledge in new ways.

> **Handoff:** Students' interests drive the learning experience with teacher guidance and the flexible choice of tools and technologies to achieve an authentic, exemplary product.

TOOLS FOR CREATIVITY	
PicMonkey	http://www.picmonkey.com PicMonkey is an online photo-editing tool that's great for helping students edit their own photos or remix images they have the rights to use.
Shadow Puppet	http://get-puppet.co Shadow Puppet is an app that lets students combine video and images and then add their own voice-over. The app enables them to make movies quickly.
Tagxedo	http://www.tagxedo.com Tagxedo is a word cloud generator. Have your students turn their writing or their reading into a word cloud and consider the meaning from another angle.
Google Story Builder	https://docsstorybuilder.appspot.com Google Story Builder lets you and your students create short video versions of what looks like characters typing on a shared Google Doc. (See plugin-powerup.com for examples.)
Dipity	http://www.dipity.com Using this online tool, students can create time lines about themselves or the subject matter of your course.
Meme Generator	http://memegenerator.net Combine a picture with some pithy text and make a statement. Then share it with the world.
Minecraft Edu	http://minecraftedu.com Setting up a Minecraft world for your students requires some technical knowledge, but your students will thank you for it.
iBooks Author	https://www.apple.com/ibooks-author It works only on Apple computers, but with this software your students can create their own interactive iBooks. (Web-based tools that work in similar ways are coming soon.)

Figure 8.5 Top Tools for Supporting Creativity and What They Do Best

We see handoff happening for our students when they take the tools we have taught them to use and leverage those tools in new ways or for their own purposes. Here are some examples:

- Several of Jen's students took the skills from their video production class and made their own video. They wanted to make a skateboarding video, but because none of them were great at skateboarding, they reverted to making a satirical video about how to walk, using all the conventions of skateboarding videos.
- Once our students learn how easy it is to collaborate in Google Drive, they leverage that knowledge in their other classes when collaboration is called for.
- One of Jen's colleagues needed to make a screencast of a presentation to share with parents because she could not attend the annual open house. Later she told Jen that is was so much easier than she had thought, and that she could see how easy it would be to make her own video lesson.

When we give our students (and ourselves) the tools and skills they need to create, they will go off to create even more with their new superpowers.

Sometimes we can create a handoff situation for students in our classrooms, and sometimes handoff happens with the projects they create outside of school. In our 1:1 classrooms, we continually find new ways to encourage imagination and creativity. We hope you have stopped often while reading this section to consider various ways of adding creative work to your classroom as well.

 **PLUG IN** Ramp Up the Imagination and Creativity in Your Classroom with These Challenges

1. **Build your own imaginative thinking skills**, or even better, work with a team by brainstorming ten ways you could add imaginative thinking and creative skill building to your next unit plan. Don't limit your ideas to things you already know how to do, and don't reject ideas because you think you don't have the tools to make them happen. Ideas breed ideas.

2. **Give your students the chance to make a list of creative ways** they could demonstrate their learning. Ask teams to generate five or ten ideas. Allow them to share their ideas and choose one to work on.

3. **Identify a digital tool for creativity** that you would like to know more about. Set aside thirty minutes just to play with it. If you have a purpose for creating something, that's great, but it is also fun just to play with the tool and then make a list of all the possible ways you could use it. Look online to find examples of how other teachers have used it. Or, better yet, ask your students to consider (and reconsider) its utility.

Innovation
Making a Dent in the Universe

If imagination is the process of conjuring up ideas that are not present to our senses, and creativity is bringing those ideas to life, then innovation is like creativity for a cause. In other ways, innovation is creativity that benefits others. Steve Jobs often quipped that the role of the innovator is to "make a dent in the universe." Innovation means breaking with the status quo; it means creating new products that respond to dynamic problems. Innovation takes creativity out of the personal space and thrusts it into the public arena. Innovation is the response to a greater call to action.

In their book *Creative Confidence* (2013), the Kelley brothers write about the conditions needed for innovation to flourish. David Kelley is the founder of IDEO (one of the world's leading design firms) and creator of the Design School at Stanford University. Tom Kelley is a partner at IDEO and a fellow at U.C. Berkeley's Haas School of Business. The heart of innovation, they suggest, is "believing in your ability to make change in the world around you" (2).

Living and working in California, we have both benefited from the innovative, entrepreneurial spirit that seems to linger in the air. With Apple and Google literally in our backyards, we have witnessed everything from start-up launches in coffee shops to beta testing on town sidewalks. Diana once had brunch in the booth next to Steve Jobs at the local diner, and Jen serves as an adviser to several ed tech start-up companies. We are surrounded by leaders and thinkers who are trying to improve the business world. As enthusiastic educators, we can't help but ask, What would happen if we harnessed that same innovative spirit and brought it into the classroom?

Thinking Through an Innovative Project

The process steps for innovation are well documented, and in the Bay Area where IDEO and the Stanford d.school have their roots, "Design Thinking" has become part of the fiber of the business culture. About five minutes down the street from these design hot spots is Diana's school. Diana's colleague Chris Chiang, a middle school history teacher, knew that his sixth graders weren't too young to embrace innovation. He figured they would thrive on the opportunity to put their creative minds to work for good. What follows is his innovative apps project, loosely based on the Stanford d.school's framework for Design Thinking. (The Stanford d.school has a whole host of Creative Commons–licensed materials available online, well beyond the scope of this section. If the process of Design Thinking interests you, we encourage you to check out the website at dschool.stanford.edu.)

Background

Chiang's history students had just finished a unit on ancient and contemporary China. They had explored the archaeological records of the Shang dynasty, discussed Confucianism and Taoism, and vicariously traveled along the Silk Road to discover its importance in trade and cultural development. Chiang situated their study of ancient China within the context of modern China, calling on students to draw connections between the two civilizations and to trace the roots of contemporary Chinese traditions in their ancient past. At the end of the unit, instead of the usual cumulative test to evaluate students' memorization of dates and leaders, Chiang pushed them to apply their understanding of development and moderniza-tion and to create their own "apps for good," phone and tablet apps that could help solve one of the challenges faced by people in China today.

Chiang outlined the origins of the project, saying, "This year, our school's focus was my favorite of [our goals]: a social awareness that impels to action. We want these kids to have this social awareness, but then how are we going to have them able to act on it? I wanted them to do something to address these issues. Along that line, I was also aware that we hadn't given our students an initial exposure to computer science. I've read research that sixth grade is a critical year at which to introduce kids to computer science, because they don't yet have these built-in stereotypes about whether it's for them or not. If we expose all kids to it, we can increase interest in computer science, especially among girls. I decided to create a unit where, after we studied the social problems in China, we'd take about three weeks and the kids would design a mobile app that addresses one of the social problems we studied. That really worked well with our China unit because Android is the most popular operating system in China, and increasingly, China is the largest app market in the world."

Step 1: Empathize

The first step of Design Thinking is to understand the problem or opportunity and, more important, the people who will benefit from the final product. The Kelley brothers (2013) explain that "connecting with the needs, desires, and motivations of real people helps to inspire and provoke fresh ideas" (22). The Stanford d.school cites three behaviors as core to empathizing: observing, engaging, and immersing. In other words, the first step to an inno-vative design is radical listening.

Because a class field trip to China was out of the question, Chiang instead helped his students empathize with their target market through academic study. He grouped students into their design teams based on areas of interest, and together students investigated issues ranging from pollution to political power. They read articles, watched news clips, and pooled as many resources as they could to understand the nature of the challenge facing their Chi-nese market.

Step 2: Define

The second step of Design Thinking is to "explicitly express the problem you are striving to address through your efforts" (Hasso Plattner School of Design at Stanford 2011). Defini-tion requires design teams to synthesize what they learned in the empathy phase and to make sense of it. Defining the problem means that teams must "recognize patterns, identify themes, and find meaning in all that [they have] seen, gathered, and observed" (Kelley and Kelley 2013, 23).

One of Chiang's design teams wanted to focus on educational access for the rural poor. From the empathy step, they knew that all Chinese students must take the *Gaokao*, or National Higher Education Entrance Exam, to determine their potential admission into Chinese universities. In the definition stage, the team decided that they wanted to address the needs of those with limited access to educational resources, those who may not have an opportunity to practice for the exam.

Step 3: Ideate

The third step of Design Thinking is "idea generation" (Hasso Plattner School of Design at Stanford 2011). Most of our students have participated in a brainstorming session before, but that doesn't mean they are good at ideating. Tom Kelley, in his book *The Art of Innovation* (2001), outlines the "secrets" to an effective brainstorm, which we like to practice with our students. It's worth noting that some of the fastest ways to kill a brainstorm—taking turns, writing everything down, or starting with a leader (or teacher)—are all fairly common practices in classrooms. Instead, Kelley calls on us to reimagine our design space (read: classroom) as a think tank and follow a few key principles, some of which are stenciled in large letters in the conference rooms at IDEO:

- Start with a clear definition of the problem. "Edgy is better than fuzzy" (56).
- Steer clear of critiquing and debating ideas . . . for now. Remember how creativity requires us to shut off the filter? Now is the time to do that.
- "Number your ideas" and "go for quantity!" (58). Both of these practices make it easier to create collective challenges such as: We won't quit until we hit fifty ideas.
- "Encourage wild ideas" (57). You never know what other ideas they'll spark.
- "Be visual" (58). Drawing ideas and mapping connections so that the brainstorm is visible to the whole team is a great way to engage spatial memory and quickly get everyone on the same page.

As a living testimony to the value of ideating, Chiang's whiteboard is covered, literally *covered*, in multicolored sticky notes, Mandarin characters, mind maps, and questions. Students had creative license (and encouragement) to think up as many different ways of reframing the problem and reimagining the solution as they possibly could. It was through the process of ideating that the design team was able to zero in on creating a learning app with built-in feedback for students to practice the essential elements of the *Gaokao* exam.

Step 4: Prototype

The fourth step of Design Thinking is to move ideas into some sort of physical form. The Kelley brothers call this the process of building "rough representations . . . that are concrete enough for people to react to" (Kelley and Kelley 2013, 23). Prototypes can be anything from storyboards to design maps to sketches of product features (Hasso Plattner School of Design at Stanford 2011). Prototyping is like asking students to outline before they write the essay, so that they can work through their ideas while paragraphs and evidence are still easy to move around and change.

Chiang's students created their actual apps during the prototyping phase because they weren't planning to redesign the product multiple times like a company might. Chiang's explanation of the process they used made building apps sound easy enough that, well, a sixth grader could do it. "We used this program, a development tool, called MIT App Inventor, which allows students to be introduced to a new programming structure using block coding," he said. "They were able to design and create a functional mobile app for an Android device. They even set up Scrum boards, which is the process that software developers use to keep track of the team, and the feedback and testing that they have to do."

Step 5: Test

The final step of Design Thinking is to implement and test the product, looking for more feedback that would help refine it further. After weeks of practicing coding and learning the basics of app design, Chiang's students pitched their projects to panels of parents (who acted as Chinese investors) and proposed reasons for why their app responded to the needs of a growing, modern China. The students fielded questions, defended design choices, and considered the panelists' suggestions for the tweaks and changes that would need to happen before launching the apps. Chiang's students were delighted to learn that their projects had made it into one of China's newswires, *36KR* (see Figure 8.6).

是的你没有看错，这是一个小学六年级的课程。不要说"九年义务教育"，不少国内大学的创业课程，恐怕都相形见绌了。与国内许多热捧的以发现市场机会和产业化潜力为目的的创业比赛不一样，课程没有刻意强调市场，客户与盈利模式，更多关注的是学生发现问题，通过现代科技可扩展地解决问题的能力（solve problem in a scalable way）。我这才意识到，原来整个硅谷的创新源动力，并非从斯坦福大学那四年突然爆发。这种从小灌输的**make things happen and solve the problem**的理念，是长大后如何恶补都恶补不出来的。所谓"天生创业者"并非天生，而是后天教育过程中传达的意识形态与价值观，一种骨子里的信念和行为方式。

Figure 8.6 Chris Chiang's students make the news in China!

In reflecting on their process of innovating, Chiang noted, "It was a really great way to build multicultural understanding and introduce globalization to the kids; they saw this rising tech and online market in China that they weren't really aware of before. [They learned] graphic design, international marketing, how to deal with cultural sensitivity in international business, and how to graphically design and code their prototypes. In the end, all seventy-two kids got to experience a very authentic, lean start-up model that shows them how software is developed."

Over the course of the project, Chiang's middle schoolers transformed from a group of in-betweeners—not quite elementary and not quite high school—to a group of innovators, inventors, and imaginative problem solvers. Their work had real-world flair, and they knew it. It's true that the Apps for Good project took time. And in the couple of weeks that students spent discussing, designing, creating, and implementing, Chiang probably could have crammed in a few more lessons about Emperor Shi Huangdi and the Han dynasty. But jamming "more stuff" into our students' heads never has been, and never will be, the core practice of meaningful learning. Rather, hands-on experience and real-world engagement is the creative space in which our students thrive.

POWER UP!   Design for a Change

1. **Want to get your feet wet with Design Thinking?** Try taking Stanford's free ninety-minute virtual crash course: http://dschool.stanford.edu/dgift/.

2. Sometimes, we want our students to practice the art of innovation, but we can't logistically see the design all the way through (because we lack either the resources or the time to dedicate to a polished product). In those cases, **ask students to engage in the process anyway**. They can usually get all the way through the steps empathy, define, and ideate, and can come up with a plan for a prototype. Practicing the skills at the heart of innovation is still valuable, even if they don't have a cool app to show for it.

3. **Take the leap! Create a project that requires your students to truly innovate**—to create something that benefits others. Have them work in design teams, and equip them to navigate the five steps, from understanding the problem to designing the solution. Then, step back and watch the creative genius flow.

CHAPTER 9
Rethinking Class Time

Time (n): *An opportune or suitable moment.*

Teacher: Diana Neebe
Class: Freshman English

If we let it, 1:1 technology has the power to radically transform how we teach and what we do with precious class time. What follows is a case study of how I rethought my ninth-grade English writing instruction curriculum and how, with a little bit of creativity, this new model of teaching and learning has allowed me to meet students' needs in new ways.

To an outside observer, day two of our *Of Mice and Men* drafting workshop must have looked like a scholastic combat zone. Sprawling teenagers littered the once-tidy room with opened books, propped-up iPads, wireless keyboards, and backpacks spewing homework and handouts from a long day of learning. In the front corner of the room sat Chris, a young man silenced by his fear of "looking dumb." He had many questions but lacked the confidence to ask them. All through middle school, Chris barely made passing scores in language arts, and in his first semester of high school, he appeared to be rapidly falling behind.

I looked down at my iPad, cued to the todaysmeet.com room I had created for questions and help requests. A new line flashed at the top:

"I think my quote is OK, but I don't know what to say about it. What do I do next?—Chris"

Seeing my rare opportunity, I beelined over to Chris, crouched down next to him, and zoomed in to his question on my screen. "Let's see this awesome quote you found and start there," I prodded.

"It's the one where Crooks says that the guys 'ain't got no right coming into [his] room.'"

"What made that line stand out to you?" I asked.

"I don't know. I tried to find something with 'weighty words' like you said in the video. The word *right* seems like it's important. But I don't know," Chris mumbled, deflated.

"Who's the speaker?" I pushed.

"Crooks."

"Why do we care that Crooks is trying to protect his space and *his* rights?" I continued.

"I don't know. Crooks doesn't really get any rights unless he stands up for them. It's sorta ironic."

"Great!" I jumped in. "Why is it ironic? How might you play off of Steinbeck's use of irony to prove your point?"

Chris and I conversed back and forth like this for a few minutes to clarify his argument before I moved on to help other students. If Chris had been in my class just a couple of years earlier, our whole-class lesson on quote selection and body paragraphs would have taken up the bulk of our face-to-face time, and Chris would have been left to write at home by himself. The notion of providing "just in time" support was nonexistent in that model. Instead, because I flipped where instruction and practice took place, I was able to work side by side with Chris, tailor my teaching to his specific writing needs, and skip that entire ugly step of Chris feeling stumped, or worse, stupid.

While I was working with Chris, his classmates were typing away, quietly asking each other questions on our backchannel and reviewing the tutorial videos I had posted the night before for homework. Because students shared their docs-in-progress with me, I was able to peek in on their papers while they wrote, and check in virtually with any students who had unanswered questions after class ended.

Of course, to free up class time for highly personalized and targeted instruction, I had to shift something. In the case of my English classes, I moved all of my writing instruction outside of class, and pulled *all* of our drafting and editing into class. This model—where guided practice is done in class, and some portion of instruction is delivered as homework—is often called *flipped teaching,* or *blended learning.*

A few compelling reasons made me consider, and eventually move to, a blended learning environment. The first is what I witnessed in working with Chris: by freeing up valuable class time, I am able to have personalized conversations with kids about exactly what they need, exactly when they need it. Beyond working one-on-one with students, shifting lecture-based instruction out of the classroom gives students more time to work with each other and engage in dynamic activities that creatively push them to apply their learning. I love that as a result, my role unequivocally shifts from the proverbial "sage on the stage" to my dream job of "guide on the side."

The second reason is that the instruction itself becomes differentiated. Moving my instruction to a video or other multimedia online source is like handing each of my students a remote control. Imagine a class period in which every student could push a button to pause, rewind, or even replay your lesson. You might have to stop every few seconds to meet every student's demands. But when instruction is delivered at home, students can loop and repeat it without ever having to raise a hand and feel embarrassed. For example, my lesson on quote selection changed from being teacher determined to student paced. As a result, students' work in class became dynamic and responsive instead of linear and prescribed.

The third reason is that instruction is archived. I didn't fully appreciate the value of having lessons saved online until I started walking around the room during our writing workshops. I was in the middle of a fabulous conversation with my freshman Carrie about race, gender, and being the outcast (conversations I didn't get to have, midpaper, with students while they were writing at home), when I turned around to see Aaron jamming on his headphones. I was about to bust him for being off task when I saw that he was rewatching my video on conclusions. I was working with Carrie while simultaneously teaching Aaron. It was as if I had cloned myself! Because the lesson was archived, Aaron was able to pull up a video from a couple of months earlier and rewatch it during his writing workshop.

The New Time Management

Diana's experience of being able to provide the right instruction at the right time is one of the beauties of blended instruction and one of the gifts we get with 1:1 technology. Instead of her lesson plans being dictated by the bells at the beginning and end of the class period, she had the freedom to listen to her students' needs and plan accordingly. The process becomes a new kind of time management.

Back in the days of the original tablet, the ancient Greeks marked the concept of time with two disparate terms—χρόνος and καιρός—*chronos* and *kairos*. They used *chronos* to describe chronological time that is quantitative and marches along like the ticking of a clock. *Kairos*, on the other hand, was reserved for qualitative measures, such as moments and opportunities. If chronos was "time," kairos was the "right time."

When we let 1:1 technology transform our classrooms, we no longer have to abide by the same rules of chronos that, in the past, governed teaching and fettered learning. Gone are the days of planning an activity simply because it's the next lesson in the sequence, or because we see our students only fifty minutes per day. Rather, by blending the types of learning experiences we do inside and outside of class, and by blurring the boundaries between what is "schoolwork" and what is "homework," we have the power to maximize our limited face-to-face time for lessons that truly require teacher support and peer collaboration. We have the keys to kairos.

The Theory Behind the Practice

Beyond anecdotal success stories, there are many other, more scientific, reasons for blending our classrooms. Bloom's revised taxonomy (Anderson and Krathwohl 2001) gives us language to discuss the types of learning objectives we have for our students. The higher up the taxonomy we go, the more in-depth and authentic student learning becomes. Many of us remember the terms shown in Figure 9.1 from our Ed School days and have thoughtfully created curriculum that moves our students up the ladder.

Create	design, develop, produce, propose, synthesize
Evaluate	argue, critique, defend, recommend, validate
Analyze	compare, interpret, deconstruct, dissect, categorize
Apply	implement, solve, experiment, illustrate, simulate
Understand	explain, summarize, infer, translate, restate
Remember	recognize, recall, define, recite, list

Figure 9.1 Bloom's Revised Taxonomy (Highest-Level Thinking at the Top)

However, higher-level Bloom's tasks are also associated with a greater demand for critical thinking and thus place a higher intrinsic cognitive load on students' working memory (Sweller 2008). It seems intuitive that students are more likely to need our support for the "tough stuff" than for the less taxing tasks of remembering and understanding. And yet, most classes are set up to frontload content (*remember, understand*) during face-to-face sessions and to send students home on their own to practice what they've learned (*apply, analyze, evaluate, create*).

In the traditional model, a math teacher during class might present a new concept, such as the quadratic formula, and give students ways to remember the process steps for problem solving. Then, those students would go home to work through a series of questions that required them to apply the quadratic formula. In a history class, students might come to class to learn about sectional crisis and the Civil War, but then go home to work on a research paper explaining one of the factors leading up to the war. In each of these instances, the work done in class with the support of a teacher is much less challenging than the work done independently. What if we flipped that sequence? What if, instead, we used technology to create a flexible classroom that allows us to support students with the most challenging tasks we ask them to do during our collaborative face-to-face time and then provide the lower-level Bloom's content outside of class through multimedia presentations?

Blending our classrooms not only is a strategic approach for igniting and supporting critical thinking but also creates a responsive pedagogy for the realities of teaching in the "flat" and connected world of contemporary education. José Antonio Bowen (2012), a music professor at Southern Methodist University, writes about the parallel shift he has experienced in the college classroom, and how technology fits into the new paradigm of teaching and learning:

The workforce of the future will always be connected to the Web, and learning how to triage information is a crucial professional skill. Life has always been an open-book exam, but life and work in the 21st century are all about who can find the right information quickly, analyze what it means, and then put it to use before anyone else can … As knowledge proliferates, the need for analysis and critical thinking will only increase. The talking head is dead. (145, 47)

We no longer need to be our students' only source of information. In fact, even if we *wanted* to be the oracle, we have to acknowledge that our students will still access and learn from a multitude of sources beyond us. The task of teaching in the twenty-first century is to be "less oracle and more curator" (Bowen 2012, 46) and for classroom time to be less us, more them.

When we make this shift from a traditional classroom to a blended one, the hidden curriculum becomes visible. We reinforce the importance of learning in community with others, and co-creating knowledge with our students. We acknowledge that there are many voices in the learning process, and that ours is neither the loudest nor the most important. We free up time for our students to engage in peer-to-peer learning, to teach each other, to grapple with the biggest challenges we can throw their way, and to share the results of their learning with the world.

The Evolution of a Blended Classroom

Moving to a blended classroom does not happen overnight. And, of course, this model works well only if all of your students have access to your lessons at home, usually via the Internet, and have the same device they use at school. If your school is beginning a 1:1 program with a cart-based model, where the devices remain in the classroom, you will have less flexibility to flip or blend your classroom. What follows is a snapshot of each step of the way—from preparing students for a blended classroom, to creating and curating media, to transforming what you can do with class time once you've made the flip.

Preparing Students for a New Workflow

For most students (and their parents), flipped instruction represents a new model for learning. Your students will probably need several lessons on how to actively engage with the content material they are using at home. Depending on the ages and experience of your students, you may have to teach them about pausing a video to take notes and have them practice the steps for accessing your course material online. You'll also want to be sure students can access any tools you are using to check for their understanding.

When Jen visited Mike Salamanca's eighth-grade math class for the first time, she received an apology: "I know you came to see flipped teaching, and today we aren't really flipping," he said. "Before I send the students home to watch videos, I want them to practice the process here in class for a few days. So this is just getting them ready for flipping." Salamanca knew he needed to prepare his students by practicing the flipped instructional process in class. It was a great opportunity for Jen to see the process from the beginning.

Because Salamanca was not giving a lesson to the whole class at once, Jen was free to wander the room and observe students closely. Each student wore headphones and had a laptop on his or her desk. Most were already watching a video about real numbers, but as they watched, students would often pause the video to solve a problem in their notebooks and then restart it to check their answer. The video lasted about nine minutes, but most students spent fifteen to twenty minutes watching the whole thing. When they had finished, they used the notes they had taken to answer some quiz questions on a Google Form that Salamanca had set up on his classroom website.

Figure 9.2 One of Diana's students practices studying with a flipped lesson.

Jen came to Salamanca's class expecting to see great teaching in action, and she did. He was not at the front of the room delivering an amazing lesson that compelled every student to pay attention. He was wandering the room as she was, checking on students who had questions, reviewing the practice problems in their notes, and helping them navigate to the next step. What was most striking to Jen was that every student heard the teacher's lesson on the video in a distraction-free way. With headphones on and their eyes glued to their screens, no one was looking out the window, poking a classmate, or making eye contact with a friend across the room. On a warm day in a classroom bungalow without air-conditioning, students were focused on learning about solving problems with real numbers (see Figure 9.2).

Once he is sure all his students know how to access his website, navigate to the right lesson, keep track of practice problems along the way, and complete the Google Form to check their understanding, Salamanca will move the video lessons to homework. (His students carry home the same laptops they use in class.) And, once students are watching the lessons at home, he can devote class time to more interesting practice problems, differentiated instruction, and projects.

Engaging Students with Dynamic Media

After we have prepared our students for the transition to a blended learning environment, we must think about how we will engage them in meaningful learning outside of school. Surely, there is a time and a place for a podcast lesson on cell division, or a screencast of the origins of geometric formula, but that is not and should not be the extent of what we ask students to watch and listen to at home. In his 2013 TED Talk on sparking student learning, teacher Ramsey Musallam said it best:

> Flipping a boring lecture from the classroom to the screen of a mobile device
> might save instructional time, but if it is the focus of our students' experience
> it's the same dehumanizing chatter just wrapped up in fancy clothing. But, if
> instead, we have the guts to confuse our students, perplex them, and evoke real
> questions, through those questions, we as teachers have information that we can
> use to tailor robust and informed methods of blended instruction.

It may be overwhelming at first to realize the nearly limitless potential of the web, but it is also liberating to know that we have options for how we instruct our students and for what actually constitutes "instruction." Trust us: our students are far more delighted to see a goofy claymation video tutorial about plural versus possessive than to listen to us drone on *again* about when to use an apostrophe, and often we find that the more diverse and dynamic the media, the more memorable the content (i.e., the more it sticks!). Sometimes the best teaching we can do is curating.

Sasha Kelly and her seventh graders were in the middle of a unit on plate tectonics, earthquakes, and volcanoes, and she wanted to teach them the difference between the major types of faults in preparation for their hands-on lab the next day. Instead of sending her students home with textbook pages to read, or a mini-lecture to listen to, she gave them an annotated video with clips of real earthquake footage. The video stopped every minute or so to provide content in context. Kelly used EdPuzzle to add audio comments to the paused video: after students saw a clip of the 1989 earthquake in California with images of the San Andreas fault, she explained how the collision of the Pacific plate and the North American plate caused an earthquake, and why it was considered a strike-slip transform fault. She then asked students a check-in question for which they had to apply their prior learning around plate tectonics to help explain why that collision would happen. The video was a far cry from a boring lecture, and it prepared the students for a collaborative inquiry-based class the next day.

Here are a few more examples from other disciplines that showcase ways to engage students by using dynamic media:

- A US history teacher looking to illustrate the waves of immigration into the
  country assigned students the interactive immigration map from the *New York
  Times* and asked them to pick two different counties from two different states
  and note their change over time. They also were to track one foreign-born
  group of people and look for trends in how they settled across the United States.

Students came to class the next day with a list of questions for their small-group discussions about potential causes for the immigration trends they noticed.

- A chemistry teacher wanted to maximize the amount of time her students would have for a lab focusing on solubility and conductivity. Instead of spending a class period on the pre-lab, walking students through a teacher-led demonstration, she created a video pre-lab of the experiment for students to watch and required them to take a pre-lab quiz before arriving the next day. A passing score on the quiz was the admission ticket to participating in the lab activity.

- The high school's band director was hoping to fast-track the acclimation process for his beginning students learning to play with one another, so instead of assigning solo practice for homework, he provided students with SmartMusic, which enabled his budding musicians to rehearse at home with a professional orchestra. By the time they showed up for class, they were ready to play together.

- A computer science teacher flipped her traditional lecture-based lesson on "how search works" to homework. That evening, students thought through an interactive infographic from Google on the story behind search (www.google.com/insidesearch/howsearchworks/thestory/), following along with a graphic organizer. As a result, the next day her students had hands-on class time during which they investigated and tested out the effects of crawling and indexing on their own search histories with their peers.

- An English teacher wanted to flip his traditional author biography background lecture on Ralph Ellison, but instead of recording himself in a podcast, he posted a short video from biography.com for his students to watch. Students found the video engaging, with its integration of images and primary sources, and their teacher was thrilled to buy back enough time to dig into a deeper discussion in class.

- A physics teacher introducing potential and kinetic energy to his students assigned a short video chock-full of real-world examples created by a fellow science teacher from Bozeman, Montana, who creates and curates his lessons on bozemanscience.com.

- Students in a women's history senior elective course were preparing for a big project in which they were to update the Seneca Falls Declaration of Sentiments and Resolutions, working in teams during class time. In preparation for their discussion around "what still needs to change," the teacher assigned a series of contemporary speeches by prominent women. Students watched a range of videos, from Sheryl Sandberg's TED Talk on "Leaning In" to Emma Watson's address to the United Nations announcing the "He for She" movement.

Holding Students Accountable at Home

At some point in the transition, many teachers notice that, without accountability tools built in, students may choose to slack a bit, and either not do the assignment ("There's nothing to turn in!") or not do it with care ("It's like watching TV!"). Dario Flores noticed that students in his Spanish 1 class were falling into these very traps. One night, he sent them home with a short video lesson explaining "*verbos como gustar,*" along with a clip from a *telenovela* that put the verb construction into play. The next day, he was surprised when students came into class foggy about how to conjugate this peculiar verb type, complaining that the video just wasn't clear. That night, he gave the exact same assignment, but this time he added a couple of checkpoints to hold his students accountable. While listening to the mini-lesson, they followed along with cloze notes, where most of the major bullet points were already written out but strategic words were left blank for students to fill in. After they had finished the lesson and watched the telenovela clip, students recorded a two-sentence summary in the target language explaining what each of the main characters mentioned liking most ("*A ella le gusta . . .*"). Then they uploaded their short recordings to Flores's learning management system (LMS) so he could review their understanding.

When transitioning to a new model of instruction, it's all too easy to forget that we used to hold our kids accountable for our lessons when we taught them face-to-face. The need for accountability hasn't changed now that those lessons are online and available at home. Truthfully, the method of holding students accountable isn't all that different, either. Here are a few simple, and likely familiar, strategies for holding students accountable for content they learn at home:

- Provide a graphic organizer to help students make sense of new material.
- Assign guided notes, cloze notes, or Cornell notes that students are responsible for as they watch or listen.
- Check for understanding after students complete the flipped content. You could use a Google Form with some open-ended questions, create a quick at-home quiz on your learning management system, or choose another method.
- Ask for a discussion question or clarifying question at the start of the next class period.
- Give a quiz in class the next day. Often, we make it easy for students to earn credit at the beginning of the year when they are just learning our blended methods. We might ask obvious questions, such as "Describe the setting for the video. Where was I standing? What details do you remember?" Or, "What did I drop during the experiment?" When we know our students have become comfortable with the process, our questions become more rigorous and content based.

Digging Deeper During Class

After more than a decade of teaching AP chemistry, Kavita Gupta had long since created and refined her "wish list" of what she would do in class if she just had more face-to-face time. She knew that students internalized content best when they had hands-on practice in a low-stakes environment. But it seemed that with the ever-increasing list of content to cover to prepare students for the national AP exam, the labs and projects that she yearned to include kept getting cut from the jam-packed calendar, and class time had become a cycle of lecture-quiz-review-test.

When Gupta's school moved to the bring-your-own-device model for 1:1 technology, she realized that she had the tools she needed to free up precious face-to-face time for collaborative inquiry. She started by flipping just one unit—the hardest one for students to understand. At night, students went home to a series of brief podcasts, video lectures, and interactive readings from an e-book that Gupta had created to preview the various types of chemical reactions: synthesis, decomposition, single replacement, double replacement, combustion, redox, and complexation. During class, instead of listening to Gupta's lectures, students worked in teams to investigate and explain the reactions they witnessed in the experiments that Gupta had presented, or to identify the differences between net ionic equations and predict the type of reaction based on the equation.

Over a cup of coffee after the unit came to a close, Gupta reported with a smile that her students fared better than ever before on their unit tests. "What we ended up doing in class was more like what real-world scientists do: ask questions, make predictions, test assump-

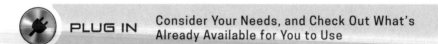

PLUG IN Consider Your Needs, and Check Out What's Already Available for You to Use

1. **Identify the friction points in your classroom.** What takes up time but doesn't include the payoff of student engagement and construction of knowledge? Are there any types of lessons you wish you could shift out of class?

2. **Make a wish list of student-centered lessons and activities** that really require face-to-face time to be effective. If you had all the time you would ever need, what kind of peer teaching and collaboration would you most want your students to have? Which activities and lessons seem to get cut most often when you run out of time?

3. **Watch a lesson about a subject you are interested in.** Start by searching the Khan Academy (https://www.khanacademy.org/), a nonprofit that publishes thousands of videos on a variety of subjects for grades K–12. Access is free, and each video lesson is about ten minutes long. There are thousands of videos on YouTube if you search [flipped lesson + subject], or peruse the YouTubeEDU channel (www.youtube.com/education).

tions, collaborate with a team of researchers," she said. "Every kid was engaged in figuring out how to apply what they had learned the night before. I loved it!"

Moving to a blended classroom offers countless opportunities for crafting instruction that engages students in real-world learning. Gupta's transformative experience is but one of many that we've heard from teachers who are thrilled with the flexibility and creative license that 1:1 technology affords them.

Thinking Through a Blended Unit: *Their Eyes Were Watching God*

Teachers: Diana Neebe and Fehmeen Picetti
Class: US Literature

When I first heard about the "flipped classroom," I thought it sounded like a great idea . . . for math and science. In those disciplines, it intuitively made sense to me for teachers to push their instruction to homework and pull in guided practice as classwork. But what about a discipline where the boundaries are a bit more fuzzy? I couldn't imagine the application being relevant or beneficial in an English class. For years, English teachers have refined the tried-and-true pattern of asking students to read at home and discuss in class. My own experiences in English class had been rooted in this seminar-style model. How could I possibly flip discussion? Or reading, for that matter?

I was unconvinced until I met my fourth-period class. They were an energetic crew with loads on their plates beyond academics. Most students in the class participated in sports after school, and many didn't get home to start homework until 8:00 p.m. on a regular basis. Between balancing multiple courses and fighting off exhaustion, required reading was often last on the list, and was either attempted by half-asleep teen zombies or replaced by a cursory glance at SparkNotes. At the start of the year, the majority of my fourth-period students were self-professed loathers of reading, and a few even mentioned to me with a grin that they had yet to complete an assigned novel for school.

At this point, I was fairly certain that the old "read at home, discuss in class" model would simply perpetuate a cycle of fake reading and yield a number of class periods that could only be described as "bull sessions." To complicate matters further, our department had just adopted a new text—a beautiful, compelling, and complex novel that had the power to challenge and enchant strong readers but the potential to leave struggling readers (like many of mine) in the dust. As I embarked on teaching Zora Neale Hurston's *Their Eyes Were Watching God* for the first time, I knew I would need to try something different.

Ultimately, my teaching partner, Fehmeen Picetti, and I settled on a meet-in-the-middle, blended (or partially flipped) approach. Some of our reading would be done at home, but most would take place in school. We applied the same strategy to discussion, writing, and direct instruction. At each step of the way, we made decisions about what "stayed" (in class) and what "went" (to homework) based on what we thought students needed the most help to complete. At the beginning of the unit, we knew they needed our support to understand the complex dialect in the novel and make sense of the characters. By the end of the unit, when they had a stronger grasp on the novel and were actually engaged enough in the story to read it independently, we focused our class time around face-to-face discussion and writing practice.

With Bloom's taxonomy firmly planted in our minds, we designed, produced, curated, and facilitated a fully blended unit that was custom-built for our students. What follows are the questions we had to think through along the way.

Step 1: Designing a Blended Unit

Jen and I have said it before, but I'll say it again: good teaching is good teaching. With or without technology, our end game is meaningful student learning, and that means we must start with the end in mind. Beyond the general questions about learning objectives and outcomes that we ask with any unit, Fehmeen and I wanted to consider how we could leverage technology to expand what we could each achieve in class. We wanted to move up Bloom's taxonomy, and from coverage to *uncoverage*.

In his book *Creating Significant Learning Experiences* (2003), Dee Fink expands on Bloom's taxonomy of higher-order thinking, and includes six elements that make for "significant learning" for today's young generation:

- Foundational knowledge: understanding and remembering information and ideas
- Application: critical, creative, and practical thinking skills, managing projects
- Integration: connecting ideas, people, and realms of life
- Human dimension: learning about oneself and others
- Caring: developing new interests, feelings, and values
- Learning how to learn: becoming a better student by inquiring about a subject and directing one's own learning (34–36)

In crafting this particular unit, we asked ourselves questions about our goals and how we could best help students reach them. We drew upon prompts posed by curriculum design classics (Wiggins and McTighe 2005; Fink 2003) as well as the central ideas presented in previous chapters of this book (engagement, collaboration, audience, differentiation, assessment, creativity), and each of us considered the following questions during our design process:

- What core skills will students need to be proficient in by the end of the unit? How can I draw upon their already-established reading, writing, and discussion skills to prepare them for new skills?

- What background knowledge will they need to be successful with this novel?
- How does this unit fit in with previous and forthcoming units of study? How can I help students integrate this unit into the broader arc of their learning and make explicit connections to other courses and disciplines?
- How will I authentically assess their learning, such that the audience matters and the skills are relevant to their lives beyond my class? Along the way, what formative data will I collect to help me understand my class's needs for differentiation?
- What do I anticipate will be the biggest hurdles for students in this unit? Where (and when) will they most need my support to be successful?
- What do I want students to do when they are together for face-to-face meetings? What is the role of our learning community in stretching their individual learning processes?
- What bigger life questions do I want students to grapple with? How do I hope this unit shapes my students as thinkers? As developing young adults?
- How can I best use our 1:1 technology to move myself out of the classroom as much as possible and build our face-to-face time so that it is student centered, collaborative, and hands-on? In other words, how do I make class time "less me, more them"?
- How can I best use our 1:1 technology to engage students outside of our face-to-face time? How will I foster connections between students beyond the four walls of our classroom?

One glance at this list may be enough to make your head spin. It would be a tall order to succeed in each of these areas, and I can honestly say in hindsight that we did not. But it is important to start with our ideal in mind. It helps with the design process and keeps us anchored during the unit itself. Then, we teach. We make adjustments, trim, adapt, and deal with all the curve balls that come with working with teenagers.

What follows is an overview of the completed unit for *Their Eyes Were Watching God* (see Figure 9.3). Each chunk of the unit is labeled with the corresponding category from either Bloom's or Fink's taxonomy. What we loved about this blended approach is that the work we did in class allowed us to increase the rigor of work done at home as the unit progressed, and by sustaining higher-order thinking at home, we were able to take students even further in class. Blending instruction, reading, and discussion made both our face-to-face time *and* our independent time more meaningful.

	IN CLASS—FACE-TO-FACE	OUT OF CLASS—FLIPPED
Week 1	**Building Foundational Knowledge** • Cultural Anthropology Museum Day: historical background for the setting of the novel through a QR code museum. • Preview African American English vernacular language of the novel by reading Hurston's short story, "Sweat," together as a class. • Practice discussion norms for face-to-face discussion to prepare students for flipped discussions.	**Connecting and Reflecting Personally** In the past, we used journals as "bell work," or warm-ups, for class. Instead, we flipped a series of reflective "connect" journals and made them homework for students to submit via our LMS. They wrote about everything, from the relationships in their lives to their hopes and dreams for the future, all as a way of prethinking about the themes in the novel. Writing about personal experiences is a great way to preview content while keeping that affective filter low.
Week 2	**Working on "Understanding"** • Guided, teacher-led reading of Chapters 1–4 using an audiobook to help tune the ear to the novel's vernacular language. • Modeled types of questions that strong readers ask before, during, and after reading, and demonstrated strategies for getting "unstuck."	**Building Understanding in Community** Typically, all of our discussion of a text would happen in class because we had no other viable option. At this point in the unit, we turned to online discussion boards to flip our conversations about the text out of class so that we would have time in class to lift the heaviest cognitive load: reading an unfamiliar text with complex diction.
Week 3	**Applying Skills in Community** • Students worked in reading teams to debrief the chapter from the night before, check for understanding, clarify confusion, and make connections. Teams discussed teacher-created "after-reading" questions. • Reading teams also previewed the next chapter by writing "before-reading" questions and starting the chapter.	**Building Understanding Independently** We knew we wanted to move our class sessions back to a student-centered model where they spent most of their face-to-face time working collaboratively. This meant that our guided reading instruction would have to happen at home. For Chapters 5–10, we recorded a series of "think-alouds" to accompany the readings, so that with each chapter, there was a passage that we unpacked and explicated in five minutes or less.

Figure 9.3 Blended Unit At-a-Glance

	IN CLASS—FACE-TO-FACE	OUT OF CLASS—FLIPPED
Weeks 4–5	**Analyzing and Evaluating in Community** • Reading teams generated and asked their own questions about the text. • Using the video think-alouds as a model, reading teams guided whole-class think-alouds of selected passages. • Students evaluated the novel through a Socratic seminar and creative project to consider contemporary connections to race in America and Hurricane Katrina.	**Applying Skills Independently** Gradually, we removed the scaffolds of teacher-guided reading and replaced the video think-alouds with the pared-down reading guides that students created in their reading teams. These guides prompted students to consider a series of before-, during-, and after-reading questions. They read the second half of the novel this way. On nights that students weren't reading, they previewed the contemporary content we would discuss and debate in class the next day.
Week 6	**Analyzing and Evaluating Independently (with Teacher and Peer Support)** • Essay drafting in class, with built-in teacher conferencing time and ongoing feedback through Google Docs. • Peer instruction through brainstorming buddies and editing partners.	**Reviewing Foundational Writing Skills** The culminating analytical assignment for the unit was to write a thematic response to the literature. To clear up time for students to draft their papers in class, we flipped our review of writing instruction and brainstorming time to homework. Students watched a series of mini-tutorials on thesis statements, body paragraph organization, introductions, and conclusions, and outlined their "plan of attack" for the next day.

Figure 9.3 Blended Unit At-a-Glance (continued)

Step 2: Curation and Organization

Ask any librarian: curation is an art. Regardless of whether you create your own resources or direct your students to resources that are already available, you will need a system for storing and organizing your flipped content.

For my unit on *Their Eyes Were Watching God*, I turned to my YouTube channel to curate all of my videos. I created a new playlist for the unit and added my own videos first. Then, I copied the URL for each of the preexisting videos and added those to my playlist as well. Now, when I go to teach that unit again, all I will have to do is pull up the playlist: all of my resources are in order and ready to go. For my nonvideo flipped resources, I leaned on my learning management system to host everything from discussion boards to audio recordings to image galleries. Just to stay organized, I have links to all of my resources saved in a spreadsheet in my Google Drive. Jen inspired me to organize that way when she showed me the spreadsheet she shares with her grade-level team.

Step 3: Production of Online Resources

To support the blended model of teaching and learning for this unit, Fehmeen and I knew we would have to create a handful of online resources for our students. For the contemporary connections, we planned to search for videos on Hurricane Katrina and remix a CNN documentary called *Black in America*. Those videos would be easy to find and just as easy to host on my YouTube channel as a part of our unit playlist. We felt fairly comfortable with the writing tutorials we would need for the end of the unit; I had already created three of the videos for my students over the course of the year and would only need to make the video on conclusions; I knew I could get my partner teacher to help me on our common prep, and we already had a couple of handouts on conclusions that we could work from. The most time-consuming part of gathering our "flipped" resources would be creating the video think-alouds for the early chapters in the novel.

Step 4: Facilitation

The last major piece to figure out in planning our blended unit for *Their Eyes Were Watching God* was how to facilitate and assess the work that students were doing at home. The biggest departure from our traditional teaching repertoire was the discussion board. Our students hadn't participated in one before, and we had no idea what to expect from them in terms of posts, replies, or even the potential for inappropriate or insensitive comments.

As a class, we started by brainstorming a list in class of what makes for a good discussion. Students said everything from "Ask interesting questions" to "Actually listen to what your peers are saying so that you are replying to their comments instead of just waiting to say your own." Our next step was to think about how these elements would transfer to an online forum. It seemed logical that we should practice what that would look like, and debrief. We set up a discussion board in class that day, and I gave the students twenty minutes to silently participate and think about the "dos and don'ts" of online discussion.

What follows is our top ten discussion board dos and don'ts, adapted in part from American University's online library resources (see Figure 9.4). For more on facilitating online discussions, see Chapter 3.

Step 5: Reflection

As with any unit, there is a lot I would go back and change in hindsight. But a lot about it worked, and I will gladly repeat those parts. By blending our instruction, Feehman and I know that our students did significantly more reading—some even reported that it was the first

Do think before you post. Complete the reading or preparation work before you write.
Do post your response early to give your classmates more time to reply. Check back later to see what comments have been added.
Do explain your opinion and use examples to help others understand your points.
Do post something that furthers the discussion and shows depth of thought. The best part of a discussion board is that you get lots of think time before you post. Use it.
Do reply to several of your classmates' posts, adding examples or asking questions.
Do remember that it is harder to tell when something is a joke online. Use humor sparingly.
Don't agree with everything you read. It makes for a really boring conversation. Politely disagree when you have a difference of opinion.
Don't reply to the same people each time. Try to bring in other voices.
Don't get personal. Focus your criticism on ideas and arguments, not on your classmates.
Don't bring the outside in. No inside jokes, references to people who aren't in the conversation, or comments you wouldn't say face-to-face.

Figure 9.4 Top Ten Discussion Board Dos and Don'ts for Students

"school book" they read in its entirety. They also complained less. The workload at home was less arduous, and they got the support they needed when they needed it. Often the flipped lessons took less time, which meant more sleep for my teen zombies. Most important, the process was more collaborative and more "about them." When the bell rang for class, students knew they would be working with peers to examine pieces of the novel, apply skills, ask questions, debate ideas, and draw contemporary connections . . . but they certainly wouldn't show up to listen to their teacher talk for fifty minutes or their classmates shoot the bull in response (see Figure 9.5). As far as I'm concerned, that's a huge success.

Behind the Scenes: The Nuts and Bolts of Blended Instruction

We know what you're thinking: that's great, but how do I actually *do* all of those steps in my own classroom? Let's go back and take a behind-the-scenes look at the nuts and bolts of blending instruction.

Figure 9.5 Diana's students make the most of face-to-face time.

Curating Your Resources

There are a few key principles to follow when curating online content to ensure that you won't have to start your entire search process all over again the next time you want to use that one perfect video.

Adopt a naming convention. Our "go-to" convention is Unit_Content_Source, where the unit is what we are teaching, the content title is a description of the file, and source is where we found it. For example, if we have an image for a video on conclusions with the title Writing_ConclusionFunnel_FlickrCC, we know just by looking at the file that it goes in our writing curriculum, it's an image of a funnel for teaching conclusions, and we found it on Flickr in their Creative Commons search area.

Create a master document. You might include a spreadsheet with links to online content and file names, a page on your blog or website, or an online curation site where you store bundles of resources. In all cases, it will be helpful to have a central hub that links you to all of the content you plan to use with a particular unit and includes titles and descriptions of those resources. There are fabulous curation tools available online (see Figure 9.6), which also allow teachers to connect with each other, share resources, and save time.

Creating Your Own Online Content

For any videos we create—the most frequent being a screencast recording of a slide deck—we go through the same process and follow similar design rules.

1. *Create a concept map.* What do you need your students to understand, and how can you explain that concept in a meaningful way? We like to start by determining a story arc, angle, or metaphor to connect students to content.

2. *Storyboard.* The slides in the slide deck are fabulous for this purpose. We label the slides with key points for starters, and then we go back and fill in with images, words, and details.

3. *Write the script.* We strongly suggest having a script. We know teachers who can record themselves talking off the cuff and have it sound totally polished. But most of us ramble without a script, and rambling leads to unnecessarily long videos.

Generally, any video that tops seven minutes is likely too long for a teenager's attention span. We use the slide notes section to write what we want to say about each slide in the presentation while we are recording.

4. *Design your visuals.* Our general rule for slides is that they need to be simple, clear, and contain an anchoring image to ground the story. We like to find images through photosforclass.com, and we use only images that are Creative Commons licensed, in the public domain, or photographs we took ourselves. Try to keep words to a minimum, unless you are analyzing a chunk of text. In that case, consider highlighting specific words and phrases with a contrasting color or font. If you are new to presentation design, we recommend picking up a copy of *Presentation Zen* (Reynolds 2012) or his follow-up book, *Presentation Zen Design* (Reynolds 2014). Slide:ology is also a great resource (Duarte 2008).

5. *Do a run-through.* Talk out your slides at least once before recording to make sure the images and script match, and that the words flow well.

6. *Record!* Launch your screencasting software, select the area of the slide on your screen, and click the red "record" button. When you are finished recording, check the video to make sure everything looks and sounds okay. Then post it where your students can find it, and link to it on your learning management system.

Video Curation	• YouTube.com (uploads from almost any production tool) • Vimeo.com (very easy to password protect)
Audio Curation	• SoundCloud.com • Spreaker.com
Image Curation	• Instagram.com • Flickr.com • Pinterest.com
Article Curation	• Diigo.com • Evernote.com
Central Hub	• Online curation sites such as Dropmark.com, BagTheWeb.com, Pearltrees.com, or Bundlr.com • Classroom blog or website • School website or learning management system • Shareable spreadsheet or document, like Google Sheets • Educlipper.net

Figure 9.6 Staying Organized

If you want to get more sophisticated, consider taking a short course in video editing. You can also search for video-editing tutorials on YouTube specific to the software you have available. Being able to edit your videos can help you feel more confident about making them because you know you will be able to fix any flubs you make while recording. Also, remember that your videos do not have to be perfect to be effective. Your live classroom teaching is not perfect, so give yourself permission to make flawed videos as you learn more about the process. And remember that videos you create are not the only source for content material. The chart in Figure 9.7 has other ideas based on your objective.

TEACHER OBJECTIVE	CURRENT LIST OF TOOLS
Bring Outside Experts In Much of the content you may want to create is already available from other sources, and often is very high quality	**Search** • YouTube • Nat Geo • PBS, Smithsonian • Bio.com • Discover Education • History Channel • Khan Academy • Bozeman Science • TED
Embed Your Lesson into Preexisting Content Fortunately, technology has evolved to equip teachers with the power to annotate preexisting videos. It's just like what you would have done while showing a video in class: pushing "pause" and pointing out an important tidbit before moving on. Now you can embed those salient points and checks for understanding right in the video as voice-overs, quizzes, and text.	**Remix** • EdPuzzle (free web-based software) • YouTube Video Editor (free web-based software)

Figure 9.7 Flipped Lesson Objectives and Tools

➡ For an updated list of our favorite tools, check out pluginpowerup.com.

TEACHER OBJECTIVE	CURRENT LIST OF TOOLS
Quick Mini-Lesson Record the action on your computer or tablet screen with your voice (but not your face) included so that students can watch at home or at school. Some apps give you a blank whiteboard or image to "ink" on while you record your voice. This type of video is particularly effective for demonstrating process instead of content.	**Screencast** • Screencast-o-matic (free web-based software) • QuickTime Player (built into every Mac) • Explain Everything, ShowMe, Educreations (iPad apps) • Snagit (screencast software for Mac, PC, Chrome) • Jing (free screenshot/screencast software) • Screenflow for Mac (free downloadable software) • Movenote (record yourself giving presentations, multiplatform)
Deliver Content or a Lecture Record your voice over a slide presentation you already use so students can watch it at their own pace. The easiest way to do this is with screencasting software while you progress through the slides and narrate them. We use the "presenter's notes" section of the slide deck to write out our script.	**Recorded Slide Deck** • Google Presentations • PowerPoint • Keynote • Prezi
Grab Students' Attention Make a creative version of your content using animation or stop motion to grab students' attention or show how a process works. (Also great for student projects.)	**Animation** • GoAnimate! • Stop Motion HD App • Hyperlapse • Lego Movie Maker • Telegami
Polished Tutorial Sometimes, there's a lesson you know your students will come back to over and over again. When you want to create something really impressive that you know you can get a lot of mileage out of, try cutting together multiple videos, or integrating video and still pictures for a more movielike effect.	**Video Editing** • WeVideo (free web-based software) • Camtasia Studio (paid software download) • Pixorial (online editing; great for Chromebooks) • Apple iMovie for Mac • Windows Movie Maker for PC

Figure 9.7 Flipped Lesson Objectives and Tools (continued)

Common Questions About Blended Instruction
Isn't "blended instruction" just code for "go home and watch videos"?

Understandably, any radical shift in how we approach teaching and learning will spark questions and doubts. When we disrupt the working order of "how things have always been," we naturally wonder what the trade-offs will be and how we'll navigate the shift. We had our doubts, too, and have included them throughout the remainder of the chapter.

Our first doubt was this: isn't blended instruction just code for "go home and watch videos"? No more than class time is just code for "sit in your seat and listen to your teacher lecture." We can—and should—vary the modes of instruction we provide for students, both in class and at home. For some classes, video instruction at home may be the most effective means of communicating content, but those videos will likely look different from each other. For other classes, like Diana's, a mixed-methods approach works best: some video, some audio, some discussion, and some traditional homework assignments (such as reading). Each teacher will have to be the judge of which tool is right for the job.

Regardless of what the homework looks like, the underlying goal of blending instruction is to free up valuable face-to-face time for collaboration, peer instruction, differentiation, and increased, personalized contact time with each student (Bergmann, Overmyer, and Willie 2011).

When will I have time to create all these flipped resources?

It's true that creating flipped resources, whether videos, podcasts, discussion boards, or interactive texts takes time. A lot of time. And there is a learning curve that comes with any new software program we use. But creating resources is an investment: you pay up front and accrue the benefits over time. We would not recommend making a set of mini-lecture videos for a unit you never plan to teach again or for a concept you don't plan to return to. We invest our energy in resources we know our students will return to this year and that we are likely to reuse next year. We also consider how other teachers might use the same resource and benefit students beyond our own classes.

So, when will you have time to create these resources? The answer is *over time*. Diana made her first two writing mini-lessons at the beginning of the year for one unit; then she added to it over the course of the school year. Jen has been known to use an app to record her lesson while she does it live, and then use it for a flipped lesson the next year. (It also helps students who were absent.) Some teachers make a set of videos during a break or over the summer and wait until their next break to add to their playlists. Other teachers use only videos that already exist online for the first year or so and then dabble in creating their own resources once they have seen the process work for their students.

Doesn't all this online teaching make me kind of replaceable?

We actually think all this online teaching makes us less replaceable. Try this: The next time you are about to teach a concept, start by asking your students to do an online search about that concept. Ask one of them to read the definition they found or share some of the information they encountered in the search. Then ask the student to connect it to something else you have studied or apply it to a new situation. We find that most of the time, our students can't connect and apply the information they find in their searches without our scaffolding and guidance. Jen likes to joke that this is job security before she goes on with her lesson. At the end of the period, she circles back to that found definition and asks students to read it again. "Oh, this makes sense now" is the common response.

Think back to the quote from Bowen (2012) earlier in the chapter—"The talking head is dead." Students can find content with or without us. We don't need to spend our precious face-to-face time delivering information that they can find elsewhere. Rather, the more we make class time student centered instead of teacher centered, the more valuable that time becomes. We spend our class time making sure students have the context and scaffolding to understand their online learning. We become irreplaceable and our students learn more when we create authentic, engaging experiences in a dynamic learning community that students couldn't get anywhere else.

Shooting for the Moon: A Final Thought

Advances in technology are never easy. Transition always takes time. Imagine what the streets of New York were like a hundred years ago as horse-drawn wagons shared the roads with early automobiles. For a few decades they coexisted uneasily, and then gradually, the horse-drawn carts became fewer and trucks took over deliveries. But both the wagons and the trucks needed drivers. It was the horses that were replaced, not the humans. We absolutely still need teachers, but we need teachers who can cope with change, adapt to new pedagogy, and creatively innovate their way through the next few decades of transition.

Back in 1913, just before those trucks took over from the horses, Thomas Edison said this to a newspaper reporter from the *New York Dramatic Mirror*: "'Books,' declared the inventor with decision, 'will soon be obsolete in the public schools. Scholars will be instructed through the eye. It is possible to teach every branch of human knowledge with the motion picture. Our school system will be completely changed inside of ten years.'"

Using 1:1 programs *does* have the potential to completely change our school system inside of ten years. We have seen far more change in pedagogy and instruction after the introduction of 1:1 devices than we did from rolling in a television cart or strapping a screen to the wall. Edison, it's worth noting, was looking forward to this change—but Edison could walk into many of our classrooms today and not see much difference. Diana teaches at a school founded in 1898, and in a brick building that has been standing since that first school year. If Edison walked the halls without students there, he could think nothing had changed in the world of education. Bring in the students and their devices, though, and he would see the beginning of what he had hoped for: an education system that is dynamic, visual, technologically driven, and open to innovation.

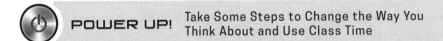

POWER UP! Take Some Steps to Change the Way You Think About and Use Class Time

1. **Expand your lesson library by curating multimedia content** to accelerate or remediate instruction. Think of a topic that you currently deliver in a "traditional" way. Now go online and look for other means to the same end. Are there YouTube videos, Ted Talks, photographs, audiobooks, apps, or games that communicate what your go-to lesson does? Start a spreadsheet of links for easy repeat use, or create a YouTube channel of your own with saved playlists.

2. **It's time to get brave and test your skills at creating your very own flipped lesson.** It can be a one-minute screencast showing students how to submit work on your LMS, or even a brief refresher on a couple of equations to help students study for an upcoming algebra test. Plan your content in advance, write out your script, and click "record." See the tools listed in Figure 9.7 for software suggestions.

3. **What are you going to do differently** in class once you have moved some of your instruction into the homework space? Think through a unit you are planning with blended instruction in mind. How can you move understanding and remembering tasks to homework and move practice, analysis, and synthesis into your class time?

CHAPTER 10
Becoming a Connected Educator

Con·nec·tion (n): a relationship in which a person, thing, or idea is linked or associated with something or someone else.

Teacher: Diana Neebe
Class: Twitter

Toward the middle of the second semester, as my mind was gearing up to plan capstone projects and write the final exam, my school brought in author Alfie Kohn to speak about homework and assessment overload. It's no secret that high school students in the Silicon Valley (or anywhere, really) are stressed out, overscheduled, and often overassessed. As I listened to Kohn, all I could think about was that I was guilty as charged. That final I was about to write? Just another exam in students' battery of high-stakes tests. At the break, I sought out a couple of like-minded colleagues to reflect on an idea for revamping my assessments.

"What do you think about doing a digital portfolio instead of the regular final?" I asked.

"That could be cool," one colleague agreed.

"Ooh, I like that!" my partner teacher chimed in.

"They could even use it for college apps if they wanted," added the college counselor.

"So," the voice of reason asked, "how do we do that?"

All eyes turned to me, the "tech mentor," in hopes of a solution. But, truth be told, I had never assigned digital portfolios before and had no idea where to start. My network at school was enthusiastic and supportive, but we didn't have the answers. I knew then that I would need to learn more, but who could help me?

Later that afternoon, I posted an appeal to my colleagues on Twitter and tagged my plea (see Figure 10.1) for help to three different professional learning networks (PLNs) that I actively follow: California Ed Chat (#CAEdChat), English Chat (#EngChat), and Ettipad (#Ettipad). I wrote, "Looking for resources on building digital portfolios with my 9th–10th English Language Arts students like they do at High Tech High. Ideas?"

Before the start of the next school day, I had a slew of how-to blog posts, sample portfolios, rubrics, and resources from colleagues everywhere, from the next town all the way to Australia. Thanks to my tech network, my digital portfolio alternative final exam went off

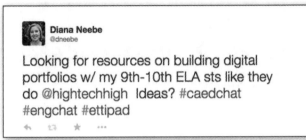

Figure 10.1 Diana tweets for help from her PLN.

without a hitch. How comforting to know that a mere 140 characters away, a brain trust of fellow educators is ready to share their work and offer their wisdom to us!

The Power of Loose Links

As we mentioned in the acknowledgments, this book exists in large part because we are connected to a wider community of excellent teachers who are creatively transforming their classrooms. The professional learning we have gained from the generous teachers on social media networks helped us innovate in our own classrooms and take on responsibilities for mentoring our colleagues. You are holding this book because we learned enough to write it.

In *The Tipping Point*, Malcolm Gladwell (2000) writes about the power of loose links, the benefits we get from being loosely connected to a wide network of people. Maybe you need a job or you're looking for a new babysitter or you wonder who has tried that new restaurant in the neighborhood. You reach out to your professional or personal contacts, colleagues, friends, or neighbors—someone can probably help. Now apply that network idea to your teaching. You still have the colleagues, but your friends and neighbors probably can't help you figure out how to share a Google Doc with your students or decide which blogging platform will work best for your class. What if your colleagues don't know either? You need a wider network.

Plenty of other professions subscribe to the networking philosophy of doing business. But for some reason, teaching has historically been one of the most isolated careers. It's quite the paradox when you think about it. In a profession where the typical secondary teacher sees about 180 students each day, isolation and alienation rank among the top reasons for early attrition (Dodor and Hausafus 2010). Back in the mid-1980s, researcher Dan Lortie published an often-cited sociological study of the teaching life, describing schools as being organized like egg crates, in which the "architecture ... of schools reinforce the divisions that physically separate teachers" (quoted in Flinders 1988, 19). We can recall entire school days going by without interacting with another adult. Many of us may be the only teacher at a particular grade level or the only one focusing on a particular course, leaving us with little opportunity to plan curriculum or talk shop with a colleague down the hall.

Yet we also know the power of participating in supportive communities of practice (Lave and Wenger 1991; Wenger 1998). It's why attending conferences leaves us on a learning high, or why reading a great professional development text makes us feel empowered to sharpen our skills and expand our repertoires. At the core, communities of practice link us to others who share our occupation and can lighten the load of the work we do. It comes as no surprise, then, that these communities of practice have shifted over time and are found in increasing numbers online (Hur and Brush 2009). Virtual communities, such as the professional learning networks we have found on Twitter, can transcend the rigid structures of school buildings, bells, and teaching assignments to create the loose links among educators that were not possible before. Our friend and colleague Adam Bellow reflects on this concept (see Figure 10.2).

Adam Bellow reflects: I was reminiscing with Tom Whitby (one of the founders of the popular #EdChat on Twitter) at a conference recently about what it was like "in the early days" of Twitter—the days when I would read every tweet that had the word *education* in it or *edtech* and then go to sleep and scroll back a few tweets to see what I had missed. It seems that today—only a handful of years later—we are in a totally different world. There is so much incredible information from so many connected educators who are looking to connect, share, and learn that it can feel a bit overwhelming—especially to those getting started today. That said, I truly believe it is better to drink from the firehouse than wander an endless desert looking for sustenance, which is what I felt like I was doing before I became connected. I must have reinvented the wheel every week in my classroom, and didn't even realize it.

All this goes to say that there is incredible power in becoming a connected educator. Whatever your level of experience, there is always something to bring to or get from the conversations. Imagine the best faculty room you have ever been to. Or dare I say it is far better than that—it is the faculty room you have always dreamed of: people lining up to help you, support your projects and passions, and play the devil's advocate role when your ideas permit some workshopping. There is much written about how to be a connected educator—people talk about the role of a "lurker" and then slowly becoming engaged in the conversation. I think there is a lot of merit in that. Be present. Drink from the "fountain of knowledge"—and be sure to contribute when you are ready or asked to.

Some people have questioned how much time I spend in connected spaces, whether that be face-to-face environments like EdCamps or conferences or online ones like Facebook, Twitter Chats, Voxer, or even my own creations, eduTecher and eduClipper. My answer has been the same for the past few years and it is quite true. The time and effort I put into building my personal learning networks is far surpassed by what I get from the group. It has made me a better educator, a better learner, and a better human being.

Figure 10.2 Adam Bellow: Founder and President of eduTecher

Often when we share something new with colleagues, or present at a conference, people ask us, "How do you know all this?" It's not a secret; we have a superpower. We call it social media, and it really works. Social media provides us with a way to access the hive mind of educational innovators. We learn from them, test ideas in our own classrooms, and share what we discover. Chris Anderson, founder of TED, calls this "crowd-accelerated innovation" (2010). When innovators have access to each other, they create better and faster. This inspirational process happened in Italy during the Renaissance, and it is happening today in education because social media is connecting teachers and administrators who want to provide students with the best possible educational experience. See Figure 10.3 for author Troy Hicks's reflections.

Troy Hicks reflects: Since I began connecting with other educators on Twitter, I have participated in some great hashtag-based chat sessions, ongoing dialogue with individuals and small groups, and been able to share my own work more widely. Most important, Twitter allows me to stay in touch with K–12 colleagues who are teaching digital reading and writing every day, finding out more about their curriculum, teaching, and students' successes.

For instance, Gerard Dawson (@GerardDawson3), a high school English teacher from New Jersey, contacted me this past April just to say thank you for the many examples I had shared in one of my books. Since that time, we have exchanged numerous tweets and e-mails where he has shared exemplary student work with me, and we had a conversation via Skype on how he could try to integrate web-based RSS reading [see Appendix C] into his students' independent reading time. We continue to communicate, and perhaps someday we will write a blog post, article, or chapter about our collaboration. Even if we don't write about our collaboration, I am a much better teacher and teacher educator for having spent the time getting to know Gerard and learning about his classroom.

Thus, when I begin and end my professional development sessions, I share my Twitter name and e-mail address with teachers in the audience, and I asked them to please stay in touch. I am thankful to teachers like Gerard—and dozens of others—who take up my invitation and choose to continue the conversation. Without their insights, examples, and questions, I would not be able to engage in the research, writing, and teaching that I do. For that, I am thankful to the network of educators that Twitter has enabled me to grow.

Figure 10.3 Troy Hicks: Author and Associate Professor of English at Central Michigan University

Moreover, as Meenoo Rami (2014) explains in her book *Thrive*, in an age in which "we expect our students to be active, responsible, and independent digital and global citizens," it is particularly critical that we act as "models for them" (16). We couldn't agree more. See Figure 10.4 for additional insights from Rami.

Jen's Story: Getting Connected

I joined Twitter in 2009. The first person I followed was my friend Hillary, who was a deejay for a local radio station. A few weeks later I presented at a conference and met several amazing educators, and I added them to the list of people I was following. Mark Wagner was among those I met. At the time, he was the coordinator for the Google Certified Teacher program. Because I was following Mark, I heard about the application for the Google Teacher Academy coming up in July 2011.

Meenoo Rami reflects: In an ever increasingly interconnected and interdependent world, our students need us to model the empathy, curiosity, and tenacity required to solve complex problems. We don't need our students to wait till they graduate to begin their work in the world; our very classrooms can be places where they hone these skills. Our students often need more than us to do the work they want to do. By opening them up to our network and teaching them to connect with others in doing meaningful work, we're helping them launch their own networks. Our work as teachers essentially is to become unnecessary. We need to empower students to locate resources, connect with collaborators, and begin the work they're meant to do in this world. Our passion and commitment to our students' independence and agency will ultimately be the force behind rethinking and reshaping our practices.

Figure 10.4 Meenoo Rami: Author of *Thrive*

At the same conference where I met Mark in 2009, I also learned about Prezi, which was then a very new kind of web-based presentation tool. I wrote a blog post about how the use of Prezi was spreading at my school. I tweeted a link to the post, and the folks at Prezi saw it. They retweeted the link to my post, and for the first time my fledgling blog saw visitors from all over the world.

Now I see and often respond to teachers asking all sorts of questions on a daily basis. I've recommended memoirs that work well for middle school students, books to help content-area teachers prepare for Common Core reading expectations, and blogging platforms for a fifth-grade class, as well as which restaurants to try in San Diego. The people, information, and opportunities I have found through Twitter have made me a better teacher and a more informed educator.

Diana's Story: Staying Connected

I joined Twitter in 2012 because Jen told me to. (This is actually how a surprising number of my experiences with technology begin.) One day in November, we were waiting for a colleague to join our Google Hangout so that we could plan our upcoming presentation for the National Council of Teachers of English (NCTE). I was excited about the conference, which was just a few weeks away. I couldn't wait for the opportunity to reconnect with colleagues from other schools and other states with whom I could discuss new ideas, challenge assumptions, and explore the possibilities of teaching English language arts in a twenty-first-century classroom.

As Jen and I made small talk, she asked me how things were going. There was no way around it: I was frustrated. I explained to Jen that I felt isolated and alone when it came to teaching with 1:1. I loved my English department colleagues dearly, and I knew that they pushed me to grow in many other ways. But I was often considered far "outside the box" for my incorporation of technology. As a result, I did not have anybody to collaborate with to create a technology-rich English curriculum. I was tired of going it alone, experimenting with ways to use the iPad in my classroom all by myself.

Jen's response was pretty firm. She told me that my school colleagues were great but simply couldn't be the extent of my network. It was time for me to get on Twitter. I was resistant at first, thinking that Twitter was where people posted celebrity gossip or stupid cat videos from YouTube. "Are you kidding me?" Jen interjected. "Just trust me. I'll show you." I clicked over to start a screen share, and Jen walked me through the steps of creating an account, adding a bio, and getting rid of the telltale newbie egg picture that automatically pops up when you first hatch an account. By the time our colleague joined the hangout a few minutes later, I was already following my first ten people on Twitter. Needless to say, I'm now very glad our colleague was running late that day. (See Figure 10.5 for J R Ginex-Orinion's thoughts on being a connected educator.)

> **J R Ginex-Orinion reflects:** The educators on Twitter that I've connected with in the past two years have been instrumental in shaping my philosophies and attitude toward approaching my profession. I can honestly say that I am a better educator today because of Twitter. And not because I hear about the newest applications or technologies I can use in my classroom. It's the ongoing, meaningful *conversations* I have with fellow teachers that make Twitter a powerful tool for professional development in education.

Figure 10.5 J R Ginex-Orinion: Digital Learning Coach and Cofounder of #CAEdchat

Creating Loose Links
Getting Started: Some Practical Tips

We know that becoming a connected educator is really helpful for those making the transition to teaching in a 1:1 setting. This book is just the tip of the iceberg of what you can learn from colleagues through loose links on social media. If the fifty most interesting educators you know were going to be speaking at a conference in your town, wouldn't you go to hear them and meet them? What if you could follow them all on Twitter or Google? You get to pick whom you follow, and they don't have to follow you back for you to read what they post. People you admire in education are already online. Teachers who teach the same material you do are already there too. They are sharing and collaborating to make themselves better teachers. You will find networks of educators ranging from art teachers and AP history teachers to high school Mandarin teachers, as well as information about local education camps and national conferences.

We are active on both Twitter and Google, but some teachers tell us they have a strong preference for one or the other. It's fine to start with whatever makes the most sense to you. Social media networks will ebb and flow throughout your teaching career; the important part is finding a way that works for you to be connected to a larger community of educators. We hope what follows will help. Our advice is aimed at new Twitter users, but much of it will apply to any social media account.

In Figure 10.6, we illustrate a sample Tweet. In addition, consider the following crash course on Twitter lingo and how to get started.

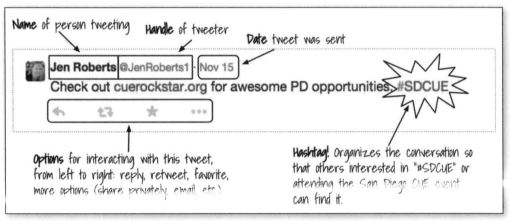

Figure 10.6 Understanding the anatomy of a tweet can help you get started with Twitter.

Create an account: Choose your handle (online name) carefully. It will represent you professionally online. For Twitter, especially, we recommend selecting a short handle, because your name will be included in any tweet that is quoted or retweeted, and you get only 140 characters.

Add a profile photo: We are always wary of profiles with no photo because they are often associated with spammers. If you want to make connections online, you need to add a picture to your account. It does not have to be your face, if that makes you nervous at first, but pick an image that represents you. If you are active across several networks (Twitter, Facebook, Google), try to use the same profile picture. It will help your followers know they are following the same person.

Write your bio: Many new users skip the biographical information, but people are unlikely to follow you back if you don't say anything about yourself. We suggest mentioning at least your role in education and your geographic area—a city or state works well. Including some topics you are interested in helps, too. We often look to connect with colleagues in teaching contexts similar to ours (for example, 1:1, humanities).

Edit your notification settings: Most social media platforms have a plethora of notification options. Unfortunately, the default setting for all of them is usually "on." Navigate into your account settings and look for notifications. We suggest you leave on only those that let you know when someone specifically mentions you or sends you a direct message. Most of the rest will probably just clog your inbox, but read the options carefully and decide what works for you.

Check your privacy settings: Many users initially want to set their accounts to be private while they test the waters. We recommend you keep your Twitter and Google accounts public, so that others can follow you and see the things you share. It is very difficult to be part of the larger educational community online if your account is private. If you keep your account professional and avoid mentioning specific personal details, there won't be a reason to make it private.

Play it safe: Twitter is public, and anyone can see your posts if they know what to search for—even if they are not actually following you. Don't post anything that you wouldn't say publicly in a professional setting. Avoid complaining, and focus on the positive. Never post about specific students or colleagues. When in doubt, follow the social media guidelines of your employer.

Learn the lingo: Social media has definitely added some new words to our vocabulary. Part of the reason we lurk at first is to get used to the genre of social media. Often things are abbreviated because characters are limited. We've included a chart of some of the current popular abbreviations (see Figure 10.7). Hashtags are a way of adding a short link to a tweet that will connect your message to similar messages. Try clicking on a tweet that has a word with a # in front. Click the tagged word and it should give you a list of content with the same tag.

Building Your Network: Figuring Out Whom to Follow

Start with people and organizations you already know. Most social media platforms will recommend people to follow as soon as you sign up. This is typically a rather random list of news organizations, celebrities, and advertisers who may or may not interest you. You do not have to follow any of the recommended people. Instead, search for the names of some people you know professionally, such as the authors of a recent book you've been reading. Then, look into the professional organizations you may belong to and the educational organizations you trust. You can also allow the site to have access to your e-mail contacts. It will look to see which of your existing contacts are already on that social network, and then you can follow people you know.

TWITTER LINGO IN PLAIN ENGLISH	
#	Hashtag: A "tag" to organize conversations by topic or theme. See Figure 10.10 for a list of common educational hashtags.
@	Public Mention: If you start a tweet with @ it gets seen only by people who follow both you and them. Use .@ to mention someone and have all your followers automatically see it.
Retweet	Reposting someone else's message to your timeline so your followers can see it too. Use the circular arrows to retweet.
Quote Tweet	You can also quote a tweet and add your own thoughts to it. Use the same circular arrows icon but choose "quote tweet."
Direct Message	A private message between one or more users who follow each other. You can also set your account to accept direct messages from anyone (not recommended).

Figure 10.7 Common Twitter Terminology with Definitions

The stereotype that social media is just for people who want to follow celebrities is only partially true. We follow celebrities, but our celebrities are the educational rock stars who are innovating in their classrooms. We get starstruck when meeting our educational heroes, and we get to learn from them all the time. Find your educational heroes and follow them. A good starting goal for any network is to follow at least fifty people. Don't expect that they will all follow you back, and don't worry about that.

The idea of loose links inspired David Jakes to start a blog connecting educators in conversation about pedagogy and technology (www.strengthofweakties.org). We don't know David very well. We follow him on Twitter, read the articles he shares, and see him at conferences from time to time. But we do know that he is a leader in educational innovation, and we are certain that we want to learn more from him. The good news is that we know how to find him and the countless other leaders in our profession who are sharing their research and writing online. Figure 10.8 shows some of the folks such as David whom we were thrilled to follow from the start, and other organizations that would make great additions to your professional learning network. For even more suggestions about which leaders and organizations to add to your learning network, visit pluginpowerup.com.

Education Leader	You Know Him/Her From . . .	You Can Find Him/Her @
Adam Bellow	Adam Bellow, founder and president of eduTecher and eduClipper and our favorite keynote presenter	@adambellow
Kylene Beers	Author and adolescent literacy expert. A great source for reason and wisdom.	@KyleneBeers
Jerry Blumengarten	Fantastic curator of teaching resources and part of the #Edchat team	@Cybraryman1
Lisa Dabbs	Educator, blogger, and the founder of #NTChat (New Teacher Chat)	@teachingwithsoul
Kelly Gallagher	High school English teacher, author, and literacy expert	@KellyGToGo
Troy Hicks	Associate professor of English, author of several books on digital literacy, and director of the Chippewa River Writing Project	@hickstro
Carol Jago	Literacy expert, author, and past president of NCTE	@CarolJago
David Jakes	Digital strategist and designer for CannonDesign and The Third Teacher Plus	@djakes
Chris Lehman	Founding principal of the Science Leadership Academy	@chrislehmann
Dan Meyer	Math teacher and Stanford researcher studying math education	@ddmeyer
Diana Neebe	Author, teacher, ISTE Outstanding Young Educator, Google Certified Teacher	@dneebe
Meenoo Rami	Educator, author of *Thrive*	@MeenooRami
Julie Ramsay	Educator, author of *Can We Skip Lunch and Keep Writing?*	@JulieDRamsay
Jen Roberts	Author, teacher, blogger, Google Certified Teacher	@JenRoberts1
Sir Ken Robinson	Internationally recognized leader in the development of creativity, innovation, and human resources in education and in business	@SirKenRobinson
Eric Sheninger	Principal, author of *Digital Leadership*	@NMHS_Principal
David Theriault	Innovative English teacher, reflective blogger, and a #CAedchat moderator	@davidtedu

Figure 10.8 Jumpstart Your Network

Tom Whitby	Founder of #EdChat, education professor	@TomWhitby
Grant Wiggins	Author of Understanding by Design and others	@GrantWiggins
Rick Wormeli	Author on differentiation, assessment	@RickWormeli2
Organization	**You Know It For. . . .**	**You Can Find It @**
ACTFL	American Council on the Teaching of Foreign Languages	@ACTFL
ASCD	Learning, teaching, and leading in education	@ascd
CUE	Educational technology leaders and professional development	@cueinc
Edudemic	Education technology tips for teachers	@Edudemic
Edutopia	George Lucas Foundation for Education	@edutopia
ISTE	International Society for Technology in Education	@iste
Khan Academy	Nonprofit dedicated to free online education	@KhanAcademy
KQED MindShift	From NPR and KQED, trends in education	@MindShiftKQED
NAfME	National Association for Music Education	@nafme
NCSS	National Council for the Social Studies	@NCSSNetwork
NCTE	National Council of Teachers of English	@ncte
NCTM	National Council of Teachers of Mathematics	@nctm
NSTA	National Science Teachers Association	@nsta
NY Times Education	*New York Times* blog for news in teaching	@NYTimesLearning
Smithsonian Edu	Educational resources from the Smithsonian Institution	@smithsonianedu
STEM Connector	"One-stop shop" for STEM information	@STEMConnector
TED Talks Education	"Ideas worth spreading" about education	@TED_ED

Figure 10.8 Jumpstart Your Network (continued)

Now What? Start Reading.

Twitter starts off like a stream. As people post their thoughts, articles, and ideas, tweets will begin to populate your feed. The more people you follow, the more tweets you will see and the more insights you will be able to access. But as you start to follow more people, the stream will become a river. You don't need to absorb all of it. You don't need to see or read every tweet that goes by. In fact, you really can't. For now, just check it a couple of times a day. Leave it open on your computer at work and see what has popped up every now and then. Before long, someone will share something you will want to know more about.

 PLUG IN   Get Yourself Online and Start Building Your Network

1.   **Sign up for a Twitter account.** Go back through our "getting started" list and set up your Twitter handle, biography, picture, and notification settings.

2.   **Start by adding twenty people you know** or know of. These could be personal contacts, colleagues, organizations, or authors you read. (Bonus: you get two obvious choices—@jenroberts1 and @dneebe.)

3.   **Add ten more people you want to know** through connections to the first twenty. This is the process of creating loose links, and how your network grows.

Joining the Conversation

It may be a cliché, but our profession needs your voice in the conversation about teaching and learning in the age of 1:1 computing. As educators, we need to share what's working and work together to solve what isn't. That process can happen only if dedicated teachers come to the table to offer their ideas, experiments, victories, and challenges. We want you to be connected for your own sake; we want you to join the conversation for the sake of the group.

We know what you're thinking: *When will I have time for this?* Just like changing an exercise routine or deciding to cook more frequently, adding another daily "to-do" can seem daunting at first. We both went through the early phase of asking ourselves how we could possibly squeeze in one more thing. Making regular connections to our PLN is a time commitment. But we find so much value in the connections and information from our social media that we don't mind giving it a few minutes of our day.

In their book *Reading in the Wild* (2013), Miller and Kelly remind us about the power of creatively using "edge time." Inevitably, we have a handful of otherwise-unused minutes sprinkled into our day—time on the edge of time. Sometimes we snag a couple of minutes to check in with our PLN while waiting for the department meeting to start, or for a child's soccer practice to end, or for the pot of water to come to a boil for a mug of tea. It's a few minutes here and a few minutes there, but it's actually enough to keep us connected. On days when we feel like we could really use the support, or have a great story to offer to our PLN, we carve out ten minutes or so to read Twitter as our morning paper or to get caught up with our cyber-colleagues during a prep period in the middle of the day.

Although Twitter has become one of our primary sources of professional development, we certainly didn't start off by regularly participating in chats and rapidly tweeting quotes during conferences. We started off by lurking, but our participation grew from there. In Figure 10.9, Alyssa Black shares some of the baby steps you might take toward full participation in the online professional community of teachers.

Alyssa Black reflects: I was a connected educator before I even knew what the term meant, and it was a powerful factor in my decision to seriously pursue education as a career. I harbored this fear that being an educator was going to be too solitary and that I wouldn't be creative enough or confident enough to provide for the students in my room. My mentality began to shift almost immediately when a teacher I was observing sent me to Twitter to browse educational hashtags, where people all over the world are sharing, brainstorming, and providing strength to each other almost instantaneously. Above all, these educators are learners first. They embody the growth mind-set we want for our students, and are endlessly giving each other ideas, thoughts, tricks, and tips.

I'm not exaggerating when I say Twitter is where I learned that everyone has something to contribute and that we as educators can do more if we do it together. Connecting with teachers in this way pushes my thinking, and my teaching, far beyond where I ever thought it could go and challenges me to be better. I'm learning how to ask the right questions, share my thoughts, and surround myself with positivity. Nothing is more valuable to me as an educator.

Figure 10.9 Alyssa Black: Preservice Teacher

Step 1: Lurking

Just as people learning a new language go through a silent period, most educators spend a period of time observing online before beginning to post regularly. We fully support the silent period; this is a great time to work on settling into a routine around reading professional development materials. When we first got on Twitter, we each observed a period of radio silence in which we read ferociously and learned the ropes. But at some point, we jumped into the conversation. So, go ahead and lurk around a bit, but push yourself to work toward engagement.

Step 2: Responding

The next step is to let others know you are there. If you see a post you agree with, that intrigues you, or that you don't want to forget, click the "favorites" button at the bottom of the tweet.

The person posting will be notified that you marked it as a favorite, and that person may respond by following you back. Go through this process a few times and you will start to grow your network.

Another easy way to join the conversation is by retweeting or replying to the posts other people make. Add your ideas, resources, or links to other pieces you've read that might support or sustain the discussion.

Step 3: Asking a Question

As Diana did when she was getting ready to start a new project, post a question for your PLN about an upcoming unit or assignment that you might like some help constructing. Be sure to hashtag the question so that it is directed toward people who likely are interested in similar topics. Remember, collaboration comes in all forms.

Step 4: Sharing a Success

Try posting about something great happening in your classroom or a link to a useful article you read. Add a hashtag related to the topic. Popular ones are #eduwin for classroom successes and #edchat for anything educationally related. Sometimes you'll end up with a great idea or a fantastic lesson purely because of your online network. Not everyone sticks with social media. But we know that those who do almost always have a story about a moment of serendipity, finding just the right resource at just the right time, connecting with someone they admire, or just connecting with someone they can collaborate with. Making social media into your superpower can take persistence, but we think it is very worth it.

Perhaps our favorite aspect of social media is when we meet people we follow and people who follow us in person. We often get to skip right to our shared interests because we already know each other through the loose connection started online. Those connections are strengthened in person, so that online acquaintances quickly become friends. Over time, we can leverage those loose links to advance our practice and expand our influence. Recently, Jen met with her son's first-grade teacher and offered to help him set up some video calls with other classrooms. He said, "Oh, yeah, you must know a lot of teachers in San Diego." Jen was surprised that he was thinking so locally when she was already calculating time zones globally. She explained that because of her network of teachers, she could easily arrange some kind of global exchange; he was amazed. That is just part of the success story of social media.

Step 5: Participating in a Twitter Chat

Twitter Chats, or Tweet Chats, happen when a professional learning network tweets about a specified hashtag or topic at a regular time each week. For example, we both participate in a Twitter Chat for California educators called #CAEdChat. Colleagues across the state (and some folks from out of the state) meet each Sunday at 8:00 p.m. Pacific Standard Time to discuss a range of topics such as implementation and assessment of the Common Core and favorite professional texts. Usually, chats have a moderator who is responsible for asking a series of questions and keeping the conversation moving. Retweeting is a common way to show support of an idea or agreement with a colleague in the chat. Truthfully, chats can be a bit overwhelming at first, as the flow of content is instant and rapid. We recommend using an app like TweetDeck or a site like hootsuite.com to manage the conversation. Figure 10.10 shows some of the useful professional Twitter chats that happen through Twitter. Visit pluginpowerup.com for an updated list of educational Twitter chats and hashtags.

Hashtag #	In Plain English	Weekly Chat
#CAEdChat	California Education Chat	Sunday 8–9 p.m. PST
#EdChat	Education Chat	Tuesday noon–1 p.m. EST, 7–8 p.m. EST
#EdTechChat	Educational Technology Chat	Monday 8–9 p.m. EST
#ELLChat	English Language Learner Chat	Monday 9–10 p.m. EST
#EngChat	English Chat	Monday 7–8 p.m. EST
#FlipClass	Flipped Classroom Chat	Monday 8–9 p.m. EST
#LangChat	Foreign Language Chat	Thursday 8–9 p.m. EST
#MSMathChat	Middle School Math Chat	Monday 9–10 p.m. EST
#MSChat	Middle School Educators Chat	Thursday 8–9 p.m. EST
#MusEd	Music Education Chat	Monday 8–9 p.m. EST
#NTChat	New Teacher Chat	Wednesday 8–9 p.m. EST
#SciChat	Science Chat	Tuesday 9–10 p.m. EST
#SpedChat	Special Education Chat	Tuesday 8:30 p.m. EST
#SSChat	Social Studies Chat	Monday 7–8 p.m. EST
#YALitChat	Young Adult Literature Chat	Wednesday 9–10:15 p.m. EST

Figure 10.10 Top 25 Weekly Twitter Chats and Popular Education Hashtags

Making the Journey

In the first chapter of the book, we asked the question you might have asked yourself at some point. That is, We have 1:1; now what? The answer, really, is this: now, anything is possible. We wrote this book because we believe in the power of technology to transform education. From flipping the classroom, to connecting our students in meaningful collaboration, we know that 1:1 technology equips us to make our learning more personal, our time more purposeful, and our environment more malleable. We believe in placing that power in the hands of our students, so they can push down the walls of the classroom. When the audience for learning is extended to the real world, education becomes more authentic. We believe in leveraging technology's power for connection, reflection, and learning from colleagues around the world, and for collaboration, experimentation, and participation in the dialogue that is shaping our profession. We believe in empowering educators to harness the current of change. We have witnessed the progress that is possible when we place powerful tools in the hands of innovative teachers and set them free. We hope this book will help you experience success for your students with the technology now at their fingertips.

There is an African proverb that says, "If you want to go fast, go alone. If you want to go far, go together." The journey from here is your own, but you get to make it with a host of connected educators who will support your learning and cheer on your progress.

So, we all have 1:1. Great! Now let's get to work.

 POWER UP! Expand Your Network and Dive into the Conversation

1. **Ask a question you have, and hashtag it to a PLN**. #Edchat and #Edtechchat are always good places to start.

2. **As you read what your "loose links" have to say, mark as favorites** the comments that resonate with you. Pick a post and respond to it using the "reply" button.

3. **Feeling brave? Participate in a Twitter chat**. There's at least one chat every day of the week, so find one that works for you. It's okay to just "lurk" for the first time.

4. **Connect with us (@JenRoberts1 and @dneebe)** and share a success story. We'd love to hear how teaching in a 1:1 environment has enriched, extended, and transformed learning for your students. Hashtag your comment with #PowerUpEd.

Copyright, Creative Commons, Public Domain, and Fair Use

When students have access to a whole world of digital content, it becomes easy—sometimes too easy—for them to lift images, audio, video, and text and use these elements illegally. Most of the time, students are unaware that being able to download a file doesn't mean that they can *legally* download and then use the file. We find ourselves frequently reminding students that having "access" to something isn't the same as having "rights" to something.

At the risk of oversimplifying a very complex and ever-changing topic—copyright law—we have outlined four major types of "rights" that help us explain what's legal and what is not legal to our students. In a nutshell, creators of intellectual property can protect their work in many ways. Knowing the rights of the creator is critical to knowing what type of permission a student has to use that creation.

Copyright

Copyright is the most stringent of the intellectual property rights and is outlined extensively (and we mean *extensively*) in US Code, Title 17. Copyright law has a constitutional provision: "The Congress shall have power to . . . promote the progress of science and useful arts, by securing for limited times to authors and inventors the exclusive right to their respective writings and discoveries" (Article 1, Section 8). Copyright protects the person who created the intellectual property by giving him or her exclusive rights to reproduce, distribute, display, or sell a creative work. In general, we tell students that if something is under copyright, do not download, do not pass go, and do not collect $200. Just walk away.

Creative Commons

Creative Commons is much more flexible than copyright. The licensing options work like a menu, and creators of intellectual property can select as many or as few of the components as they like. All of the definitions on the following page can be found at creativecommons.org/licenses. The components are as follows:

- Attribution: "This license lets others distribute, remix, tweak, and build upon your work, even commercially, as long as they credit you for the original creation."
- Share Alike: This license requires that other creators using your work also "license their new creations under the identical terms. This license is often compared to 'copyleft' free and open source software licenses."
- No Derivatives: This license requires those using your work to make sure that your work "is passed along unchanged and in whole, with credit to you."
- Non-Commercial: This license means that the person using your work may not use it for commercial use. "Commercial use is one primarily intended for commercial advantage or monetary compensation."

Public Domain

Works in the public domain technically belong to the public, usually because the copyright has expired or because the creator of the work "dedicated" it to the public domain. Shakespeare's plays are a great example of creative works in the public domain. Anyone can access, use, and share these plays, because Shakespeare's rights to his intellectual property have long since expired. Typically, works under copyright move into the public domain seventy to one hundred years after the death of the author or creator. These dates are fuzzy and actually change based on the country of the original copyright. Gutenberg.org is a great place to start for books in the public domain.

Fair Use

Educators tend to throw around the term *educational fair use* as a catchall phrase that suggests we can use any content we like, anytime we like. But that's not how fair use works. Let's review some important factors of fair use. The first factor is whether the use is truly educational. Our friend Diane Main often gives this example: A teacher wants to reward her students for being really good this week. She shows the Disney movie *Aladdin* as a fun Friday treat. Educational? Nope. But let's say that same teacher decides to use specific clips of the movie as part of her unit on contemporary world issues and the portrayal of people from Middle Eastern countries in the media. Educational? Absolutely.

The second factor in determining fair use is how much of the work will be used, and how often. The reason this matters is that ultimately, copyright comes back to the "effect on the market": how will your use of this work change the value of that work? Are fewer people buying the text because you are scanning it and posting it on your learning management system (LMS)? In general, if you use 10 percent or less of a work, you're probably in the clear. The only time it is acceptable to use more than 10 percent is for the purpose of parody or satire. If you plan to use the same copyrighted story or the same article year after year, you should probably get permission or have your school purchase a text containing what you need. Obviously, fair use does not apply if you plan to use the material for commercial purposes or plan to post copyrighted works on the open web. Teachers often mistakenly post material to their school website for student use without realizing that by making copyrighted material available to the world, they are violating copyright laws. If you need to share copyrighted material with your students digitally, you will need to share that file privately through your password-protected LMS. If students have to log in to access the material, then it is limited to your class.

If you are interested in digging deeper into copyright, Creative Commons, public domain, and fair use, and getting a better understanding of the differences among the four and how they affect your classroom, we recommend the book *Copyright Clarity: How Fair Use Supports Digital Learning* by Renee Hobbs (2010). Also, check out commonsensemedia.org for helpful and free resources that you can use with your students. We have included a set of links and resources to help you make sense of all these laws on our website, pluginpowerup.com.

Teaching Search Skills

Having access to the Internet, and all of the resources available online, is one of the biggest perks of a 1:1 classroom, just as making sure students know how to access that information effectively is one of our most crucial responsibilities as educators. We want our students to be confident in their knowledge of how to find and apply any information they might need in the future, whether it's the perfect poem to read at a family event, the directions for repairing a dishwasher, or the details of a municipal ordinance. We use the language and content of our courses as a starting place, but we are conscious that teaching students how to search effectively is a vital and highly transferable skill.

What to Teach

Once we accept that teaching search skills is critical in a 1:1 classroom, it helps to know what to teach.

1. There is more than one search engine. In an era dominated by Google, some students don't even realize there are other ways to search the web. The next time your class is looking for something, ask some students to use Bing and others to try Yahoo. Depending on the subject, Wolfram Alpha may have relevant results. Next, take a moment to compare what students found. How are the results similar or different?

2. Teach students how to "read" a URL. The address of a web page can provide a lot of information if students know what to look for. Every address is made up of a domain name and an extension. Pluginpowerup is our domain and .com is our extension, so pluginpowerup.com takes you to our site. Domains can identify a company, an organization, or an individual. The extensions include .com, .org, .edu, .gov, and many others. Students looking for reliable data may want to be sure they are looking at a site whose name ends in .edu or .gov.

3. Show students how search engines work. Adding a few simple pieces of punctuation can change search results dramatically. (We use [square brackets] to denote what one might use in the search box. It helps to imagine the brackets as representing the box.)

- A minus sign will filter some things from your search. Search for [Jordan] and you will find lots of information about Michael Jordan. Search for [Jordan -Michael] and your results will mostly be about the country of Jordan.

- Quotation marks enable you to search for an exact phrase. If you search [men who have been to the moon], you will get results with many of those words but not linked together in a single phrase. Search ["men who have been to the moon"] and you get fewer results that all have those words used together as a single phrase. Using quotation marks can help you search for an exact quote or to look for people by their first and last names.

- Use an asterisk to represent an unknown word in a phrase. For example, if you search for ["a * in time * nine"], you will probably get results that say "a stitch in time saves nine." This process comes in handy when you remember part of a phrase or quotation but need help with the rest.

- For a complete list of the formatting and punctuation that affect search results, try searching [online search operators].

4. Teach students to search for what they expect to find. Often students phrase their searches as questions [Why does the sun go down in the evening?] rather than as keywords [explain sunset]. The difference in the results can be striking. The trick to effective searching is to search for the words you want to see on the page you are looking for. In other words, imagine the result you want, and then search for words that would be on that page.

5. Teach students to validate what they find. Just because the same information appears in more than one place does not make it accurate, but checking for multiple sources is one step in the validation process. Also show students how to validate information through different forms of media. There are many maps online that show the voyage of the *Beagle*, but you can check the accuracy of those maps by comparing them to the table of contents for *On the Origin of Species* by Charles Darwin. The book is organized geographically, validating many of the maps.

6. Show students how to access and search through any subscription-based online resources that your school or district may already be paying for. This material is vetted and specifically prepared for students. Although they may need to take some extra steps and use additional passwords, they likely will find more consistently high-quality material thorough subscription-based resources.

There are fantastic resources online for teaching students about searching effectively. Do your own search for [teach students to search the Internet] for the most current information, videos, and lesson plans.

Glossary of Technology Terms

➡ *In these definitions of highly technical terms, we emphasize what each term means, what you need to know about it, and why you should care.*

1:1: The ratio one-to-one means there is a computing device for every student.

Acceptable Use Policy (AUP): A document that you and your students sign to acknowledge understanding of the rules and expectations for using the computers, network, and Internet access provided by the school or district.

Backchannel: An online space for communication during a face-to-face discussion or presentation. See Chapter 6 for examples.

Backup: An extra copy of digital files kept in another location. For example, you may save a document on your computer but also save a copy to a cloud storage service such as Google Drive or Dropbox. External hard drives and flash drives are other forms of backup.

Blended Learning: Leveraging technology to move some activities to online spaces, which frees up classroom time for guided practice and collaboration. Learning becomes a blend of face-to-face and virtual environments.

Blog: Website content that is updated regularly by one or more authors, usually in short narrative or informational segments. *Blog* is an abbreviation for *web log*.

BYOD: Bring Your Own Device is a model for integrating technology that encourages all students to bring their own computers or tablets to school.

Cloud: A large online "warehouse" that stores your data for you. Many online services (Flickr, Google, Dropbox, Amazon, iCloud) provide "cloud" storage for your data. Using one of these services can be a good way to create a backup of your important files.

Dongle: A cable or adapter that attaches to your computer. For example, you will need a dongle to attach your iPad to a VGA cable, so you can project it. We suggest avoiding the term *dongle* in the classroom when students are present. Try *adapter* instead.

Embed: To take content from one website and insert it into another location. Many creation sites offer embed codes, a bit of HTML code that sits inside angle brackets < > that you can use to make that content appear directly on your website instead of as a link.

Export: The process of transferring your creation to a format that can be accessed by others. If you create a movie in video-editing software, for example, you will need to export it as an MP4 file so that others can view it. In some programs, you use "Save as" to change the type of file, such as converting a Word document into a PDF.

File Type: The extension on a file name tells you its file type. A Word document has the extension .doc or .docx. A photo file might be .png or .jpg. Knowing what kind of file you are working with can help you edit, adapt, or share that document with ease.

Hashtag: A word with a # symbol in front of it. Technically, the hashtag is just the symbol, but when the # comes attached to a word, it often becomes a link. Common on social media sites such as Twitter and Instagram, hashtags help users find similar content. If you see #edtech, for example, you are probably reading a tweet about educational technology. Click on the #edtech to see more tweets on that topic.

HDMI: High-Definition Multimedia Interface. Most modern projectors are going to have an HDMI input. This means a better picture for your content, but you also might have to jump through some hoops to connect things. HDMI also provides an audio channel, which means you get picture and sound with one connection.

Java: A programming language that website developers use to make their websites run better. You need some software called the Java Runtime Environment (JRE) on your computer to make those websites work the way they should. Keep your JRE up to date for security purposes.

LMS: A learning management system is a protected website that your and your students can use to exchange information digitally. You can use the LMS to post assignments and collect student work. Many LMSs offer discussion boards, internal blogs, and other fun virtual classroom activities.

Mirroring: Making the image on one computer or tablet appear on another computer or tablet. With the right software, you can mirror a tablet screen to your computer. Search [mirroring software] for some options that will be compatible with your devices.

Open Source: Noncommercial software created by a community and available for free. The Firefox browser is one example.

Platform: The type of device or operating system you use. Mac and Windows are two common but different platforms. Tablet devices are another common platform. When someone asks you what platform you are using, answer by explaining the device and the operating system, such as "My students are using laptops running Windows 8" or "My students have iPads, and they just upgraded to the latest iOS." Sometimes the platform will determine your options.

PLN: A personal learning network refers to the group of people you interact with and learn from on a regular basis.

QR Code: A quick response code is a square with lots of pixelated black dots. When scanned with an app, the code usually becomes the address to a website and then takes you there. QR codes can be a great way to help your students get to information fast.

Refresh: To reload a web page. The icon usually looks like a circle with an embedded arrow. Refreshing the web page is often the first thing to try when it isn't working right. (Trying a different web browser is the next step.)

RSS: Really Simple Syndication works as a way of collecting posts from various blogs and news sites in a single reading location. Lots of reading apps such as Flipboard and Feedly rely on RSS feeds to collect reading material.

Screencasting: A video recording of your computer screen, which also records your voice. Screencasting is a great way to make video lessons for your students and is easier than you think. Search [screencasting] for easy software options.

Screenshot: A picture taken from your computer screen or tablet screen. Use a screenshot to show your students what they should be doing, or capture a piece of content you want to keep.

Settings: Most apps, websites, and programs have settings, which are usually found by clicking the icon that looks like a gear. When you are learning about a new app, website, or program, you should always explore the settings to see which features you can and can't change, including privacy, sharing, and backup options. Notification settings are particularly important to adjust to eliminate messages you really don't need.

Social Media: Online communication platforms such as Twitter, Facebook, Instagram, and Google+. Social media enables large numbers of people to exchange information online.

Storage Space: The amount of space a file takes up on your computer. A simple text document might use only a few kilobytes, whereas most photographs require a few megabytes. One thousand megabytes equals a gigabyte; about fifteen minutes of video recorded on your phone will take up a gigabyte of storage space. One thousand gigabytes equals a terabyte. The trend toward larger capacity and less expensive storage is expected to continue.

Sync: Short for *synchronize*, *sync* means to match the contents of one device to another. If you have an account with a cloud storage system, you can use it to sync your data across your devices.

Tabs: Multiple windows open within the same web browser. They appear across the top of your screen like tabs in a three-ring binder. Each tab will display the name of the web page it is holding. Click on the name to switch between pages easily. This is often called *tabbed browsing*.

Undo: To go back a step. Lots of programs offer an undo option. Look for an arrow pointing backward. You can press the Control key and the *Z* key at the same time to undo the last thing you did. Ctrl+z is the common abbreviation for this process. On a Mac, the undo option abbreviation is Command+z. (We use this a lot.)

Update: To make sure your software or apps are the most current versions. You can also update a blog or a web page by adding new information to the page. If you see "technical difficulties" displayed on a page, you may need to update software or apps.

Upload: To move a file from your computer to a website. Sometimes students will upload their work to your LMS.

URL: The "universal resource locator" is the specific address of any web page. It always begins with http:// or https:// if it is a secure site.

USB: The Universal Serial Bus is a flat rectangular port on your laptop that enables you to plug in a mouse, a remote clicker, or an external hard drive, among other things. Most of the things you plug into your computer will temporarily go into the USB port.

Username: The name an app or website uses to identify you. To be safe, we recommend that students avoid using a full first and last name as their usernames.

VoIP: Voice and video calls over the Internet, such as through Skype and Google Voice.

Webcam: A camera built into your device or attached by USB that sends a video signal over the Internet. When you make a Skype call or participate in a Google Hangout, you will use a web camera to send the images.

Wi-Fi: Internet access without wires. Wi-Fi works through a radio signal. It is usually slower and less reliable than a wired connection, but unless you are downloading large files or having a video call, you probably won't notice the difference. Wi-Fi problems are among the most common sources of technical problems that occur in a 1:1 classroom. Getting thirty-six students online at once means you need a Wi-Fi access point that can handle the load.

Wiki: A website that can be edited by the users of that site. Wikipedia is the most famous version of this.

Workflow: The process of moving digital material from one platform or app to another, such as sending or receiving materials to and from students and colleagues. Another form of workflow is the process or steps you take to accomplish a task digitally.

References

Anderson, C. 2010. "How Web Video Powers Global Innovation." *TEDGlobal*. http://www.ted.com/talks/chris_anderson_how_web_video_powers_global _innovation?language=en.

Anderson, L., and D. Krathwohl, eds. 2001. *A Taxonomy for Learning, Teaching, and Assessing: A Revision of Bloom's Taxonomy of Educational Objectives*. Boston: Pearson.

Avrith, T. 2014. "ReBrand Digital Citizenship—Get Ignited!" Edtechschools.com. http://www.edtechschools.com/rebrand-digital-citizenship-get-ignited/.

Beers, K. 2003. *When Kids Can't Read: What Teachers Can Do*. Portsmouth, NH: Heinemann.

Behrmann, M. 1998. "Assistive Technology for Young Children in Special Education: It Makes a Difference." *Edutopia*. http://www.edutopia.org/assistive-technology -young-children-special-education.

Belanger, J., and P. Allingham. 2002. "Using 'Think-Aloud' Methods to Investigate the Processes Secondary Students Use to Respond to Their Teachers' Comments on Their Written Work." Technical Report. The University of British Columbia. http://faculty.educ.ubc.ca/ belanger/thinkaloud.htm.

Bellow, A. 2013. "You're Invited to Change the World." Closing keynote presented at the Annual Meeting of the International Society of Technology in Education (ISTE), San Antonio, TX, June 26, 2013.

Bergmann, X., Y. Overmyer, and Z. Willie. 2011. "The Flipped Class: What It Is and What It Is Not." *The Daily Riff*. http://www.thedailyriff.com/articles/the-flipped-class -conversation-689.php.

Borko, H. 2004. "Professional Development and Teacher Learning: Mapping the Terrain." *Educational Researcher* 33 (8): 3–15.

Bowen, J. 2012. *Teaching Naked: How Moving Technology Out of Your College Classroom Will Improve Student Learning*. San Francisco: Jossey-Bass.

Bronson, P., and A. Merryman. 2010. "The Creativity Crisis." *Newsweek*, July 10. http://www.newsweek.com/creativity-crisis-74665.

Burke, J. 2011. "Preparing Today's Students for Tomorrow's World: Using Technology with Students and Teachers." Keynote address presented at Promising Practices, San Diego, CA, October 29, 2011.

Buzzeo, T. 2008. *The Collaboration Handbook*. Santa Barbara, CA: Linworth.

Casner-Lotto, J., L. Barrington, and M. Wright. 2006. "Are They Really Ready to Work? Employers' Perspectives on the Basic Knowledge and Applied Skills of New Entrants to the 21st Century U.S. Workforce." New York: The Conference Board. http://www.p21.org/storage/documents/FINAL_REPORT_PDF09-29-06.pdf.

Cavanaugh, K. 2013. "The Benefits of Working Collaboratively for Both Employees and Business." *The Atlantic*. http://www.theatlantic.com/sponsored/ibm-smarter -workforce/benefits-working-collaboratively-both-employees-and-business/27/.

Cho, K. 2004. "When Multi-Peers Give Better Advice Than an Expert: The Type and Impact of Feedback Given by Students and an Expert on Student Writing." Doctoral diss. University of Pittsburgh, 2004. *Dissertation Abstracts International* 65 (10): 3688.

Cornally, S. 2012. "Deeper Learning: Performance Assessment and Authentic Audience." *Edutopia*. http://www.edutopia.org/blog/making-assessment-relevant-students -teachers-shawn-cornally.

Cothran, D. J., and C. D. Ennis. 2000. "Engagement for What? Beyond Popular Discourses of Student Engagement." *Leadership and Policy in Schools* 3 (1): 59–76.

Dodor, B., and C. Hausafus. 2010. "Breaking Down the Walls of Teacher Isolation." *Journal of Family and Consumer Sciences Education* 28 (1). Also available online at http://www.natefacs.org/Pages/v28no1/v28no1Dodor.pdf.

Duarte, N. 2008. *Slide:ology: The Art and Science of Creating Great Presentations*. Sebastopol, CA: O'Reilly.

Dweck, C. 2007. *Mindset: The New Psychology of Success*. New York: Ballantine.

Edutopia. 2008. "Why Integrate Technology into the Curriculum? The Reasons Are Many." *Edutopia*. http://www.edutopia.org/technology-integration-introduction.

Ender, S. C. 1985. "Study Groups and College Success." *Journal of College Student Personnel* 26:469–471.

Fink, D. 2003. *Creating Significant Learning Experiences: An Integrated Approach to Designing College Courses*. San Francisco: Jossey-Bass.

Fisher, D., and N. Frey. 2012. "Making Time for Feedback." *Educational Leadership* 70 (1): 42–46.

Flinders, D. 1988. "Teacher Isolation and the New Reform." *Journal of Curriculum and Supervision* 4 (1): 17–29.

Fluckiger, J. 2010. "Single Point Rubric: A Tool for Responsible Student Self-Assessment." Connection.ebscohost.com. http://connection.ebscohost.com/c/articles/52418300 /single-point-rubric-tool-responsible-student-self-assessment.

Freeman, D., and Y. Freeman. 2007. *English Language Learners: The Essential Handbook.* New York: Scholastic.

Gilbert, E. 2014. "Where Does Creativity Come From?" *National Public Radio TED Radio Hour.* http://www.npr.org/2014/10/03/351554044/where-does-creativity-come-from.

Gladwell, Malcolm. 2000. *The Tipping Point: How Little Things Can Make a Big Difference.* New York: Little, Brown.

Graff, G., and C. Birkenstein. 2009. *They Say, I Say: The Moves That Matter in Academic Writing.* 2nd ed. New York: W. W. Norton.

Griffiths, A. J., E. Lilles, M. Furlong, and J. Sidhwa. 2012. "The Relations of Adolescent Student Engagement with Troubling and High-Risk Behaviors." In *Handbook of Research on Student Engagement*, ed. S. Christenson, L. Reschly, and C. Wylie. New York: Springer.

Harvey, S., and H. Daniels. 2009. *Comprehension and Collaboration: Inquiry Circles in Action.* Portsmouth, NH: Heinemann.

Hasso Plattner School of Design at Stanford. 2011. *Bootcamp Bootleg.* http://dschool .stanford.edu/wp-content/uploads/2011/03/BootcampBootleg2010v2SLIM.pdf.

Hattie, J. 2012. "Know Thy Impact." *Educational Leadership* 70 (1): 18–23.

Hobbs, R. 2010. *Copyright Clarity: How Fair Use Supports Digital Learning.* Thousand Oaks, CA: Corwin.

Hur, J., and T. Brush. 2009. "Teacher Participation in Online Communities: Why Do Teachers Want to Participate in Self-Generated Online Communities of K–12 Teachers?" *Journal of Research on Technology in Education* 41 (3): 279–303.

Hurley, R. 2014. Presentation for the Google Apps for Education Summit (GAFE). Coronado, CA.

International Society for Technology in Education. 2007. *ISTE Standards for Students.* http:// www.iste.org/docs/pdfs/20-14_ISTE_Standards-S_PDF.pdf.

Jago, C. 2005. *Papers, Papers, Papers: An English Teacher's Survival Guide.* Portsmouth, NH: Heinemann.

Jenkins, H., K. Clinton, R. Purushotma, A. Robinson, and M. Weigel. 2006. "Confronting the Challenges of Participatory Culture: Media Education for the 21st Century." MacArthur Foundation. http://www.macfound.org/media/article_pdfs/JENKINS_WHITE _PAPER.PDF.

Jerald, C. 2009. *Defining a 21st Century Education.* Center for Public Education. http://www.centerforpubliceducation.org/Main-Menu/Policies/21st-Century/Defining -a-21st -Century-Education-Full-report-PDF.pdf.

Johnson, L., S. Adams Becker, M. Cummins, V. Estrada, A. Freeman, and H. Ludgate. 2013. *NMC Horizon Report: 2013. K–12 Edition.* Austin, TX: The New Media Consortium.

Kajder, S. 2003. *The Tech-Savvy English Classroom.* Portland, ME: Stenhouse.

Kelley, T. 2001. *The Art of Innovation.* New York: Currency.

Kelley, T., and D. Kelley. 2013. *Creative Confidence: Unleashing the Creative Potential Within Us All.* New York: Crown Business.

Klopfer, E., S. Osterweil, and K. Salen. 2009. *Moving Learning Games Forward.* Cambridge, MA: Massachusetts Institute of Technology. The Education Arcade. http://education.mit.edu/papers/MovingLearningGamesForward_EdArcade.pdf.

Kohn, A. 1993. "Choices for Children: Why and How to Let Students Decide." *Phi Delta Kappan* 75 (1): 8–16, 18–21.

_____. 1999. *Punished by Rewards: The Trouble with Gold Stars, Incentive Plans, A's, Praise, and Other Bribes.* Boston: Houghton Mifflin.

Lamott, Anne. 1994. *Bird by Bird: Some Instructions on Writing and Life.* New York: Anchor.

Lattimer, H. 2003. *Thinking Through Genre.* Portland, ME: Stenhouse.

Lave, J., and E. Wenger. 1991. *Situated Learning: Legitimate Peripheral Participation.* Cambridge, UK: Cambridge University Press.

Limb, C. 2010. "Your Brain on Improv." TEDxMidAtlantic. http://www.ted.com/talks/ charles_limb_your_brain_on_improv?language=en.

Magaña, S., and R. Marzano. 2014. "Using Polling Technologies to Close Feedback Gaps." *Educational Leadership* 71 (6): 82–83.

Marzano, R. 2006. *Classroom Assessment and Grading That Work.* Alexandria, VA: Association for Supervision and Curriculum Development.

McDowell, Fredrick H., Jr. 2013. "Technology's Impact on Student Engagement in Urban Schools: Administrators', Teachers', and Students' Perspectives in Urban Schools." Education Doctoral Theses. Paper 100. http://hdl.handle.net/2047/d20003034.

McGilchrist, I. 2011. "The Divided Brain." TED Talk. https://www.ted.com/talks/iain
_mcgilchrist_the_divided_brain.

Meyer, D. 2014. "Capturing, Sharing, and Resolving Perplexity." Kickoff keynote presented
at CUE Annual Conference, Palm Springs, CA, March 20, 2014.

Miller, D., and S. Kelly. 2014. *Reading in the Wild.* San Francisco: Jossey-Bass.

Moeller, B., and T. Reitzes. 2011. *Integrating Technology with Student-Centered Learning.*
Quincy, MA: Nellie Mae Education Foundation.

Moffett, J. 1968. *Teaching the Universe of Discourse*. Portsmouth, NH: Heinemann.

Mosley, V. 2013. "Qualitative Study: Why Technology Is Underutilized in K–12 Education."
In *Proceedings of Society for Information Technology and Teacher Education International
Conference*, ed. R. McBride and M. Searson. Chesapeake, VA: Association for the
Advancement of Computing in Education.

Musallam, R. 2013. "3 Rules to Spark Learning." TED Talks Education. http://www.ted.com
/talks/ramsey_musallam_3_rules_to_spark_learning?language=en.

November, A. 2013. "Why Schools Must Move Beyond 'One-to-One' Computing." *eSchool
News*. http://www.eschoolnews.com/2013/01/29/why-schools-must-move
-beyond-one-to-one-computing/?.

Partnership for 21st Century Skills. 2014. "Framework for 21st Century Learning."
http://p21.org.

Project Tomorrow. 2012. "Speak Up 2011: National Findings K–12 Teachers, Librarians and
Administrators." Tomorrow.org. http://www.tomorrow.org/speakup/pdfs/SU11.

Rami, M. 2014. *Thrive: 5 Ways to (Re)Invigorate Your Teaching.* Portsmouth, NH: Heinemann.

Reynolds, G. 2012. *Presentation Zen: Simple Ideas on Presentation Design and Delivery,*
2nd ed. Berkeley, CA: New Riders.

_____. 2014. *Presentation Zen Design: A Simple Visual Approach to Presenting in Today's
World*, 2nd ed. Berkeley, CA: New Riders.

Richardson, W. 2012. "Preparing Students to Learn Without Us." *Educational Leadership*
69 (5): 22–26.

Robinson, K. 2011. *Out of Our Minds: Learning to Be Creative*. West Sussex, UK: Capstone.

Slagle, P. 1997. "Getting Real: Authenticity in Writing Prompts." *The Quarterly,* 19 (3).
National Writing Project. http://www.nwp.org/cs/public/print/resource/882.

Smith, F. 1913. "The Evolution of the Motion Picture: VI—Looking into the Future with
Thomas A. Edison." *The New York Dramatic Mirror*, July 9.

Steinberg, A. 1997. *Real Learning, Real Work: School-to-Work as High School Reform*. New York: Routledge.

Stix, A., and F. Hrbek. 2006. *Teachers as Classroom Coaches: How to Motivate Students Across the Content Areas*. Alexandria, VA: Association for Supervision and Curriculum Development.

Sweller, J. 2008. "Human Cognitive Architecture." In *Handbook of Research on Educational Communications and Technology*, ed. J. M. Spector, M. D. Merrill, J. J. G. van Merriënboer, and M. Driscoll. 3rd ed. New York: Lawrence Erlbaum.

Tomlinson, C. 2014. *The Differentiated Classroom: Responding to the Needs of All Learners*. 2nd ed. Alexandria, VA: Association for Supervision and Curriculum Development.

Tomlinson, C., and E. Javius. 2012. "Teach Up for Excellence." *Educational Leadership* 69 (5): 28–33.

Vogel, C. 2009. "A Call for Collaboration." District Administration Magazine. http://www.districtadministration.com/article/call-collaboration.

Wenger, E. 1998. *Communities of Practice: Learning, Meaning, and Identity*. Cambridge, UK: Cambridge University Press.

Wiggins, G. 2009. "Real-World Writing: Making Purpose and Audience Matter." *English Journal* 98 (5): 29–37.

_____. 2012. "Seven Keys to Effective Feedback." *Educational Leadership* 70 (1): 10–16.

Wiggins, G., and J. McTighe. 2005. *Understanding by Design*. Alexandria, VA: Association for Supervision and Curriculum Development.

Wormeli, R. 2013. *The Collected Writings (So Far) of Rick Wormeli*. Westerville, OH: Association for Middle Level Education.

Index

Page numbers followed by *f* indicate figures.